D1523268

ANNALS OF COMMUNISM

Each volume in the series Annals of Communism will publish selected and previously inaccessible documents from former Soviet state and party archives in a narrative that develops a particular topic in the history of Soviet and international communism. Separate English and Russian editions will be prepared. Russian and Western scholars work together to prepare the documents for each volume. Documents are chosen not for their support of any single interpretation but for their particular historical importance or their general value in deepening understanding and facilitating discussion. The volumes are designed to be useful to students, scholars, and interested general readers.

Silence Was Salvation

*Child Survivors of Stalin's Terror
and World War II in the Soviet Union*

Cathy A. Frierson

Yale UNIVERSITY PRESS
New Haven and London

Yale University Press books may be purchased in quantity for educational, business, or promotional use. For information, please e-mail sales.press@yale.edu (U.S. office) or sales@yaleup.co.uk (U.K. office).

Set in Sabon type by Newgen North America. Printed in the United States of America.

Library of Congress Cataloging-in-Publication Data
Frierson, Cathy A.
   Silence was salvation : child survivors of Stalin's terror and World War II in the Soviet Union / Cathy A. Frierson.
      pages   cm. — (Annals of communism)
   Includes bibliographical references and index.
   ISBN 978-0-300-17945-3 (hardcover : alk. paper)   1. Political prisoners—Soviet Union—Interviews.   2. Political prisoners—Soviet Union—Biography.   3. Soviet Union—Politics and government—1936–1953.   4. Stalin, Joseph, 1879–1953.
5. Political purges—Soviet Union—History.   6. World War, 1939–1945—Soviet Union.   7. Soviet Union—Social conditions—1917–1945.   8. Soviet Union—Social conditions—1945–1991.   9. Communism—Social aspects—Soviet Union.
I. Title.
   DK268.A1F75 2014
   365'.45092530947—dc23

                                                                                2014026669

A catalogue record for this book is available from the British Library.

This paper meets the requirements of ANSI/NISO Z39.48–1992 (Permanence of Paper).

10 9 8 7 6 5 4 3 2 1

Yale University Press gratefully acknowledges the financial support given for this publication by the John M. Olin Foundation, the Lynde and Harry Bradley Foundation, the Historical Research Foundation, Roger Milliken, the Rosentiel Foundation, Lloyd H. Smith, Keith Young, the William H. Donner Foundation, Joseph W. Donner, Jeremiah Milbank, the David Woods Kemper Memorial Foundation, and the Smith Richardson Foundation.

To the Good Samaritans, especially the teachers

And, behold, a certain lawyer stood up, and tempted him, saying, Master, what shall I do to inherit eternal life?

He said unto him, What is written in the law? how readest thou?

And he answering said, Thou shalt love the Lord thy God with all thy heart, and with all thy soul, and with all thy strength, and with all thy mind; and thy neighbour as thyself.

And he said unto him, Thou has answered right: this do, and thou shalt live.

But he, willing to justify himself, said unto Jesus, And who is my neighbour?

And Jesus answering said, A certain man went down from Jerusalem to Jericho, and fell among thieves, which stripped him of his raiment, and wounded him, and departed, leaving him half dead.

And by chance there came down a certain priest that way; and when he saw him, he passed on the other side.

And likewise a Levite, when he was at the place, came and looked on him, and passed by on the other side.

But a certain Samaritan, as he journeyed, came where he was: and when he saw him, he had compassion on him.

And went to him, and bound up his wounds, pouring in oil and wine, and set him on his own beast, and brought him to an inn, and took care of him.

And on the morrow when he departed, he took out two pence, and gave them to the host, and said unto him, Take care of him; and whatsoever thou spendest more, when I come again, I will repay thee.

Which now of these three, thinkest thou, was neighbour unto him that fell among the thieves?

And he said, He that shewed mercy on him. Then said Jesus unto him, Go, and do thou likewise.

—Luke 10:25–37 (*The Holy Bible, Containing the Old and New Testaments Translated Out of the Original Tongues and with the Former Translations Diligently Compared and Revised By His Majesty's Special Command. Appointed to Be Read in Churches. Authorized King James Version.* [London and New York: Collins' Clear-Type Press], n.p.d. [before 1939, when this copy was given to my father, John Witherspoon Frierson, V])

Contents

Acknowledgments

My deepest debt is to the child survivors of Soviet political repression who shared their life histories with me. They entrusted me to convey them to you, and I have tried to be worthy of that trust. They agreed to revisit traumatic episodes in their past and to respond to questions whose content they did not know beforehand. Their goal was to enlighten future generations. Their memories now reside in my memory, too. Their childhood hunger inhabits my kitchen; their childhood lack of warm clothes haunts my routine of dressing for winter walks. Their expressions of gratitude to those individuals who extended a hand to them in their pariah status as children of "enemies of the people" remind me daily to be generous.

Institutions and funding organizations supported the research for this project. The National Endowment for the Humanities supported the translations and research. The Davis Center for Russian and Eurasian Studies of Harvard University twice provided an institutional home for me as a senior fellow. The National Council for Eurasian and East European Research and the International Research Exchanges Board supported my travel. The University of New Hampshire (UNH) provided generous funding through endowments for faculty research in the College of Liberal Arts, History Department, Graduate School, and Center for Humanities. In Russia, Vozvrashchenie (The Return) and the Memorial centers in Moscow, Saint Petersburg, and other cities provided contacts, research materials, and wise counsel.

Colleagues in the United States and Russia enriched this project. Judith Moyer, Jehanne Gheith, and Anika Walke shared expertise on oral history. In Russia, Semyon Vilensky, Irina Flige, and Tatyana Morgacheva oriented me in the survivors' networks. Peter Greenleaf and Melissa Stockdale created nurturing domestic spaces in Russia. Jeffry Diefendorf, Mary Malone, Jennifer Lee, Pey Yi Chu, and David Pillemer commented on the introduction. Elena Vetrova and Valerie Wattenberg refined the translations. Dee Ann Dumas assisted with the computerized aspects of manuscript preparation, and Thea Dickerman proofread the results. Jonathan Brent, Vadim Staklo, and Christina Tucker were supportive editors at Yale University Press. The two readers for the manuscript offered astute criticism, detecting errors in translation. An author's most critical partner in the final stages of producing a book is the copyeditor. My good fortune is to have had Jeffrey Schier as that partner on this book. I thank him for his linguistic precision and meticulous attention to all the complexities of transliteration, translation, and composition that were required to bring these Russian oral testimonies to the English-reading public. All remaining errors are, of course, my own.

The child survivors of Soviet political repression most wanted *students* to read these recollections. It is thus appropriate that UNH students actively contributed to this book. Two UNH history majors did research and preliminary editing for the introduction: Ella Nilsen and Karen Cue. A third UNH student, majoring in history and geography, Eric Pugliano, prepared maps for most of the interviews. The UNH Hamel Center for Undergraduate Research supported these students' participation in the project.

My sisters and son read and commented on sections of this manuscript. Eleanor Frierson, who in the 1950s taught me to read and write, joined Claire Frierson, Lily Frierson, and Isaac Josephson in supporting my efforts here to bring other families' intimate histories to the English-reading public. And for that, I am truly grateful.

Author Note

Punctuation, Names, and Abbreviations

In these interviews, unbracketed ellipses of three dots indicate that the child survivor paused briefly during his or her narrative. When the word "pause" appears thus—[*pause*]—the speaker paused for several seconds or longer. An ellipsis of four dots indicates cuts I have made in my questions or a survivor's responses.

In Russian culture, a person's full name includes a first name, patronymic, and last or family name. The patronymic is the name of the individual's father, plus a suffix to indicate the person's gender. The polite form of address includes both the first name and the patronymic. Referring to a person or addressing a person in this form indicates respect. Because one of the goals of this anthology of interviews is to restore dignity to these survivors of Soviet repression and humiliation, I refer to them in this form. It seems especially important to do so, because including the patronymic also retains in the historical record the name of the father whom the Soviet government took away from the child and tried to erase as anyone other than an "enemy of the people."

In formatting the interview transcripts, I have denoted the child survivors by the initials of their first name and patronymic. Thus, Aleksandr Yudelevich Zakgeim appears as AYu; Inna Aronovna Shikheeva-Gaister appears as IA, Valentin Tikhonovich Muravsky appears as VT, and so forth. I denote my questions with the initials of my first and last names—CF.

I have also included some brief explanation of transliterated terms within the text in brackets, e.g., *Pravda* [central Communist Party newspaper].

Maps

Darya Oreshkina prepared the map of Valentin Muravsky's life originally for Cathy A. Frierson and Semyon S. Vilensky, *Children of the Gulag* (New Haven: Yale University Press, 2010).

Eric Pugliano prepared all other maps for this anthology. Each map focuses on the most relevant years of the survivor's life as recounted in the interviews. Most survivors' maps include as well the journey of the survivor's mother and/or father. The goal of the maps is to display the families' separations and displacements, illustrating the geographic aspects of political victimization in the Soviet Union.

Silence Was Salvation

Introduction: I survived. I speak.

his book introduces ten people who were survivors of childhood trauma during the Soviet era and who were still living
in Russia in 2005–2007. The Soviet government created their
suffering when it orphaned them in the 1930s and 1940s by arresting one or both of their parents, whom the state then imprisoned,
exiled, or executed. The children subsequently endured social, political, and economic stigmas as offspring of "enemies of the people" or
"traitors to the motherland." These categories excluded them for life
from many opportunities their peers enjoyed as unstigmatized Soviet
citizens. When World War II began in Poland in 1939, the horrors on
the Eastern Front of Soviet-occupied territory made these fatherless,
and sometimes motherless, children more vulnerable than others to
hunger, exposure, violence, homelessness, and death. And yet they
survived. They agreed to share their stories with me, believing that in
doing so they would make an important contribution to the history
of the Soviet Union, Soviet terror, and the Soviet network of penal
institutions known as the Gulag. Unwittingly, they were also offering
lessons in survival.

Survival and resilience are not new to the history of the Gulag. One
of the first Gulag memoirs to be published in English, Evgenia Ginzburg's *Journey into the Whirlwind,* offered readers several illustra-
tions of these phenomena.[1] As a university student in the 1970s, I was
struck by one reminder of survival which Ginzburg may not have an-
ticipated: simply the presence of her name as author. The publisher of
the English translation placed two words—"Evgenia Ginzburg"—at

the top of every right-hand page. This printed name framed her descriptions of degradation with the implicit message: "I survived. I speak." And two pages later, again, "I survived. I speak."

But what of the children left behind when Evgenia Ginzburg and other mothers like her entered the Gulag? Did they survive? What remained to sustain those children when their mothers were forced to walk out the door under escort by security police? Typically, their fathers had already disappeared. What became of such child victims of Soviet political repression? Ginzburg herself raised this question, when she recalled hearing elderly peasant women ask it.[2] The scene was a railroad station in late summer 1939, "deep in the Urals," where Ginzburg's prisoner transport train stopped en route to Siberia. On the platform, women selling produce realized it was a "convict train," and their "ancient peasant eyes filled with tears and pity." Ginzburg heard one woman comment, "And think of all their poor little children left at home, no better off than orphans."[3]

In December 1989, Maya Rudolfovna Levitina introduced me to the anguishing history of these children's experiences. Serendipity landed me that winter in her apartment in Smolensk, where she quietly told me about losing her parents to the Great Terror—her father in 1937, her mother in 1939. Her Soviet horror story left me pondering this question: Which is most astonishing, most fantastic? Her childhood deprivations? Her survival into late adulthood? Or her willingness to share her tale with an unexpected guest from the United States? By then, Mikhail Gorbachev's policy of transparency—*glasnost*—had opened the way for state archivists and individuals alike to release evidence and memories they had guarded or suppressed for decades. I found myself relating to the incredulousness Ginzburg experienced when she first heard the life stories of her fellow "camp women" in the far eastern reaches of the Gulag. She found them "fantastically improbable, and yet true" when she heard them during her first three days in the camps.[4]

The collapse of the Soviet Union in December 1991—two years after I met Maya Rudolfovna Levitina—opened the floodgates of memory. Over the next decade, innumerable personal memoirs of Soviet life appeared in Russian.[5] Aleksandr Nikolaevich Yakovlev,[6] who, under Boris Yeltsin, was chairman of the President's Commission on the Victims of Political Repression, rose to the challenge of assembling data on the Soviet system's victims. Nongovernmental organizations in Moscow, Saint Petersburg, and regional cities had already formed to bring survivors together, gather documentation and testimonies, publish martyrologies and memoirs, commemorate the victims, and lobby for social welfare benefits for survivors. The most important was then—and still remains—Memorial.[7] Historians and officials in Russia and the West expanded the categories of persons recognized officially as victims of Soviet state repression to include others besides Stalin's Bolshevik rivals who were repressed in the 1930s. The list also came to include "former people" of the propertied classes before the revolution; priests and religious believers; peasants subjected to deku-lakization and forced collectivization; members of national and ethnic groups deported by force to remote, undeveloped regions; citizens or soldiers captured by the Axis powers as prisoners of war or slave laborers during World War II and who were arrested upon return to the USSR; still more political victims from 1945 to Stalin's death in 1953; and those targeted by his "last purge" in early 1953—Jewish citizens of the USSR.[8]

Maya Rudolfovna Levitina's tale turned out to be not at all un-usual in its traumas. She was one of millions of such children, a fact which the Soviet state's own records and other evidence had amply demonstrated by 2002. In that year, Semyon Samuilovich Vilensky, a Gulag survivor, journalist, poet, and editor, joined with archivists and historians to publish a compendium of state documents, letters, and survivors' memoirs under the title *Children of the Gulag*.[9] Roughly ten million Soviet children up to age sixteen, the age of legal majority, had parents who were targeted in Stalin's campaigns. The children became collateral victims.

Children entered the Gulag as wards of state orphanages, minors accompanying their parents into exile or to special settlements, visi-tors to their imprisoned parents, or residents in the regions where their parents served out their sentences and were forced to remain after release as "freely hired laborers." I define the Gulag broadly here to include the entire network of detention facilities; transit prisons; long-term prisons; execution chambers and fields; forced labor camps; and "special settlements" run out of the Commissariat of Internal Affairs (NKVD), renamed the Ministry of Internal Affairs (MVD) in 1946 and the Committee of State Security (KGB) in 1954. The Gulag also includes the network of NKVD institutions for children: so-called child receiver-distributors, orphanages, and labor colonies. The youngest Soviet citizens who entered this vast network thereby became "children of the Gulag."

This volume presents Maya Rudolfovna Levitina's memories and those of other child survivors as they recounted them to me in oral history interviews between 2005 and 2007. Like Ginzburg's memoir in the 1970s, their oral testimonies offer the implicit refrain, "I survived. I speak."

Legal Repression

The Soviet state's laws and regulations prescribed the punitive actions to be taken against individual men and their wives, children, and other relatives when they were deemed dangerous to the system. It was thus perfectly legal for state agents to target children as young as twelve months for separation from their families to be raised by the Soviet state, and to place teenagers in labor colonies for "correctional labor."

Soviet law explicitly protected the state and society, not the individual citizen. Article 58 of the Criminal Code, which defined crimes against the state, had the most frequent impact on these children. The first eleven of the twelve original chapters in the article covered these crimes: armed uprisings; assistance to international bourgeois enemies; undermining state industry, transportation, or trade; terrorist acts against state officials; destroying or damaging the transportation or communications systems; disseminating propaganda calling for overthrowing, undermining, or weakening Soviet power; preparing such acts or being part of an organization that prepared such acts; failing to report such acts or planning; and "counterrevolutionary sabotage" through a failure of duty or carelessness in fulfilling a duty. Finally, even in the absence of any counterrevolutionary intent, Article 58 stated, "Any act shall be considered a crime against the administration if . . . it nonetheless leads to a disturbance of the regular activities of the agencies of the administration or of the national economy." The article then spelled out what an act of omission in this category would be: "Any omission, by any person having certain knowledge of the matter, to report any counterrevolutionary crime that is in preparation or has been committed, shall entail: deprivation of freedom for a period of not less than six months."[10] The most severe punishment prescribed was execution by shooting, along with confiscation of property. As readers will see below in the children's eyewitness accounts, the state's confiscation of property often meant seizure of everything the accused had possessed, leaving any surviving relatives only the barest minimum of clothes. This also meant that many children who were left behind lost their homes.

After Sergei Kirov, the leader of the Leningrad Communist Party organization, was shot dead inside the Party's central building in Leningrad on December 1, 1934, Stalin penned a decree that permitted summary trial and execution. This decree authorized the procedure by which so many children of enemies of the people lost their fathers, especially when mass arrests spread in 1937 in what has come to be known as the Great Terror. The text of this decree is reproduced in Appendix I.

The key decree launching the "mass operations" against broad swaths of Soviet society was NKVD Operational Order No. 00447 of July 30, 1937. It called for a campaign against "former kulaks and socially dangerous elements, . . . Members of anti-Soviet parties (SRs [Socialist Revolutionaries], Georgian Mensheviks, Dashnaks, Mussavatists, Ittihadists, etc.), former Whites, gendarmes, bureaucrats, . . . sectarian activists, church officials . . . criminals." The order provided quotas of persons to be arrested, shot, or exiled in each geographic region of the empire. It also instructed officials on what to do with the families of those arrested. Potential fates included transfer to "camps and labor settlements," restrictions about where family members could live in the Soviet Union, and placement thenceforth under "systematic observation" by the security police (see Appendix II).

The party-state refined even further the operations for punishing wives and children of ascribed traitors through NKVD Operational Order No. 00486 (see Appendix III). This lengthy decree provided instructions on how to carry out arrests of wives of "traitors to the motherland," search their homes, seize their possessions, and sentence them. It also ordered the separation of child from mother if the child was beyond average breastfeeding age. As for those who had yet to reach that age, Article 17 decreed, "Wives of traitors to the motherland who have nursing children shall be . . . sent immediately to the camp without being taken to prison." Children above nursing age were to be sent to "camps, to NKVD correctional labor colonies or to special regime orphanages." The state saw very young children as being educable in the Stalinist orthodoxy.

Article 29 of this order reveals the state's determination to appropriate not only the children themselves as living, breathing, thinking, feeling beings by taking them away from their mothers, but also all the documents which relatives who were not arrested might use to establish the children's identity. Article 23 permitted relatives to take in stigmatized children of so-called enemies of the people or traitors of the motherland. This article implicitly acknowledged the state's lack of institutional capacity to achieve its ambitions of "reforging" all such children into model Soviet citizens. This loophole proved to be the salvation for some children whose relatives were determined to keep them in their extended families rather than have the children face the bitter fate of being a ward of the Soviet state.

The Interview Method and Questions of Memory

I conducted interviews with child survivors in Russia beginning in April 2005 in Moscow and concluding in November 2007 in Smolensk. An oral history interview is "an exchange between *two* subjects: literally a mutual sighting," and therefore an "intersubjective encounter" between historian and subject.[11] The settings for the interviews in this volume varied. The optimal location was the survivor's home, where I was able to see his or her photographs and other mementos and to encourage a more personal approach to reminiscences. The exceptional value placed on hospitality in Russian culture, and the custom of talk around the kitchen table for intimate discussion, heightened the importance of interviewing subjects in their homes.[12]

Alessandro Portelli asserts that in an oral history interview, "The two interacting subjects cannot act together unless some kind of mutuality is established."[13] The richest interviews were those in which the survivors and I established the greatest degree of mutual exchange and understanding over several hours or days; and, in the cases of Valentin Tikhonovich Muravsky, Irina Andreevna Dubrovina, and Maya Rudolfovna Levitina, years.[14] For example, our common experiences as parents or teachers often opened the way for communication. I located prospective interviewees initially through the Russian nongovernmental organizations Vozvrashchenie (The Return) and Memorial. I also drew on contacts from my previous research and exchange experiences in the Soviet Union and Russia. I tried to identify survivors from as many categories of victimization living in as many cities and towns in European Russia as funding for research permitted. Survivors in this volume lived in Moscow, Saint Petersburg, Staritsa, Vologda, and Kotlas. Their parents ranged from peasants to leaders of the Bolshevik Party, from manual workers to intellectuals.

I designed each interview to include three major sections: the interviewee's childhood before his or her parents' arrest, the experience of partial or full orphanhood, and the individual's life as an adult Soviet citizen after Stalin's death. Within each of these sections, there were some standard questions. Questions about the children's living arrangements before their parents' arrest elicited information about how Soviet families lived during the 1920s and 1930s as well as about the individual child's beginnings. Relations with teachers and fellow schoolchildren after the parents' arrest opened the way for discussion of stigmatization. World War II was a defining experience for all of these children; several questions related to that period. I asked survivors what they recalled about Stalin's death. A series of questions addressed how their status as children of enemies of the people influenced opportunities for higher education and employment.

The Communist party-state cultivated an insistently collective public culture during these survivors' lives in the Soviet Union. These children were taught to remember certain things, from Lenin's love of children to the outbreak and sources of victory in World War II, to collective and highly public mourning after Stalin's death.[15] These interviews reveal that parents and older relatives scrupulously imparted and nurtured *only* those memories that were socially and politically approved as a way to protect their children from political or social harm. Against this background, influential work of the French sociologist Maurice Halbwachs on collective memory seems especially compelling. Halbwachs argued that all memory depends upon the individual's social experience, his or her membership in a collective. He went so far as to argue that only the act of reminiscing with others via conversation or commemoration ensured that a memory remained in the individual's mind.[16] He saw even autobiographical memory as "always rooted in other people. Only group members remember."[17]

Even so, as a recent review of research methodologies using personal narratives concluded, "To put our point bluntly: Individuals are shaped by their contexts but never reducible to them."[18] In these interviews we detect the survivors' movement back and forth between different realms or layers of public, collective, and individual memory. David Pillemer, an expert on the psychology of memory, offers the term "personal event memory" in his work on the psychology of "momentous events" and their influence on how individuals subsequently live their lives.[19] I heard evidence of collective and individual memory in these interviews; I concluded that each type of memory contributes to our understanding of the "momentous events" and their lifelong legacies.

Personal events did occur within the larger collective experience of terror and repression for these children, and most survivors did go on to share those memories in adulthood with fellow survivors. Yet, some moments in these interviews seem to issue from the individual's personal memory more than from the collective memory of child victims of Soviet repression. My method was to allow each person to describe specific moments, emotions, or reflections as fully as he or she desired. This means that the questions may have been the same, but the resulting interviews differed in emphasis in the survivors' understanding of what happened and what those events meant in their lives and the history of the Soviet regime.

A survivor would frequently signal his or her move away from historical or public memory toward more intimate, affective domains of memory by making a transition in the interview. This transition was not just emotional and mental; it was physical and linguistic for both the interviewee and me as interviewer. Robert Kraft observed similar shifts in Holocaust survivors' physical and mental stances when he watched videos of their oral testimonies. "Sometimes . . . while providing testimony, these survivors appear immersed in visualizing the events, where the outside world dissolves and the survivors reexperience the events of the past."[20] In my experience with child survivors of Soviet trauma, when the interviewees retreated further into memory, some broke eye contact and seemed to travel far from the place where we sat. At these moments in the interviews, the survivors transitioned from formal, Soviet-trained, upright posture to a more internal shape; typically their faces gradually turned toward their laps as they leaned slightly forward into themselves. Their voices often dropped. In their language, they moved from the past tense to the present tense. The shift to the present tense mid-narrative may strike the reader as jarring, but it signals the survivor's emotional return to a highly charged moment in his or her memory.

As interviewer, I also retreated as much as possible during these moments, becoming absolutely still physically, lowering my voice, and sometimes even shifting from the formal "you" form used with adults in the Russian language to the familiar "you" form an adult would use with a child. My impression was that these were the most vulnerable moments for the survivors. I resisted pressing for more information that might enrich the historical record, wary that doing so might cause the survivor destabilizing distress. One linguistic choice I found myself making as the survivors moved into this vulnerable memory state was to adopt the words they were using for their parents, as they shifted from "my father" and "my mother" to the more familiar Papa or Mama. These violations of Russian verbal etiquette on my part resulted from my effort to join the memory realm they had entered and to signal beneficence. Most interviewees responded in kind, signaling mutuality by addressing me in the familiar you—"*ty*"—form and calling me by a diminutive of my first name ("Katen'ka" rather than "Katya").

I was careful to conclude each interview with the survivor fully returned to the present and his or her adult persona. I often ended the interview with the question, "What are you most proud of from your life?" Their answers usually focused on work and family, two crucial factors in their well-being.

A few words about recent research on memory are in order. Studies on autobiographical memory indicate that the child survivors' memories are more valid as sources on their personal histories than one might initially expect, given their advanced age and the time that had elapsed since the events they described in the interviews. Several generations of psychologists have shown that individuals are more likely to recall negative events in greater detail the further removed they are in time from the negative event. In addition, the more intense the emotions infusing the original event, the more likely the individuals are to recall it accurately and vividly.[21]

Often the memories are visual. The testimonies of these survivors of childhood trauma are indeed highly visual. The objects of their attention to their surroundings during critical events varied in their recollections of such moments as their parents' or their own arrests. Some of those visual memories remained vivid into their old age, as in the case of Aleksandr Yudelevich Zakgeim, who recalled the distinctive color of the sweater his mother was wearing, and of Inna Aronovna Gaister, who recalled exactly how her nanny was holding her baby sister while security police searched their apartment. You might see these visual images as clues to the emotions the child was experiencing most intensely at vulnerable moments. This visual record in memory suggests how children processed their "entirely new and utterly horrifying reality."[22]

Deborah Davis and Elizabeth Loftus offer the intriguing hypothesis that the type of emotion experienced influences what the mind focuses on in an unexpected, stressful situation. Will someone under threat focus primarily on the source of the threat? Or will stress and fear broaden one's attention and force it to shift rapidly among various images from the scene? Davis and Loftus argue for the latter scenario, stating that "during real-life stressful events there are often multiple central concerns and therefore multiple pulls for attention, some internal and some external—such as the need to monitor threatening

persons, the need to control one's own reactions and plan strategies
for survival, concerns regarding vulnerable children or the elderly,
searching for and monitoring opportunities for protection or escape,
and so on."[23] These findings seem most relevant to child survivors'
descriptions of their parents' arrests.

Studies on memory and aging have also established that the neuro-
physiology of aging favors memory with emotional content, because
its storage center in the brain—the amygdala—undergoes the least de-
terioration of all brain regions during aging.[24] Mara Mather has concluded that "in contrast with functioning in the physical and cognitive
domains, emotional functioning does not deteriorate with age. Instead,
if anything, it actually grows more effective across the life span."[25]

Child survivors of Soviet repression often include positive memories
and express positive emotions in their testimonies, with the most frequent positive emotion being gratitude to those persons who helped
them survive and succeed even as stigmatized victims. This may sur-
prise readers expecting a relentless recitation of losses and traumatic
episodes. The very fact that they lived to tell the tale may encourage
them to look for factors that contributed to their resilience and survival. This cohort of Soviet citizens was also the age group most thoroughly indoctrinated in mandatory gratitude to the Communist Party,

Classroom in Stalingrad, early 1940s (Private collection of Irina Dubrovina)

the Soviet state, and Joseph Stalin. They had to read and repeat the expression "Thank you, Comrade Stalin, for my happy childhood!" much as an American child has to repeat the Pledge of Allegiance.[26]

Expressing gratitude was a well-practiced skill; these survivors transferred the object of their gratitude from the Party and Stalin to those who saved them from the Stalinist system. We might also explain these survivors' positive memories as a product of this group's peculiar perspective as a tiny minority of child victims of Soviet political repression who survived well into old age and recognized fully their exceptional good fortune in having done so.

Research on how memory forms in childhood and endures into adulthood raises questions about this group as individuals who grew up in the Soviet, Stalinist political and educational system. In one sense, most of these children should have been "memory-disabled" because their traumatic experiences were taboo topics from the 1930s, when they occurred, until the late 1980s, when Gorbachev's policy of glasnost enabled them to join in the national reexamination of Stalin's terror. Based on studies of children undergoing painful medical procedures or natural disasters, it seems that the more children talk about their feelings shortly after the trauma, the better they subsequently remember it. Moreover, their emotional coping mechanisms improve if they have been able to discuss their feelings about trauma in detail with a parent or other caring adult: "The way in which children make sense of their stressful experiences, often through participating in joint reminiscing with their parents, helps them to place these stressful experiences in an appropriate context, in which children develop a sense of control over their life experiences through the ability to understand and regulate their emotional reactions."[27]

This was rarely an option for child victims of Soviet political repression. As Irina Dubrovina and other child survivors of Soviet traumas so frequently declare, "Silence was salvation." Not only were Soviet children often instructed never to discuss their parents' arrest outside their apartments, but the remaining adult caretakers also maintained silence about arrests in an effort to protect the children and themselves from further hazard. Any revisiting of the event and processing of its emotional impact was most likely to take place within the child's own mind.

However, these children had highly trained memory skills. The Soviet educational system in the 1930s and 1940s did much to ensure that children's minds would have far greater memory resources than children in more affluent or less authoritarian societies. Memorization was a core pedagogical method. Memorization of poetry had a long history in Russian culture in the nineteenth century. Because of chronic shortages of paper, books, and other school supplies, as well as the endurance of the pre-Soviet tradition of memorization, much learning in Soviet schools took place via memorization, oral repetition, recitation, and oral exams. Children memorized not only multiplication tables, but also Pushkin's poetry and everything else in the school curriculum. Oral exams required highly developed memory skills. Although rote learning through incessant memorization might not encourage creativity, it surely made memory a disciplined capacity for Soviet schoolchildren.[28] Indeed, a former Soviet teacher justified the practice of requiring kindergarteners to memorize fifteen poems by explaining, "Once a child becomes accustomed to memorizing brief poems, he will be able to memorize big textbooks and scientific problems more easily. In that sense, we regard memorization as a technical skill to be learned early."[29] Even without the opportunity to share their memories with others well into their adult lives, the child survivors retained their memories. Maya Rudolfovna Levitina offers an explicit description of the irruption of these memories into her consciousness, even when she was engaged in highly sociable activities. Tamara Nikolaevna Morozova also states explicitly that she was conscious both of her highly developed memory as a twelve-year-old, and of her determination to hold onto key episodes in her memories of childhood.

Finally, the conversations these survivors had with each other as adults in the 1980s, and for some of them as early as the 1950s during Khrushchev's rule or the 1970s during the dissident movement, nurtured the memories they possessed. These conversations provided opportunities to compare notes, share details, and assess similarities and differences. Because core memories of trauma had endured, they had a reservoir of "gist" memory to tap into once they were able to enter into conversation or research their parents' files in KGB archives.[30] Halbwachs would recognize the resulting recitations, repetitions, and commemorations of their experiences precisely as collective memory, which secured the memories through the collective association and discourse. Indeed, the motivation behind civic organizations committed to capturing the personal memories of the Soviet system's victims—Memorial, Conscience, and The Return—was largely to establish an authentic collective memory of victims' histories to contest the official, public memory promoted by the Soviet party-state. The Narodnyi Arkhiv (People's Archive) established at the same time did not restrict itself to victims of the Soviet system, but rather invited any member of the community to deposit his or her story there.[31]

I believe that these interviews illustrate a dynamic relationship between individual memory and collective memory, with each reinforcing the other.[32] Real things happened to these children, often catapulting them into overwhelming mental and emotional solitude. Many of the episodes the survivors recall have other people in them, yet a striking number of episodes involve no other human beings, from the isolation cell in an NKVD detention center to the open fields of exile locations. Fellow survivors may have been able to reinforce and influence such recollections by describing similar incidents in their lives at group meetings of Memorial or The Return or through published memoirs, but the original event, its immediate processing, and its recollection were often singular, neither social nor collective.

This leads us to the question of individual victims' memories as evidence or historical sources. The Holocaust shaped much of the debate about victims' voices in the historical record of twentieth-century Europe. Cold War politics enabled German historians to exclude pathos and victims' narratives from scholarship on the Holocaust in the name of scientific objectivity until the mid-1980s. In the United States, the historiography of slavery and the experience of Native Americans have displayed an analogous trajectory toward the inclusion of victims' voices and their pathos in the historical record. In the historiography about the Soviet era, much in the contentious debates through 1991 about Leninism and Stalinism focused on the legitimacy of personal, subjective testimonies, primarily in memoirs, as historical evidence.

After the collapse of the Soviet party-state and Soviet empire in 1991, the flood of personal testimonies swamped the barricades that Soviet and many Western historians had erected against victims' narratives, subjectivity, and pathos. Few historians would now disagree with Saul Friedlander's or James Young's position that victims' voices through personal testimony are not only legitimate, but indeed necessary to understand the full story. More than a decade ago, Young acknowledged the ability of a survivor-historian such as Friedlander to violate and thereby undermine "two of the traditional taboos of rational historiography: the sound of the historian's voice and the memory of the eye-witness."[33] The interviews in this volume violate those taboos by making explicit the historian's presence and possible influence in the research process and by presenting the eyewitnesses' memory in transcription as a legitimate gateway to learning what happened to children of politically repressed parents, how the survivors recall what happened, and what implications each survivor drew from the recollection of his or her childhood experiences.

The testimonies in this book are what child survivors remembered in 2005–2007 about events that had taken place seventy or more years earlier. The child survivors in this volume ranged in age at the time they lost one or both parents to the Gulag from not-yet-born (Tamara Nikolaevna Morozova) to age twelve (Inna Aronovna Gaister). Their memories were consequently partial, sometimes emotionally intense, and in some cases influenced by family conversations over the years. Readers may well ask, "Did this really happen?" and "Is this account solely the product of this one person's memory, or the product of other, collective narratives?" Other forms of evidence inspire confidence that the events survivors describe did indeed happen. For such details as the dates of their parent or parents' arrest, official documents were at hand to confirm memory. The fragmentary descriptions of arrest scenes given by survivors who were old enough at the time to remember such scenes conformed to the instructions in Operational Order 00486, accounts in other interviews, and descriptions in many other published memoirs and oral history records.[34]

Perhaps collective memory influenced what they remembered, but details were unique to survivors' experience. Within archives of the Soviet party-state, numerous "secret" and "top secret" memoranda and internal communications also demonstrate that state officials were observing the same events survivors later recalled.[35] Survivors themselves sometimes paused to explain that their descriptions were either very murky or the product of "analyzing here, not just remembering." Their very caution in limiting their descriptions to what they were confident they could actually recall offers some reassurance that any departures from what happened were involuntary or unconscious. Some descriptions convince us of their authenticity through a small but vibrant detail, such as a scent or a color. And sometimes confirmation came in almost fantastic encounters later in life with fellow participants in major life episodes. Maya Rudolfovna Levitina had what must surely be the most remarkable such encounter of all of the survivors in this volume. As an adult in Smolensk, she met the woman who had arrested her father before her eyes in Leningrad in 1938. It seems all the more fantastic that Maya Rudolfovna Levitina then became the teacher of the child of the very woman who had taken her own father away from her as a schoolgirl.

Even with these sources of confidence in the survivors' recollections of *what happened,* it remains true that these oral testimonies are most trustworthy as evidence of *how* these survivors of childhood trauma *remembered* episodes in their lives. We undoubtedly learn much about the private spaces and previously unrecorded or unremarked moments in the personal experiences of the youngest stigmatized members of Soviet society in these interviews. But we learn even more about the various ways child survivors understood and interpreted what happened to them, and subsequently how they expressed their memories and the lessons they had taken from them on how to live as citizens of the Soviet state.

The Transcribed Interviews as Texts and Narratives

Russian native speakers transcribed the taped interviews into text. In preparing the translations, I have referred both to those texts and to the taped interviews themselves to recapture intonation, breaks, sighs, laughter, and weeping. I have included some of these stutters in a few of the translations to convey the interviews' emotional content. Such interruptions in narration remind the reader that oral testimony differs from written testimony.

When composing written memoirs, survivors have the opportunity to arrange, edit, and control their memories of traumatic experiences. As they do so, they also are likely to align their representation of past events and their meanings with the dominant narrative. They are likely to hew to the conventions of collective memory. When survivors speak during interviews for which they have not received the questions in advance, such conscious composition or unconscious adaptation to prevailing narratives is less possible. Lawrence Langer, a specialist on the literature of the Holocaust, identified such differences between oral and written testimony when he viewed videotaped interviews with Holocaust survivors in the Fortunoff Video Archive for Holocaust Testimonies at Yale University in the United States.[36]

He observed that the people conducting the interviews followed the dominant Holocaust narrative of the "survival of the human spirit" not only in their questions, but also in their reaction to survivors' responses. Often the interviewers would cut off a survivor's testimony about permanent degradation and deadening of the human spirit as a legacy of traumas; in some cases, the interviewers went so far as to end the interview altogether by turning off the taping equipment.

Langer concluded that the persons asking questions could not tolerate answers that undermined the great heroic myth of the survival of the human spirit in the Holocaust. Saul Friedlander warned historians of the Holocaust not to seek "redemptive closure" of this kind by preempting the distressing challenge that individual survivors' testimony often presents to such comforting notions as "the survival of the human spirit." Rather, in arguing for survivors' testimonies as a key element in understanding the Holocaust, he urged historians to facilitate "working through" trauma. Friedlander recognized the particular power of oral testimony as an antidote to "redemptive closure." "Working through means confronting the individual voice in a field dominated by political decisions and administrative decrees which 'neutralize' the concreteness of despair and death. . . . Working through ultimately means testing the limits of necessary and ever-defeated imagination."[37] Although survival and resilience resound throughout most of the interviews you read here, the volume concludes with an interview that verbally displays brokenness rather than triumph of the human spirit.

Langer's analysis inspired me to allow interviewees to talk at length without interruption, as well as to permit them to hesitate, pause, and sometimes fall silent for full minutes as they wrestled with an invasive memory. When I have included these narrative breaks in the translations, they enable readers to detect memories' irruptions. For these survivors of Soviet repression, memories of hunger were most likely to cause them to stumble verbally, fall silent, or weep. One colleague with whom I have discussed these breaks concluded that there is a tight emotional and subconscious connection between loss of the father and mother—emotional hunger—and the physical hunger these children experienced. I agree.[38]

Soviet Echoes in Post-Soviet Reminiscences

Scholars of Soviet culture, especially of the Stalinist period, have explored the ways Soviet citizens inscribed themselves into the Soviet narrative in their diaries and the autobiographical statements they wrote when applying to join Communist Party organizations, enter institutions of higher education, or get a job. These studies demonstrate that Soviet citizens internalized rhetorical practices, interpretative structures, and values promoted by the Soviet regime. Even these child survivors of Soviet political repression internalized Soviet values and rhetorical practices. For the children of founding activists in the

Bolshevik Party, the tension between the values their parents had originally proclaimed and their fate at the hands of the regime they had helped to construct was especially acute. The most obvious example of this tension in the interviews included here is the betrayal felt by children of Jewish Old Bolsheviks who had imbibed the socialist ideal of internationalism but in the late 1940s became victims of Stalin's official anti-Semitism.

Born in the 1920s and 1930s, these child survivors lived the first sixty or seventy years of their lives inside Soviet culture, instructed in its regulations, attuned to its rhetoric, and disciplined to play by the Soviet government's rules as stigmatized supplicants whose opportunities were always conditional, rather than guaranteed. One of the most frequent interview experiences involved the disjunction between their Soviet understanding of history as a social science and the questions I asked as a U.S. oral historian interested in affective history and factors in survival and resilience. Most interviewees thought that their primary role in the interview would be to provide evidence about the state's actions against their families. They expected to contribute to the political history of the Soviet system. Questions about the personal or emotional impact of state policies perplexed them. "I have a document," they would say as they described their parents' arrest, imprisonment, exile, or execution. If a question stimulated an affective memory, they might hesitate to express the emotion or, as in Aleksandr Yudelevich Zakgeim's case, cautiously ask permission to share such details.

Irina Paperno has explained that part of this impulse has its origins in the Russian—as opposed to the purely Soviet—historicist tradition. From the 1830s, when Russian intellectuals discovered Hegelian historicism, through the Soviet era of an even more monolithically deterministic Marxist historical materialism, Russian, Soviet, and post-Soviet memoirists composed what Paperno calls "a paradigmatic Russian story: the story of a man forged by history."[39] In this worldview, history shapes individuals and is thus the most highly valued frame. Paperno concluded that the multitude of "memoirs and diaries published en masse at the end of the Soviet epoch tend to tell stories of intimate lives shaped by catastrophic political and historical forces, with the terror and the war figuring as the defining moments and organizing metaphors."[40] The survivors in this anthology display the effort to "align selves, in the presence of the community, across the historical and political divide of Stalinism."[41] Added to this Russian and Soviet cultural attunement to grand political narratives, the

survivors' decades of being discreet about private matters as a matter
of cultural practice and family survival complicated their discussion
with me, a foreign researcher, about the emotions they experienced as
children or adults.

At least two other Soviet legacies contributed to interviewees' dis-
comfiture over the gap between what they understood to be legitimate
evidence and my queries about feelings. The first was Soviet official
denigration of sentimentality or pathos in the Bolshevik hierarchy of
values. The Bolshevik version of socialism was insistently "scientific"
rather than what they deemed the inferior "utopian" or sentimental
variant.[42] Bolshevik revolutionaries and leaders in the Soviet government were expected to exhibit *tverdost'*—toughness, firmness, even
ruthlessness.[43] Private emotions and attention to the human costs of
building the first model Socialist society were at best indulgences,
and at worst signs of reprehensible weakness. The demands of World
War II reinforced this value system, as did the overwhelming challenges of reconstructing all that the war destroyed. The Soviet era was
replete with campaigns, struggles, battles, and fronts. Consequently,
a good Soviet citizen was always a civic or military warrior who displayed a soldier's emotional self-discipline and fortitude.

Another obvious Soviet legacy that influenced interviewees' rhetorical impulses was their experience as petitioners to the Soviet regime for rehabilitation of their parents after Stalin's death, usually in
the 1950s, as well as their own application to the post-Soviet Russian
government in the 1990s for the legal status of victim of unjustified
political repression as children of repressed parents. Rehabilitation
for their parents, both those who were executed or died in the penal
system and those who survived their sentences, became possible as
early as 1953. Most parents received (often posthumously) rehabilitation after Nikita Khrushchev's denunciation of Stalinist repression at
the Twentieth Congress of the Communist Party in 1956.[44] The small
slip of paper—the certificate of rehabilitation—that they received for
their parents' rehabilitation proved to be essential decades later. In
the 1990s, children gained the right to see their parents' dossiers in
state archives, including transcripts of their interrogations, but only
if they could provide a parent's rehabilitation certificate. "I have a
document," was the first requirement in receiving the Soviet and the
post-Soviet Russian government's acknowledgment of what had happened to them and their parents. And what mattered in those state
documents were dates of arrest, sites of imprisonment, locations of
exile, and records of interactions with official institutions to prove a

child had accompanied a parent into exile to a "special settlement."[45] Details about physical and emotional trauma were not required or even desired as evidence.

Readers will detect some commonly held values among this group of post-Soviet citizens of the Russian Federation that we may attribute to Soviet culture. First is the universal view that higher education, preferably in the sciences, was essential. Second is an aversion to ethnic or national prejudice—an aversion that some survivors attribute explicitly to Marxist internationalism. Third is a sense of responsibility to entities larger than themselves, a collective commitment nurtured through Soviet education, membership in Communist Party youth organizations, and employment in Soviet institutions as adults. Some or all of these values played in the survivors' decision to participate in an interview. They saw their interviews as a way to contribute to the international record of Soviet history.

How Representative Are These Interviews?

In a small volume such as this one, ten survivors out of a community of ten million child victims of Soviet repression cannot represent the entire group. I had several criteria in choosing these ten interviews. The categories or campaigns against "enemies" into which their parents fell was the first, and came to include prerevolutionary gentry, former imperial military officers, Socialist Revolutionaries, the scientific intelligentsia, forced deportees from the western borderlands on the eve of World War II, persons accused of spreading war rumors in June 1941, slave laborers returned to the USSR from German captivity after World War II, high-ranking Old Bolsheviks, and opponents of Stalin in the intraparty struggle for succession after Lenin's death in 1924. I also tried to include survivors who lived outside Moscow; at the time of their interviews, they lived in major cities, regional capitals, and small towns.

The national identity of the children's parents or as stated on their own Soviet passports was still another criterion in my selections. These ten include Russians, Poles, and Jews. Parents' "class" origins or occupations here include high Party officials, prominent scientists, professors, physicians, and workers of peasant background. Finally, I sought to include as much variety of attitudes toward the Soviet era and Marxism-Leninism as possible.

Much about these men and women makes them exceptional among their fellow ten million child victims. First, they physically survived into adulthood, when so many did not. Among even this small group, several lost siblings or cousins to childhood death, some in special settlements, most to the widespread hunger, tuberculosis, and typhus of World War II, and the famine of 1946–1947. The men included here were in their late sixties, seventies, and eighties at a time when male life expectancy in the Russian Federation hovered around fifty-eight years.[46] Second, all of these survivors lived in European Russia; seven had spent most of their lives in Moscow (four) or Saint Petersburg (three). They thus do not represent the survivors in non-European Soviet republics.[47] Survivors in post-Soviet Ukraine, Kazakhstan, Belarus, and the Baltic states might recall the traumatic episodes of family destruction described here in much the same ways, but their reflections on their adult lives as Soviet citizens until 1991, and as citizens of newly independent states thereafter, about the long-term political and personal meanings of those common traumas would likely differ. Third, these survivors are exceptional in their psychological well-being, lengthy marriages, steady work lives, and post-Soviet civic activism.[48] Most constructed satisfying personal and professional lives.

The persons whose lives you will enter in this volume often thanked me at the end of each interview for listening to their stories. They survived. They spoke. In their name, I thank you for taking the time to read what they had to say.

Notes

1. Evgenia Semyonovna Ginzburg, *Journey into the Whirlwind,* trans. Paul Stevenson and Max Hayward (New York: Harcourt, 1967).
2. Soviet authors often presented elderly peasant women as the embodiment of Russian truth questioning Soviet power. Two influential examples were Aleksander I. Solzhenitsyn, "Matryona's Home," in *The Solzhenitsyn Reader. New and Essential Readings,* ed. Edward E. Ericson and Daniel J. Mahoney (Intercollegiate Studies Institute, 2009), and Valentin Rasputin, *Farewell to Matyora,* trans. Antonina Bouis (Northwestern University Press, 1995).
3. Evgenia Semyonovna Ginzburg, *Journey into the Whirlwind,* trans. Paul Stevenson and Max Hayward (San Diego, New York, London: A Harvest Book. A Helen and Kurt Wolff Book. Harcourt, Inc., 1995), 304.
4. Ibid., 337.
5. See Irina Paperno, *Stories of the Soviet Experience. Memoirs, Diaries, Dreams* (Ithaca, New York: Cornell University Press, 2009).
6. Yakovlev was the primary Communist Party architect of *glasnost* and *perestroika* under Gorbachev.
7. See Nanci Adler, *The Gulag Survivor. Beyond the Soviet System* (Transactions, 2004) and Kathleen E. Smith, *Remembering Stalin's Victims. Popu-*

lar Memory and the End of the USSR (Ithaca, New York: Cornell University Press, 1996).

8. "Dekulakization," an official policy from the end of 1929, targeted prosperous peasants—so-called kulaks—for expropriation, forced resettlement, and sometimes execution. On the "Doctors' Plot" see Jonathan Brent and Vladimir Naumov, *Stalin's Last Crime: The Plot Against the Jewish Doctors, 1948–1953* (New York: Harper Perennial, 2004).

9. S. S. Vilensky et al., compilers, *Deti GULAGA 1918–1956* (Moscow: International Democracy Fund; Hoover Institution of War, Revolution and Peace, Stanford University, 2002).

10. In the event, "deprivation of freedom" meant imprisonment under the watch of NKVD officials in prisons, camps, and special settlements.

11. The description of the interview as a mutual sighting comes from Alessandro Portelli, *The Death of Luigi Trastulli and Other Stories: Form and Meaning in Oral History* (Albany: State University of New York, 1991), 61, as quoted in Mary Jo Maynes, Jennifer L. Pierce, and Barbara Laslett, *Telling Stories: The Use of Personal Narratives in the Social Sciences and History* (Ithaca, New York: Cornell University Press, 2008), 120. Maynes, Pierce, and Laslett also use the phrase "intersubjective encounter," especially in Chapter 4, 98–125.

12. Many works discuss the kitchen-table phenomenon. The most extended discussion of the late-Soviet and post-Soviet period is in Nancy Ries, *Russian Talk: Culture and Conversation During Perestroika* (Ithaca, New York: Cornell University Press, 1997). See also Svetlana Boym, *Common Places: Mythologies of Everyday Life in Russia* (Cambridge, Massachusetts: Harvard University Press, 1995).

13. As quoted in Maynes, Pierce, and Laslett, *Telling Stories,* 120.

14. I secured the interviewees' formal consent as required by U.S. federal regulations on the protection of human subjects in research.

15. Nina Tumarkin, *Lenin Lives! The Lenin Cult in Soviet Russia* (Cambridge, Massachusetts: Harvard University Press, 1983); Tumarkin, *The Living and the Dead: The Rise and Fall of the Cult of World War II in Russia* (Cambridge, Massachusetts: Harvard University Press, 1994); Boym, *Common Places.*

16. Lewis A. Coser, "Introduction," in Maurice Halbwachs, *On Collective Memory,* ed. and trans. Lewis A. Coser (Chicago: University of Chicago Press, 1992), 24.

17. Ibid.

18. Maynes, Pierce, and Laslett, *Telling Stories,* 67.

19. David B. Pillemer, "Can the Psychology of Memory Enrich Historical Analyses of Trauma?," *History and Memory* 16, no. 2 (Fall/Winter 2004): 147; and Pillemer, *Momentous Events, Vivid Memories: How Unforgettable Moments Help Us Understand the Meaning of Our Lives* (Cambridge, Massachusetts: Harvard University Press, 1998).

20. Robert N. Kraft, "Emotional Memory in Survivors of the Holocaust: A Qualitative Study of Oral Testimony," in *Memory and Emotion,* ed. Daniel Reisberg and Paula Hertel (Oxford and New York: Oxford University Press, 2004), 354.

21. Mahzarin R. Banaji and Curtis Hardin, "Affect and Memory in Retrospective Reports," in *Autobiographical Memory and the Validity of Retrospective*

Reports, ed. Norbert Schwarz and Seymour Sudman (New York: Springer-Verlag, 1994), 71–86.

22. The phrase comes from James Young's reflections on memory in the history of the Holocaust.

23. Deborah Davis and Elizabeth F. Loftus, "Expectancies, Emotion, and Memory Reports for Visual Events," in *The Visual World in Memory,* ed. James R. Brockmole (Hove and New York: Psychology Press Taylor and Francis Group, 2009), 190–195.

24. Mara Mather, "Aging and Emotional Memory," in *Memory and Emotion,* ed. Daniel Reisberg and Paula Hertel (Oxford and New York: Oxford University Press, 2004), 276–277.

25. Ibid., 294.

26. See Jeffrey Brooks, *"Thank You, Comrade Stalin!" Soviet Public Culture from Revolution to Cold War* (Princeton, New Jersey: Princeton University Press, 2001). On Soviet childhood overall, see Lisa Kirschenbaum, *Small Comrades: Revolutionizing Childhood in Soviet Russia, 1917–1932* (New York: Routledge, 2000); and Katriona Kelly, *Children's World: Growing Up in Russia, 1890–1991* (New Haven: Yale University Press, 2008).

27. Robyn Fivush and Jessica McDermott Sales, "Children's Memories of Emotional Events," in *Memory and Emotion,* ed. Daniel Reisberg and Paula Hertel (Oxford and New York: Oxford University Press, 2004), 266.

28. Mikhail Gronas has recently argued that the Russian and Soviet tradition of memorizing poetry is a core aspect of Russian cultural memory and the Russian literary tradition. Mikhail Gronas, *Cognitive Poetics and Cultural Memory: Russian Literary Mnemonics* (New York: Routledge, 2011), especially Chapter 3.

29. Quoted in ibid., 90.

30. "Study after study has shown that memory for peripheral detail suffers while memory for gist or thematic content improves with heightened emotionality." Jessica D. Payne, Lynn Nadel, Willoughby B. Britton, and W. Jake Jacobs, "The Biopsychology of Trauma and Memory," in *Memory and Emotion,* ed. Daniel Reisberg and Paula Hertel (Oxford and New York: Oxford University Press, 2004), 107.

31. On the history of Memorial, see Nanci Adler, *Victims of Soviet Terror: The Story of the Memorial Movement* (New York: Praeger, 1993); Smith, *Remembering Stalin's Victims*; on the People's Archive, see Paperno, *Stories of the Soviet Experience.*

32. For some of these child survivors, such communities of victims who could support individual memories and create a collective memory of their shared experiences dated to the late 1950s, during Khrushchev's de-Stalinization campaign.

33. James E. Young, "Between History and Memory," *History and Memory* 1 (1997): 51.

34. See, for example, Orlando Figes, *The Whisperers: Private Life in Stalin's Russia* (New York: Metropolitan, 2007).

35. S. Vilensky, *Deti Gulaga, 1918–1956,* includes these documents in Russian; Cathy A. Frierson and Semyon S. Vilensky, *Children of the Gulag* (New Haven: Yale University Press, 2010), presents many of them in English translation.

36. Lawrence Langer, *Holocaust Testimonies: The Ruins of Memory* (New Haven: Yale University Press, 1993).

37. Saul Friedländer, "Trauma, Transference and 'Working Through' in Writing the History of the Shoah," *History and Memory* 4, no. 1 (1992): 39–55. Dominick LaCapra also advocated a process of "working through" by the German public and intellectual elite in confrontation and mourning of the Holocaust, including victims' suffering in the process. See his "Revisiting the Historians' Debate: Mourning and Genocide," *History and Memory* 1 (1997): 80–112.

38. Elizabeth Ransome Stine, comment during a research talk I delivered at the Center for the Humanities at the University of New Hampshire in 2008.

39. Paperno, *Stories of the Soviet Experience*, 11.

40. Ibid., 56.

41. Ibid., 41.

42. The founding fathers, Karl Marx and Friedrich Engels, distinguished their program from French Utopian Socialism, employed scientific metaphors and patterns of argument, and explicitly contrasted Scientific and Utopian Socialism.

43. Barbara Evans Clements, *Bolshevik Women* (Cambridge, Massachusetts: Cambridge University Press, 1997).

44. See Adler, *The Gulag Survivor*, and Smith, *Remembering Stalin's Victims*.

45. On special settlements, see Lynne Viola, *The Unknown Gulag: The Lost World of Stalin's Special Settlements* (New York: Oxford University Press, 2007).

46. See Tamara Men, Paul Brennan, Paolo Boffetta, and David Zaridze, "Russian Mortality Trends for 1991–2001: Analysis by Cause and Region," *BMJ: British Medical Journal* 327, no. 7421 (October 25, 2003): 964–966.

47. See, for example, Vieda Skuldans, *The Testimony of Lives: Narrative and Memory in Post-Soviet Latvia* (New York: Routledge, 1997).

48. Adler, *The Gulag Survivor*, and Katharine G. Baker and Julia B. Gippenreiter, "The Effects of Stalin's Purge on Three Generations of Russian Families," *Family Studies* 3, no. 1 (1996): 5–35.

CHAPTER ONE

"If you are interested in this kind of detail, I have remembered for all these years the smell of the perfume she was wearing and the color of her blouse"

ALEKSANDR YUDELEVICH ZAKGEIM

Moscow

April 17, 2005

Transcribed by Elena Vetrova

Introduction

Born in Moscow in 1930, Aleksandr Yudelevich Zakgeim was the son of secular Jewish parents who were not members of the Communist Party. His father was a professor at Moscow State University; his mother was an economist in the trade union bureaucracy. They lived well, with a peasant nanny who had been displaced from her village by the policies of dekulakization and collectivization. Aleksandr Yudelevich Zakgeim's father, Yudel, was arrested in 1936 for reasons the family never fully understood. Family members believed that his comments about state policies during special seminars with his Moscow State University students contributed to his fate. Aleksandr Yudelevich's mother, Olga Lvovna Sliozberg, was arrested soon after her husband for being a wife of an enemy of the people. She

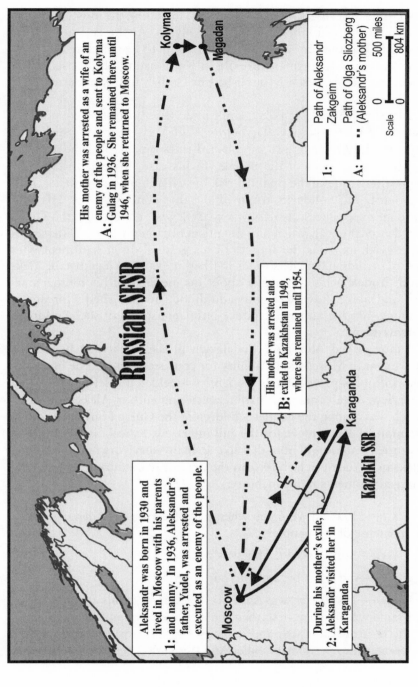

His mother was arrested as a wife of an
enemy of the people and sent to Kolyma
A: Gulag in 1936. She remained there until
1946, when she returned to Moscow.

Kolyma

Magadan

Russian SFSR

His mother was arrested and
exiled to Kazakhstan in 1949,
B: where she remained until 1954.

Aleksandr was born in 1930 and
lived in Moscow with his parents
1: and nanny. In 1936, Aleksandr's
father, Yudel, was arrested and
executed as an enemy of the people.

Karaganda

Kazakh SSR

During his mother's exile,
2: Aleksandr visited her in
Karaganda.

Moscow

Scale

	Path of Aleksandr
1:	Zakgeim
A:	Path of Olga Sliozberg
	(Aleksandr's mother)

0   500 miles

0   804 km

The journeys of Aleksandr Yudelevich Zakgeim and his mother, Olga Sliozberg, 1936–1954 (Map by Eric Pugliano) spent time in several Gulag installations, including the most notorious of Siberian forced labor complexes: Kolyma. At the end of her first term, she returned to Moscow in 1946, only to be rearrested in 1949 and sentenced to permanent exile in Kazakhstan. She subsequently wrote a memoir, recently published in English in full under the title *My Journey.*[1]

Aleksandr Yudelevich Zakgeim's interview illustrates one possible fate for children of the Gulag before August 15, 1937, at which time Operational Order 00486 established rules on the placement of the children of enemies of the people. In his case, his extended family was willing to take the political risk of saving him and his sister, feeling that family solidarity trumped all other considerations. His educational experiences also convey what Jewish children of the Gulag faced after the war, when anti-Semitism became the norm. Aleksandr Yudelevich explains the sources of his gradual disenchantment with Stalin, including his visits to his mother in exile in Kazakhstan. Aleksandr Yudelevich's comments about his memory of his mother's arrest and about how, well into adulthood, he cherished a dream of running into his father, introduce intimate aspects of such children's bereavement.

I interviewed Aleksandr Yudelevich in the kitchen of his sister's apartment in Moscow. His affinity for concision—a trait he likely developed in his profession as a scientist—yielded a brief but revealing interview. A quiet man, brilliant teacher, and author, Aleksandr Yudelevich was among the gentlest children of the Gulag I interviewed. He maintained eye contact for the full interview, as well as a composed posture. Readers will note that like so many survivors in this volume, Aleksandr Yudelevich shifts into the present tense during emotionally charged moments in his memory.

CF—How old were you when you became a so-called child of an enemy of the people?

AYu—Six years old. This was 1936.

CF—And what became of your parents?

AYu—My father was shot six months after his arrest. And Mama was in jail at first, then she was in a camp in Kolyma, then she returned in 1946, and in 1949 she was arrested again and sentenced to permanent exile. And this ended in 1955.

1. Olga Sliozberg, *My Journey,* translated by Katharine G. Baker (Evanston, Illinois: Northwestern University Press, 2011).

CF—And did you know your father's fate immediately?

AYu—No, at first they arrested my father a month and a half earlier. And Mama said that he had gone on a business trip. . . . That was the usual explanation. Then they arrested Mama. I recall both my father's and mother's arrest. But my memory of my father's arrest is very vague, there was a search. . . . This was at home. And a month and a half later, they arrested Mama. It was April 26, 1936. And before she left, she woke me up, kissed me, and left. But our relatives' official explanation was that Mama was on a business trip. I began to suspect something, I hesitate to say when exactly, at about eight years old. But not very clearly. And I fully understood what had happened at the beginning of the war, probably, when I was more than ten years old.

CF—But you said that you remember your father's arrest. Does this mean that you were able to say good-bye to him?

AYu—I did not say good-bye to him. The thing is that the search lasted, as far as I recall, all night. . . . And afterward they took him away, and I was already asleep. Both [younger sister] Ella and I were sleeping. But when Mama left, Ella didn't wake up fully, she was four years old. But I woke up, and I remember this very well. If you are interested in this kind of detail, I have remembered for all these years the smell of the perfume she was wearing and the color of her blouse. . . . It was a kind of yellow, sort of orange, yellow, a bit closer to orange. For some reason the yellow blouse, I remembered this well, somehow it clearly stuck in my memory. And the smell of her perfume to this day. This was very cheap perfume. But to this day, if I smell something similar, I have this kind of feeling that takes me back there. . . .

CF—So, when they conducted the search at the time of your mother's arrest, she was alone at home?

AYu—At that time we had what was then called a domestic worker, a nanny. I don't remember exactly whether or not she was in the apartment at that time. Apparently she was, because we must have stayed behind with her. . . . We stayed there for only a very short time. Then we moved in with my grandmother, and after that, this was our family. And, essentially, we lived together up till my grandmother's death, then my aunt's. . . .

CF—When did your grandmother, grandfather, and mother learn about your father's death?

AYu—Definitively? In 1955. Definitively. Until then, I don't recall exactly when, but already—also in the 1950s—there had been some kind of false death certificate. But we weren't completely sure. And I should say, this may sound strange, probably until I was about twenty-five years old, and maybe even older, sometimes I imagined that I would run into my father somewhere completely by accident. That he had in fact not been killed, not been shot, and that fate had tossed him somewhere and, let's say, somewhere on a business trip that I had gone on . . . . that I would run into him somewhere. But this was the kind of, you know, there are the sort of dreams that the dreamer understands cannot come true, but all of a sudden, at some moment, they appear. . . . The family in which we lived, my mother's family, this was an exceptionally affectionate family. And so when this misfortune happened to us, they all took it close to heart. At that time, well, Mama had two older sisters still living and a younger brother. And they had their families, too. The sisters were married. The eldest sister was no longer married, she had divorced. The middle sister was married, the brother was married, and they all took us in, as, well, unfortunates, naturally. And they tried very hard to compensate for our loss with their love. Whatever else may have happened to us, we never felt like victims. . . . I must say this, we didn't feel like victims.

I can tell you about my aunt's husband. His name was Vladimir Arkadievich Tronin. . . . I think he had been a member of the Communist Party since, I believe, 1918. . . . He was active, a very active participant in the civil war, he received the Order of the Red Banner in the war. And he moved in a circle of people close to power. Tomsky[2] was a close friend of his; this man later killed himself to avoid being arrested. . . . He worked closely with Kuibyshev,[3] who died peacefully according to the official version, but Vladimir Arkadievich believed that this was not true. And furthermore, he had a rather high position. He was. . . . a mem-

2. Mikhail Tomsky was an Old Bolshevik, a leader of the trade union movement before and after the Bolshevik revolution.
3. Valeryan Kuibyshev (1888–1935) was an Old Bolshevik who joined the Bolshevik faction of the Russian Social Democratic Workers Party in 1904. He served as chair of the central economic planning agencies of the Soviet Union, the Supreme Council of the National Economy and Gosplan. He was also a member of the Politburo.

ber of the Collegium, as it was called then, which means he was a deputy minister. A member of the Collegium of the People's Commissariat of the River Fleet of Russia, the Russian Republic. That is, he was already, so to say, close to the minister. And, just in case, they arrested people in such positions on the spot, all the more so with the kinds of connections he had. And we represented mortal danger for him. But he never renounced us, nor did he, how to say this, ever try to keep us at a distance. Never. So, that was my uncle, my aunt's husband. The other uncle, my mother's brother, Mikhail Lvovich, his work was always secret. He was one of the founders of Soviet radar. . . . Therefore, all of this was also mortally dangerous for him, too. There was not a single instance when he tried to distance himself from us. For him, we were the closest of relatives. So those were the circumstances in which we lived.

CF—On this subject, how did it turn out that you stayed in the family, and weren't in an orphanage?

AYu—They tried to take us and put us in an orphanage. But my grandmother made such a terrible scene, and, apparently, they didn't have absolute orders to take us mandatorily. They didn't take everyone. The thing was that our parents weren't, well, chief among those who had been arrested, the most important people. And therefore, apparently, it was just an attempt. But Grandmother defended us with all her might, she did not let go of us. Then she went to a reception with Krupskaya.[4] Mama describes this episode with Krupskaya in her memoirs. Krupskaya said that she couldn't do anything for Mama, but if Grandmother wanted, she could set us up in a good orphanage. To which Grandmother said, "Hand over your own children to an orphanage." If you keep in mind that Krupskaya had no children, this was like an insult. . . . There weren't any reprisals. We lived with the family.

CF—And was this considered exceptional?

AYu—No. There were many for whom it was like this. It was simply that, as I understand it, such a gigantic mass of people was arrested, that it wasn't possible to send everyone to orphanages. So we were lucky.

4. Nadezhda Krupskaya was Vladimir Lenin's wife and a high Party official in her own right.

CF—Did you have classmates who also lost their parents? . . .

AYu—At that time, it was School no. 170 of the Sverdlovsk Region of Moscow. Well, by the way, at our school there were. . . . Not far from this school there was a hotel, I don't recall what it was called then, later it was named the Central Hotel. The Comintern[5] staff lived there. . . . Foreigners. Some of them studied at the same school I did. Including some in my grade. I now recall only one, sorry. That was Jan Pretel, the son of one of the leaders of the Spanish Communist Party. Of course, a large number of people there were arrested during those years. But it would seem, in any case, I don't know anything about this, it would seem that those who studied at my school, their parents avoided this fate. But I don't know for sure. It wasn't very acceptable for us to talk about this.

CF—Did you believe that you needed to hide your parents' fate?

AYu—I never hid this, *never*. I should tell you honestly that it never occurred to me. My view was, it happened—so it happened. The question of how just this was, how unjust, for me at that time, of course, that was the question. But for me, I worried about it. And so if someone had started to talk to me at that time—no one did—I wouldn't have, well, expressed myself in much detail. But I believed that it was unfair. . . .

CF—Well, how did your teachers treat you? Were there any hints?

AYu—There were no nuances of any kind. . . .

CF—And what was your attitude toward Soviet power, while your mama was in the camp?

AYu—Absolutely positive. . . . It seems that my doubts about Soviet power appeared very late, in the 1960s. . . . I joined the Komsomol.[6] I wasn't, perhaps, the very best, but I was a sincere member of the Komsomol. . . . My difficulties came with applying for higher education. But I can't even tell you why these

5. The Communist International (Comintern), based in Moscow as of 1919, was the international organization of Communist parties throughout the world, committed to fomenting world revolution.
6. Communist Youth League, the Communist Party's youth organization for children beginning from age fourteen.

difficulties arose. . . . In 1948. At that time, I don't know what could have played a role. Both that I, that my parents had been repressed, and it's completely possible that the fact simply that I was a Jew could have played a role. I tried to enter the Physics Department of Moscow State University through my gold medal.[7] And with a special certificate as the winner of a Physics Olympiad that had been organized there. Well, they didn't admit me, but they practically didn't admit a single Jewish boy or Jewish girl. . . . At that time, for persons who had that kind of medal, the application process was like this: the person would have an interview, there was no official exam, and after that, unless he proved to be completely inappropriate, they would register him without entrance exams. The assistant chair of the department conducted my interview. He was a man named Vlasov, very gloomy, a very foul person. And he simply, openly, as they say, asked me an impossible question to fail me[8] . . . . I really wanted to be a physicist. I had prepared for it, I prepared in a physics study group for schoolchildren, for several years. And he asked me, specifically, "And what branch of physics would you like to study?" I said that I would like to study optics. Perhaps that was naïve, but the substance wasn't the point. He said, "Good. Do you know Newton's theory of light?" I said, "I know it. According to Newton, light was a stream of particles." "And what distinguishes the particles of different colors from each other? Mass or speed?" I said that I thought it was by mass, but that I didn't know exactly. He said, "Well, why don't you know?" And that was the end of it.

After that, since many people in the department knew me, students, even graduate students, there was some protest. Some began to agitate on my behalf. And my uncle . . . . my uncle Sliozberg, the one who worked in radar. He went there, he spoke with the department chairman, who said, "Well! We made a mistake. He didn't present the official documents showing that he was a winner of the Olympiad. If he had, we would have admitted him.

---

7. At that time, students who had earned the highest marks in all subjects received a gold medal upon graduation from high school. Such students were supposed to have virtually automatic admission to any institution of higher education they chose.

8. In Russian, the verb is "zasypat'"—"to bury" a student during an oral exam.

Let him take the exams. If he gets even a 3 on the exams, he'll be admitted. I promise you." So I began to take the exams. The first three exams were written. On the first three exams, I got three 2s.[9] Three unsatisfactory grades. At that time, I couldn't find out why they had given me this grade. That wasn't permitted.

After that, here's what happened. At that time, there were several institutes in Moscow that were permitted to admit students like me. So, I can talk precisely about three institutes of chemistry: there were two chemical-technological institutes, and an institute of chemical-mechanical engineering I know about for sure, and there was also an institute of machine-tool engineering and instrumentation that would take students like me . . . . By the way, because of this, there was a very strong cohort of students in these institutes during these years. And I was directed to go there. I went up to one of the students who knew me well from that physics study group, he sent me to some of his relatives, and they said, "Well, we have acquaintances in the Mendeleev Chemical-Technological Institute, apply there. And if something happens, they'll put in a word for you." Well, it turned out that they didn't need to put in a word for me. I submitted my application and was immediately admitted. I graduated from that institute. And, as strange as it may be, this went even further. I graduated from the institute in. . . . 1954. And at that time, there was a process called job placement. The time came to place me. So I arrive at the commission making job placements. My adviser is sitting there, some other people are sitting next to him. And he says, "Oh, good, Sasha. We have a good position for you. The Scientific-Research Institute of Fertilizers. So, please, accept it." And some man is sitting there. As it turned out later, the chief of the personnel department, as it was then called in the institute.[10] He started to say something about me, how good I was. I signed the form stating that I agreed to this job placement. And then I went out. After five minutes, a girl who had been there came out. She walked over to me and whispered, "Ivan Nikolaevich (my adviser) told me to tell you that you should disappear from the institute immediately, and don't show your face here until

9. On a scale of 1 to 5, 5 was the equivalent of an A, 4 an equivalent of a B, and so on.

10. The personnel department, the so-called department of cadres, was the base for the security police in any given institution.

tomorrow." That was so that the director of the personnel department of the institute to which I had been assigned wouldn't come to his senses and delete me from the list. And that was in 1954! . . .

CF—What was your reaction to Stalin's death?

AYu—I reacted to Stalin's death, you know, this is a very complicated question. I didn't feel a deep sense of grief. My aunt, the one whose husband was Tronin . . . . she was terrified, it wasn't clear what would become of the country. Our leader had died. I felt none of that. . . . Not long before this, well, I had had illusions that Stalin was a very great man, that he could do a great many things well. And he was doing them. But by this point, those illusions very gradually [faded], there wasn't any acute sensation. . . . But, all the same, I went with all the students at my institute to the funeral. But I stopped within literally two hundred meters of the place where that terrible crush was, where a lot of people died. The crush of people had already made me feel ill. I left this crowd and went, by the way, to that same aunt, Polina Lvovna. I spent the night at her place. Therefore, I didn't make it to the place where Stalin was lying in state. But, in any event, I didn't have the feeling that this was a good thing. That was somehow all in doubt. Where my mama was, she was in Karaganda at that time, among those who were with her, there were mixed feelings of liberation, happiness, and fear that something even worse would follow. That now Beria[11] would seize power, this would be terrible. That's what they felt. I did not feel that either.

CF—When did you find out about Khrushchev's speech at the twentieth Party congress?[12]

AYu—You know, I won't try to tell you an exact date. The speech was in February of course. But sometime in March or April, no, in April or maybe in May, this memo began to circulate in our organizations. In a kind of semisecret atmosphere. . . . Well, in the institute where I worked. They called a general assembly and read the speech aloud. I suppose that they may have read it with deletions. I can't say. But they read it. . . . No one

11. Lavrenty Beria, then head of the security services.

12. Nikita S. Khrushchev, as General Secretary of the Communist Party, delivered a speech at its twentieth congress in 1956 outlining Stalin's crimes and calling for de-Stalinization.

discussed anything. . . . They read it and we dispersed. . . . It produced, of course, a shocking impression. . . .

CF—In what way was it shocking?

AYu—Well, for the first time it openly talked about the mass repressions. About their practically complete illegality, and of course, this was shocking. . . . I had had my doubts about Stalin somewhat earlier. And at that time he fell in my eyes once and for all. . . .

CF—And what was your attitude toward Khrushchev and Brezhnev?[13]

AYu—Khrushchev. My mother was *deeply* grateful to him for that famous speech at the twentieth congress.[14] The fact that his policies changed after that caused her great confusion and disappointment. But, nevertheless, all the way until his fall from power, she had a very positive attitude toward him. I shared this opinion. I understood that Khrushchev had done quite a few stupid things. But I did not doubt that he did something great. And I don't doubt this to this day. . . . Another person who had not been in the apparatus of repressions could not have done what he did. . . . because, well, all the leaders from that time were people who had participated in this. . . . I'm a nonbeliever, but the Christian view that a robber who has repented can become a saint, this has very strong meaning for me. I don't consider Khrushchev to be a saint, but the fact that he took this step, even though it was only a partial repentance, does him a lot of credit. As for Brezhnev, from almost the very beginning to the very end, he made me a little squeamish. . . . There is one thing I want to say. Until at least the beginning of the 1990s, both my mother and I had a very good view of Lenin. What they started to say about him, what we found out at the end of the 1980s and in the 1990s, of course, changed my opinion, but to this day, I am still not convinced that Lenin was the kind of monster he seems to be to many people. . . . I can't completely consider Lenin to be a monster. . . .

After my mother was rehabilitated, after she returned, all of the people surrounding my mama were very interesting people.

13. Leonid Brezhnev, General Secretary of the Communist Party following Khrushchev's ouster, Soviet leader 1964–1982.
14. Of the Communist Party.

Basically, those who were with her in the camp. . . . in the camp, she was with quite a few remarkable people. . . . Well, for example, a rather famous writer of those days, Evgenia Ginzburg, was with her. Then there was Mirra Kizelshtein, who was Vorobyov's mother.[15] Well, and a whole slew of people. And two of those women are still alive. I stay in touch with them. . . . I really must stress that completely remarkable people were among my mama's friends. For example, Nadezhda Adolfovna Ioffe, the daughter of one of the first Soviet diplomats—Adolf Abramovich Ioffe, he was a close friend of Trotsky.[16] She died in New York, she went there when she was already in her nineties. We spent a lot of time together, she was like living history from the beginning of the century. Because among the friends at her home was, for instance, Trotsky. Bukharin recommended her for the Komsomol.[17] She knew Lenin personally. She wasn't a close acquaintance, but she met with him and so on. Such people survived, it turns out, after all that was done to them.

CF—How to put it, your family and private life were permeated completely with political history.

AYu—Everything was permeated. . . .

CF—When you became a father, did you experience any feelings that, "Now that I am a father, I lost my father early." Were there any kind of . . .

AYu—I understand. No, it seems. There was something else. Our family raised us with the view that we all must place a premium on our parental obligations. And therefore, I always loved and still love my children and grandchildren very much. . . . We love them, and they respond with love. In short, we have a very good family. . . .

CF—How do you evaluate all of these phenomena in the history of the Soviet era? The significance of the repressions, the significance of the phenomenon of children of the Gulag, orphans of repression in the history of the Soviet Union?

15. He is referring to Andrei Vorobyov, whose interview also appears in this volume.

16. Leon Trotsky, Lenin's partner in the October Revolution of 1917, Commissar of War during the civil war, and Stalin's chief rival to succeed Lenin.

17. Nikolai Bukharin, prominent Communist Party ideologist during the revolution and economist during the first decade of Soviet power. Shared power with Stalin into the 1930s, before Stalin purged him.

AYu—If we talk about significance, why do so regarding just the repressions? It needs to start earlier. At least from the end of 1917. It was terrible. But the absolutely most important, the most frightening thing that these repressions gave birth to was not even the destruction of people, not even the sad fate of children of the Gulag. The most terrible thing was the perversion of the people. By this, I mean that the masses of people lost their moral foundations. . . .

CF—What significance do you believe the repressions in the Soviet Union have for world history?

AYu—I believe that this is very important. And most of all, and if these repressions can play any kind of positive role, the only thing is as a terrible warning to the entire world about the kind of horror that can begin if you go down this path.

CHAPTER TWO

"And we began to live there in twenty-six square meters; there were thirteen of us"

INNA ARONOVNA SHIKHEEVA-GAISTER
Moscow
April 19, 2005
Transcribed by Elena Vetrova

Introduction

Inna Aronovna Gaister was born in Moscow in 1925 to two Communist Party members who subsequently rose to high positions in the Soviet state and the Party. Both parents were Jews from the Pale of Settlement who had joined the Bolshevik Party during the civil war. Their many siblings had followed similar paths to prominence in Soviet Moscow. Aron Gaister's young family lived at Government House, the most prestigious residential address in Moscow in the mid-1930s. Young Inna Aronovna even had her own room from the time she started school, as well as a beloved nanny who cared for her and her two younger sisters. Both parents were arrested in 1937. Inna Aronovna assumed the responsibility for protecting her two sisters, initially with the help of her nanny, then later among a crowd of cousins who had also lost their parents to arrest. In the course of carrying out this duty, Inna Aronovna and her family experienced evacuation, starvation, disease, and one sister's death during World War II. Inna Aronovna was

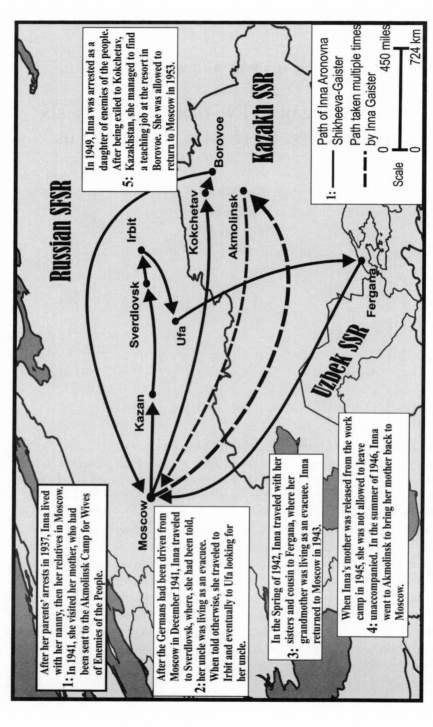

After her parents' arrests in 1937, Inna lived with her nanny, then her relatives in Moscow.
1: In 1941, she visited her mother, who had been sent to the Akmolinsk Camp for Wives of Enemies of the People.

After the Germans had been driven from Moscow in December 1941, Inna traveled to Sverdlovsk, where, she had been told,
2: her uncle was living as an evacuee. When told otherwise, she traveled to Irbit and eventually to Ufa looking for her uncle.

In the Spring of 1942, Inna traveled with her sisters and cousin to Fergana, where her grandmother was living as an evacuee. Inna
3: returned to Moscow in 1943.

When Inna's mother was released from the work camp in 1945, she was not allowed to leave
4: unaccompanied. In the summer of 1946, Inna went to Akmolinsk to bring her mother back to Moscow.

In 1949, Inna was arrested as a daughter of enemies of the people. After being exiled to Kokchetav,
5: Kazakhstan, she managed to find a teaching job at the resort in Borovoe. She was allowed to return to Moscow in 1953.

Russian SFSR

Kazakh SSR

Uzbek SSR

Irbit

Sverdlovsk

Kokchetav

Borovoe

Akmolinsk

Ufa

Kazan

Moscow

Fergana

Scale

1: ————— Path of Inna Aronovna
           Shikheeva-Gaister

    – – – – Path taken multiple times
             by Inna Gaister

0   450 miles

0   724 km

The journeys of Inna Aronovna Shikheeva-Gaister, 1937–1953 (Map by Eric Pugliano) able to enter Moscow State University in 1944, only to be arrested as a child of enemies of the people in 1949 and exiled to Kazakhstan. She returned to Moscow after Stalin's death, worked in physics, married a man whose courage, she said, "healed" her, and became a devoted mother and grandmother. With her husband's encouragement, she wrote a memoir of her life, currently available only in Russian.[1]

The section of Inna Aronovna's interview dealing with her experiences before her parents' arrests provides glimpses into the life of a privileged daughter of the Communist aristocracy. Her interview was the first to alert me to the constant displacement orphans of political repression experienced in search of stable residence. Like so many child survivors of political repression, she identifies her nanny, teachers, and school directors as the crucial Samaritans of her life after her parents were gone. Her description of her trip to visit her mother in the Akmolinsk Camp for wives of traitors to the motherland takes readers into the House of Meetings inside this Gulag installation. World War II found her in evacuation at age sixteen, caring for her younger sisters. Her repetition of the statement "We left as four. Only two returned" suggests that the loss of her youngest sister haunted her. Inna Aronovna's interview also provides a sketch of what it was like to be arrested as a young adult for the crime of being a child of enemies of the people.

I interviewed Inna Aronovna in her apartment in Moscow. The room we sat in for the interview had glass-fronted bookcases along one wall; every section of the glass had a photo of a beloved relative or friend stuck onto it. She was often impatient with my questions and looked at me from time to time as though I were a complete idiot, but she did answer even those questions she declared "primitive." I forgot one of my microphones in her apartment when I left after the interview, and she called that day to ask me to return to retrieve it. I arrived a day later to find lunch prepared and Inna Aronovna eager to be a hostess. She then confessed that she had lain awake the entire night before our interview, shaking in anxiety over having to revisit these episodes in her past.

CF—How old were you when you became a so-called child of enemies of the people?

---

1. Inna Shikheeva-Gaister, *Deti vragov naroda: Semeinaia khronika vremen kul'ta lichnosti* (Tenafly, New Jersey: Hermitage, 2003); recently republished by the publishing house Vozvrashchenie in Moscow, 2012.

IA—Let's see, Papa was arrested on June 27, 1937, and I turned twelve on August 13. So, not quite twelve years old. . . .

CF—When you were a child, in what city did you live?

IA—. . . . I was born in the city of Moscow when Papa was a student. . . . He completed the Red Professors' Department of Agronomy there. Well, and then Papa was busy. He worked with Kuibyshev[2] for a long time, then he became a member of the Commission for Soviet Control, and then in 1935, I think it was, he became the Deputy People's Commissar, dealing with agrarian questions. He was an economist. And even at that time, when there were communal apartments, we always lived in a separate apartment. At first, before I was six years old, we moved from the dormitory to Palekh Street; there we had a two-room apartment. In Government House, now it's called the House on the Embankment,[3] we moved into that same House on the Embankment, we had a four-room apartment. And there were three of us children there.

CF—So who lived in this apartment?

IA—So, we lived with Papa, we three children and the domestic worker who arrived in our family when I was two months old. Here is her photograph, even. [She points to a photo stuck onto the glass-front bookcase.]

CF—Can you tell me a bit about your parents and sisters? You said that you had two sisters?

IA—Two sisters. I was the oldest. I was born in 1925, then my sister who was born in 1930. She lives in Israel now. And my sister born in 1936; she was a year old when my parents were arrested. And she perished during the evacuation.[4] From starvation.

2. Valerian Kuibyshev (1888–1935) was an Old Bolshevik who joined the Bolshevik faction of the Russian Social Democratic Workers Party in 1904. During Inna's childhood, he served as chair of the central economic planning agencies of the Soviet Union, the Supreme Council of the National Economy and Gosplan. He was also a member of the Politburo.

3. Commissioned in 1931, Government House, or the House on the Embankment, was the showcase apartment house built for members of the Soviet elite in Moscow. Within view of the Kremlin, this modernist structure was the largest apartment building in the world.

4. During World War II.

CF—And did all of you children sleep together in one room? How did you arrange things?

IA—No, no. It was set up like this: there was my father's room, his office, where he had a lot of books. . . . There was a dining room, well, for guests who would come over, then there was a small room, with a bed and a little writing table, that was my room. And the room where one sister and the domestic help lived at first, they lived there together. And then my second sister also was put in there.

CF—This means you had your own room?

IA—I had my own little room, yes, I had my own little room. At first it was my parents' room, at first my father had a study, but then they gave it to me. First, my sister and I were with the housekeeper. And then when I started school, my parents moved into my father's study, and they gave me the room.

CF—Was your family religious?

IA—No, absolutely antireligious, and absolutely internationalist. Both Papa and Mama were the eldest in their families. They supported all of their relatives, and for that reason there was constantly someone coming to stay. We couldn't use the dining room, because someone was always sleeping in there on the couch. . . . In general, it was an open house. Which really angered the housekeeper, because she was constantly having to wait on somebody. Both Papa and Mama worked. . . . And in those years, how did they work? Josef Vissarionovich[5] loved working at night. Papa would come home at four or five in the morning. Mama also would come home really late. Mama was an economist in the People's Commissariat of Heavy Industry. And really, everything was on our nanny's shoulders, she was both nanny and housekeeper, she fulfilled every role on earth. She was fully a member of the family. When they took my parents away, she defended us, she did not let us wind up in a child receiver, she stayed with us.[6] She did not let them take us, she simply stood in the doorway and said, "I won't give them up," when they took

5. Stalin.
6. The institution was a child "receiver-distributor," where children were held until their placement in an orphanage. First they were received, then they were distributed. The term in Russian is "priyomnik-raspredelitel'." Both of these words have mechanical connotations.

Mama away. And they took Mama on August 31, the eve of the first day of school.

CF—So you said that your home was an open house, that there were always guests, there were always people who came and so on. Does this mean that you consider this to have been a very happy home?

IA—Yes, Papa was a cheerful person, yes . . . . it really was an open house, someone was always coming over. And we had a dacha in Nikolina Gora, too.[7] Our own dacha. My father joined the cooperative, and later they even asked me to join, even after the rehabilitation. . . . All these nieces and nephews, everyone on the planet gathered at the dacha. And my mother's—actually *my*—cousin, he was two months older than me. He also died during the evacuation. We departed as four and returned just two.[8] And a girl cousin, Mama's brother's children, also lived with us at the dacha. During all the vacations, all of them. . . .

CF—And what school did you attend?

IA—School No. 19. . . .

CF—Was this considered an elite school?

IA—No, no. The elite school was MOPSh—The Moscow Model-Demonstration School, and generally, children from Government House, as a rule, went there. But our school was full of hooligans . . . Later the school became very good; by later, I mean after fifth grade. But the school had one remarkable quality. They did not persecute us. If in the MOPSh children had to renounce their parents in the assembly hall, in our school, my cousin and I, he kept saying to me for a long time, "Come on, let's go tell them that our parents have been arrested." Well, it's really hard, to come in and tell them what had happened, all the more so since we were in the fifth grade. Well, in the end, we pulled ourselves together and went. Some time had already passed. They took Mama on August 31, and my uncle on September 5. My uncle also lived in Government House. So, and sometime in the middle of September we went to tell them, and the teacher very quietly said, "Well, so what. That happens. Go, children, to class." And that was it, no persecution of any kind,

7. A summer cottage community for the Soviet elite outside Moscow.
8. She is referring again to the evacuation from Moscow during World War II.

nothing, just "Go." No kind of renunciations. On the contrary. When the time came when they instituted a fee for school, I was promoted to the eighth grade, my teacher paid for me. Grandmother said that she didn't have the money, and the teacher said that she would pay, just so I would be able to go to a ten-grade school. So, the attitude toward us there was ideal.

CF—Do you know why you didn't attend the Model Demonstration School?

IA—It wasn't all so simple. I went there simply because it was closer, it was easier for our nanny that I went there. But for fourth grade, Papa decided that I needed to transfer to that school, to MOPSh. And he made arrangements, since we had spent the summer at Nikolina Gora with the head of the teaching staff at that school—Martin Lvovich, I believe, was his name. He said that the school was simply wonderful. Well, so he simply persuaded my father to transfer me to that school. And on September 1, I went there. I came home horrified. That is, I wound up in the same class with one of Mikoyan's[9] children, and someone else. I came home horrified, maybe not because it was bad there, but because it was conservative. I still remember, I was standing on the steps and straightening my stocking. Stockings back then were on elastic bands [garters], and someone's mother came by and said, "You need to do that in the washroom." Basically, I came home, sobbing, and said that I wouldn't go back to that school. And Papa said, "Well, how can that be?!"—and I really loved my father—he said, "How can this be so. If I ask you to go, you should go." Well, they were supposed to leave that day for Kislovodsk. No, I didn't go on September 2, I had an abscess on my knee, I couldn't walk, I didn't go, there were a thousand reasons. And after a couple of days, they left for a vacation in Kislovodsk. . . . This was in the fall of 1936. Standing at the train station already, to see them off, I started to cry again, saying I wouldn't go to that school. Well, my mother didn't have the heart to resist; she said, "Well, if you don't want to, don't go, don't go." . . . And the next day, I went to School No. 19. It turned out that this was the right thing to do. Really I can say: there were no renunciations of one's parents, nothing happened. . . .

9. Anastas Mikoyan was an Old Bolshevik of Armenian background who held several high positions in the party-state during the Stalin and Khrushchev eras.

Here's what happened once. For a while, we prepared parcels[10] for Mama, but then they stopped accepting them, and we hadn't had any news from Mama. So, Mama wasn't in Butyrka.[11] They stopped accepting parcels in January 1938. And we didn't know anything. Then it was May 1939, and we still didn't know anything. And suddenly, well, naturally, our situation wasn't good, as you understand. We didn't know anything—not about Papa, or Mama, or my aunt, nothing about anyone. And then in class the door opens, and the principal, Valentin Nikolaevich Postnikov, such a completely wonderful person, says, "Gaister." I went out. He's calling me out of my classroom, and he says, "Go to the office." Well, to the principal's office, you know how that is. I come in, the telephone receiver is lying there. "Pick up the receiver." He didn't say anything else. I picked up the receiver. I heard Grandmother's voice: "A telegram has arrived from Mama." Imagine! Grandmother, having received the telegram, telephoned Information, got the telephone number for the school, and called and told them. And he took me out of class, do you understand? And then, when I put the receiver down, she had told me everything, and even now it gives me goose bumps, remembering all of this. When I put down the receiver, he asked me, "Well, where will you go, home or back to class?" Understand how humane he was, to do this. . . . And so it was that kind of school where, immediately, as soon as they called, they immediately got me, immediately. So I am very grateful to the school. It really supported me. . . . These were really amazing, amazing people who in those years were not afraid to help, when everyone turned their back on us, right down to my uncle. Mama's best friends, Papa's friends, were almost all arrested. But Mama's friends, well, some of them were lucky, they got help there, but everyone turned their back on us, no one helped us. . . .

CF—Can you tell me a bit about what happened to your parents?

IA—They shot my father. They shot him on the thirtieth, the trial was on the twenty-ninth, and they shot him on the thirtieth. Well, if you can call that a trial, twelve minutes. I got the case

10. The monthly care packages relatives could send to prisoners in the Gulag.
11. Butyrka was a transit prison in Moscow; it dated back to the imperial period.

file later. The trial lasted twelve minutes. He confessed. They accused him, absolutely. Trotskyite.[12] He was never a Trotskyite. He never belonged to any kind of opposition. Well, he had been a member of the Party since 1919, he was born in 1899. Therefore, when the revolution began, he was eighteen years old. They expelled him from his classical high school for revolutionary activity. . . . And my mother was locked up as a relative of a traitor to the motherland. . . . She served eight years, in this Akmolinsk Camp for Wives of Traitors to the Motherland.[13] She worked as an economist there, too. When they released her on September 1, 1945, they didn't let her out—they wouldn't let people out without someone to accompany them. In the summer of 1946, I went for her and brought her back.

CF—Did she expect her arrest? . . . Can you describe the arrest? Were you there?

IA—They arrested Papa at work. . . . I can say only that they came, they came at night to search at the dacha. This I remember. Two soldiers were walking around, that's who I thought they were—soldiers. Both Mama's brothers were soldiers, one was a pilot, the other worked with Yakir.[14] That's who I thought they were. At first, because I was sleeping in a room with my cousin. She was living with us just then. They were opening my drawers, and this woke me up. And Mama told me, "Little daughter, Papa has been arrested." I was completely uninformed, for me, this was wildly unexpected. I knew only that just before then in May, Tukhachevsky[15] had been arrested. But I was completely unaware that these kinds of arrests were happening all over the place. We were living at the dacha. If we had been living in the city, we would have seen more of this. We were living at the dacha, and I had no idea that such arrests were going on. And in the morning, Mama said, "I'm going to the city." . . . I went with Mama. But our nanny stayed behind with my two sisters and my cousin. . . .

CF—You had no opportunity to say good-bye to your father? None at all?

12. An alleged follower of Leon Trotsky, Stalin's defeated rival in the struggle to succeed Lenin after his death in 1924.
13. Located in Kazakhstan. The acronym is ALZhIR.
14. General Jonah Yakir, Red Army officer removed in the mass purge of the Red Army command in 1937.
15. Marshal M. N. Tukhachevsky, also purged.

IA—Neither I, nor Mama, not anyone. They arrested him at work, then his secretary called Mama. . . . They sealed our apartment. When Mama and I came back, they gave us some kind of passageway as a room in a completely different sector of the complex. Mama and I moved to that place when we returned. . . . The other girls didn't wake up, and when they woke up in the morning, they stayed there with our nanny. People also arrived there and ordered them to clean up the dacha. . . . It's true that this poet Bezymianensky,[16] he behaved well, he took them as far as the station. He left them there. They sat, they waited. And they made their way back to Moscow.

CF—This means they evicted them from the dacha?

IA—They drove them out. . . . We were never at the dacha again. We tried later to get it back, through the courts, but we weren't successful.

CF—Well, after this, your mama, I'm returning to my question, after this, did your mama expect that they would arrest her?

IA—You know, she both expected it and didn't expect it. That is, she probably expected it, but she didn't say so to me. Once, in the middle of August, she was summoned to the investigator. And he told her to bring Papa's warm things. After all, Papa had left in what he had on for work, in short sleeves on June 27. She took felt boots, she took something else, and we were living at that time with Grandmother at her dacha. Grandmother had a dacha forty-two kilometers outside Moscow, we were living with her at that time. It was a kind of little hut, we were all there. We lived, we had a kind of small, small room, half a room. All five of us lived there, all three children, Mama, and our nanny, Natasha. Mama would go to work in the morning and we would stay there with Natasha.

CF—Can you describe her mood?

IA—And she came back from the investigator's so happy, thinking everything with our father would be fine, since they took winter things, to go somewhere, since he didn't have warm things. But in fact, the investigator simply wanted to know if Mama was in Moscow. . . . And the next day, at night, they came for her.

---

16. Aleksandr Bezymianensky was a popular poet of the 1920s and was associated with the Komsomol.

Yes, we moved back from the dacha and they came for her that night. And this I'm really sure of, because it was so frightening. Natalka didn't wake up, and Natasha had my little sister, like this, I recall it as if it were right now. And Natasha put her on her arm. And they searched those two rooms that they had just given us. And Mama needed to go to the bathroom. You know, the bathroom—I don't know how it is now in Government House, I don't know, I haven't gone to my apartment, ever—there was a little window in the bathroom door. And, as a rule, curtains. . . . And he pushed the curtain aside, and while Mama was sitting on the toilet, he watched. I stood behind the door and sobbed. I remember that as if it were right this minute.

CF—So, you already understood.

IA—Well, it was clear.

CF—And how many minutes passed before she left?

IA—Well, they took her away. . . . I can't say exactly. Well, I think they arrived around midnight. We were already asleep. And probably around four o'clock, they took her away. Government House, they were always taking someone away from there. You would hear screams there. They were always taking someone away there. Probably around four o'clock, they took her away. Natalka, in any case, didn't wake up, she didn't even say good-bye to Mama. Mama left.

CF—But you said good-bye?

IA—I said good-bye.

CF—Do you remember what she said?

IA—"My dear daughter, don't worry. Everything is fine. No one is guilty. Don't worry. We are not guilty. They'll figure it out." What do people say? "This is a misunderstanding." . . . This was the night before September 1. . . . September 1. Therefore, I was supposed to go to school. . . . I went. I was a star student, after all.

. . . Grandmother came in the morning. We summoned Grandmother, Grandmother arrived. Well, and she began to make arrangements to be our guardian. . . .

CF—So, you stayed for the time being in that second apartment in the same building?

IA—We shared that apartment with other people, too. It had been their former apartment. He was arrested and therefore, two of their rooms were taken from them. And we lived in those two rooms. There were also three of them: two boys . . . And the mother. The Karpovs were our neighbors.

CF—So, the mother was still there.

IA—In that family, the mother remained. Well, the mother was there for a very short time after Mama. They took her away very quickly. . . .

CF—Who took care of you then? Who looked after you?

IA—Grandfather, Grandmother.

CF—So, they moved in?

IA—No, no. It's a very long story. After that, they moved us into a different apartment. . . . In that same building. On the first floor, but no longer two rooms, only one very dark room. And, as I said, our nanny, Natasha. And so we lived there, while Grand-mother and Grandfather lived at their place, they also had only one room. And they had already, they had already arrested the husband of Papa's sister in Krasnoyarsk, and Grandmother went there and brought back two children. Therefore, at their place they had Grandfather, Grandmother, their son—Papa's younger brother—with his family, all living there, yes, all in one room, and they brought the children back from Krasnoyarsk. Therefore, there was no room for us to move in with them. So, when the government gave us one room on the first floor, that's where we lived. Well, and I went to school. The room was very dark, on the first floor. At that time, our nanny said, "Well, thanks be to God, no one will kick us out of here." We lived there . . . let me count, we lived there until February 1938. In February 1938 or in January, anyway, at the beginning of the year, they told us that they were making a dorm room for the janitors out of this room. And so they moved us again, to a completely different sector, to the eleventh floor, no, on the tenth. And we were there, and side by side with us lived the Knorin family. And Knorin was in the Comintern.[17] He was the deputy chair of the Comintern. So, there were Knorin's wife and two children. The boy was in the same class

17. Communist International, the international organization of Communist parties around the world, headquartered in Moscow.

with me at school. But the girl was younger, Maya. And so then they moved us from this apartment into still another entryway, in Entryway Number 7, and I think the chairman of the Central Committee Stetsky's apartment was there. They had already arrested him, they had already arrested his wife. So they moved us there, and a part of the apartment was also closed off. And we were in one big room, a bright, big room, and the Knorins were in the other. When we arrived there, our nanny said, "Well, we won't be here long. Everyone would like this apartment." Which was true. At the end of March or the beginning of April, they arrested the mother of these two children. And they threw all of us out into the street. They threw these two children and us out into the street. That is, they *evicted* us without providing us any place to live. And then Grandmother took in us three children, along with our nanny, at her place, in that one room. . . . And we began to live there in twenty-six square meters; there were thirteen of us.

CF—Where did you sleep?

IA—I'll tell you. This was a one-room apartment, there was a single bed, a narrow bed. We put chairs up against it, like this, three chairs. And the three of us would sleep on this. So, I would be here, Tasya, and the little one on the chairs. Well, she was already two years old at that time. And so that's how we arranged ourselves to sleep. And that's how we slept until 1941. My cousin, this was my uncle's son who lived there, he would set up a cot at night. There was a wardrobe there. Behind the wardrobe, my uncle's family lived. There was only enough room for a bed behind it. My aunt, uncle, and their two-year-old daughter slept there. And later [laughing], on June 2, 1941, they gave birth to another son and brought him to live in that very room. And our homework, homework, there was no place to do it. We did our homework in the bathroom. The bathroom there was rather narrow, so that the bathtub stood like this along the wall. So here was a wash basin, here was a little plank, where you could put your things when you were taking a bath.[18] So whoever came home from school had to be the first to get the plank, otherwise there was no place to do homework. And keep

18. In describing this setup, Inna Aronovna gestured that a board was positioned across the tub. Such arrangements were common in Soviet bathrooms well into the 1990s. Thus, a child doing homework in her grandmother's apartment was sitting in the tub to write on the plank across the tub.

in mind how many of us there were! And the people in the room next door were also arrested. There was a young couple, they arrested them, too. So they settled a family there, he worked as a waiter, he had six children. So, in a two-room apartment, there were these six children, they also needed to do their homework. So, we fought over this spot in the bathroom. One person would jump in first, in order to do his homework normally; the rest worked on their knees. Well, so it was like that. This was until the war. Well, we lived like this until the war.

CF—. . . It seems to me that you couldn't feel alone.

IA—Yes, probably I didn't feel alone.

CF—Were there some kinds of feelings of having lost your parents? Having lost your father?

IA—This was constant. I felt my parents' absence all the time. I always had to fend for myself. Well, and then I had a lot more jobs to do. I, for example, did the wash for the entire family. All the bed linens—I did all of this. I did the laundry. I remember, the first time I did the wash, I didn't rinse it out well. I had never done this before. And my aunt threw it all back into the tub for me to redo. So there was all of that. I did the bed linens for everyone. . . . Before the war, there were no laundries.

CF—And were you proud of this work?

IA—[Chuckles] No pride whatsoever. I simply felt no pride whatsoever. On the contrary, I was completely put upon that I had to do this. I wanted to play, and here I stood, washing. Well, what do you mean, what pride?

CF—What about your nanny?

IA—Our nanny left us in the fall. She couldn't live with Grandmother. . . .

CF—And how did you feel about this? Was this still another loss?

IA—Very much so. Very much so. Very much so. She came to visit all the time. Later she lived with us. Later she even died in my arms. But that was already later, in 1986.

CF—So that means you did not lose her entirely?

IA—No, no. She always stayed in touch. Later, when she retired, she came to live with me. She held both of my children in her arms. Then my husband was able to arrange for her to have a room in Tsaritsyno.[19] When she fell ill, she called us, and she lived the last ten days of her life with us. No, we never lost touch with her. And my children would go to her. She lived in Tsaritsyno in the Moscow suburbs, so that on Saturdays and Sundays, they would go cross-country skiing at her place. No, no, she was with us, when she got very ill, we gave her a bed at our place. And she died. She died literally in my arms. . . .

CF—So, despite all of these horrors, all of these displacements and so on, these separations, you succeeded all the same in maintaining this connection.

IA—With my nanny, yes, but by no means with all of my relatives. With my nanny, yes.

CF—You have already implicitly answered this question, but I want to return to it. The question is, did you have to hide your parents' fate?

IA—. . . . I was supposed to, but I, unfortunately, didn't hide it, therefore I was arrested in 1949. . . .

CF—Well, I have in mind precisely in the first years, at that time. You said that you informed them in school right away with your cousin and so on. Does that mean there were a lot of children like you in your school?

IA—A lot. They say that in my class alone, I don't know, but they say there were as many as twenty children. . . . There were a lot in our class. Those who were from our building. The thing is that this school was directly across from the Kremlin. And a bit farther down was a military dormitory. And plenty of people were arrested there, too. Besides Government House, a lot of people were arrested there, too, and therefore, evidently there were a lot. But I, the fact is that I just didn't really know, even though I was always in that class. Some hid it, some didn't hide it. As it always is in life. . . .

CF—Were you a Pioneer?

IA—Why of course! And I even joined the Komsomol. I was a very, very Soviet person. I believed that this was all a big mistake. I was *very* Soviet.

19. A suburb of Moscow.

CF—What was your opinion of Soviet power, about Stalin, and so on. Can you recall?

IA—I was kind of ambivalent toward Stalin.

CF—At that time?

IA—But about Soviet power—that was the best, that it was all correct. I, unfortunately, many people are afraid, are embarrassed to say so, some people even say to me, "How could you have been?" Well, I *was!* It seems to me that those who say things, also were. That's who I was, there was a lot I didn't understand, but I didn't permit myself to think about that.

CF—And your grandmother and grandfather?

IA—They were also very, very Soviet. The entire family was insanely Soviet.

CF—Even after these events?

IA—After both of their sons were arrested, both of their sons perished. I think that they were simply afraid to speak. . . . They were very Soviet people. Very. . . .

CF—Well, you said that only after two years, your grandmother received this telegram. A year and a half. Was there correspondence after this telegram?

IA—There was constant correspondence. Once a month. Mama wrote once a month.

CF—And do you remember this correspondence? Do you have the letters?

IA—There is nothing, because, when we left in evacuation, we destroyed everything. . . . Everything that was in that room, when we returned, it was all destroyed. Only little pieces of paper were floating around. . . . And those letters that I had after evacuation, were all burned, when I was arrested. They, they even have it in my case documents that fifty-three letters were destroyed, burned.

CF—Where was your mama?

IA—Mama was in the Akmolinsk Camp for traitors to the motherland. I visited Mama there. . . . First, the first time, well, I had to earn the money. So, while in school, I gave private lessons. And I earned money for the trip to visit Mama. And on June 22, on the day the war began, I was there. So, I arrived.

CF—So this was approximately four years after the arrest.

IA—1941, yes, yes.

CF—Was this typical, that children would make such visits?

IA—Whoever had the money could manage it, this visit.

CF—Did this happen often? For me, this seems unlikely.

IA—I can't say about everyone. But I know that a lot did. . . . When we went, I went, a certain Yasha Godlev went, he died recently. And Volodya Lyubchenko went, he perished at the front. When we arrived there, there were already children there, too. . . . So there were visits, there were, there were visits. I don't know how frequently they were granted. But the first visits began in 1940. So we went in 1941. Because it was just in 1941 that Mama submitted a request. I didn't make the request, Mama petitioned for the visit. . . .

CF—How long did the trip take?

IA—It was three full days to Akmolinsk. And the camp was forty kilometers from Akmolinsk. . . . I recall that when we went, that Mama had been approved for a visit of twenty-four hours, for a full-day visit, she wanted very much for me to come, but she did not want me to travel alone. In the eighth grade, so for the entire year—my math teacher arranged it for me—I worked, because I couldn't just go empty-handed. I needed to take her some extra food. And Grandmother said that she wouldn't give me a kopek. That she had no money. So, I gave lessons. And Mama wrote me that there was this Yasha Godlev who would be traveling with his aunt, Yekaterina Yakovlevna, that I could go with her. I wrote her. . . . And well, this Auntie Katya . . . . took the three of us, and we went. We traveled third-class for three full days. . . . So, we finished school, took our exams, and left in June, yes. And we arrived there, but this is what it was like. The camp is forty kilometers from Akmolinsk. And there was this kind of mud hut where drivers who drove back and forth stopped. . . . We walked into that little house and they told us that the truck had left that morning. We would have to wait a couple of days. . . . And we, well, eagerly went out into the steppe, to look around, to see what the steppe was. . . . But Aunt Katya stayed behind with all our luggage to chat with the owner of the house. The little house was on the outskirts of Akmolinsk, therefore, we didn't see the town itself. But the steppe, after all, we were city people, we went out into the steppe.

We came back, and Auntie Katya had a terrible expression on her face. "*War!*" In Moscow, they announced it at noon, but there was a four-hour time difference. And on her face, it was already four o'clock there, her face was pale, full of horror. "We'll go immediately to the camp." And we couldn't even understand: "We'll just go tomorrow all the same." What was there to fear? She was shaking. "We're going right now." Basically, we were idiots. So she set out for town and found a bus. And as I recall now, two hundred whole rubles for the bus. Two hundred rubles were a great deal of money at that time. Divided among the four of us, that made fifty rubles each. And I was extremely upset, because my budget hadn't planned for these fifty rubles. And she said, "You can pay me back in Moscow. We're going all the same." They gave us the bus at six in the morning; at seven thirty we were there. . . .

They announced that all visits had been cancelled. But we were already on the spot, we were in the camp. . . . And the director of the camp was decent. He said that those who had arrived, we'll give them half of the time of their visits. So, I had had twenty-four hours, I received twelve hours. This Volodya Lyubchenko had been granted sixteen hours, so, they gave different lengths of visits. It wasn't the same for everyone. . . . So Volodya had been granted sixteen hours, he received eight hours. I don't remember about Yasha. And there were already two girls there, twins, redheads. One was named Alla, I don't recall the other one's name. And there was one more with her aunt, a fifth-grader. . . . They had arrived the night before, as it turned out, she had gotten there on the very car we had missed. And we all got to have half our visits. And there we were.

So, there was this little mud hut, it stood directly in the middle of the field, well, right behind the barbed wire. They brought our mothers there. It was completely impossible to visit with each other outside, because it was so hot. Kazakhstan! Well, it is true that the escort left. He wasn't present. Well, we sat like this, shoulder to shoulder on the bed. Mama, and next to her sat Yasha, with his mama. Well, it was totally difficult for the boys. Because they aren't very affectionate, and here right in front of everybody, they had to be affectionate with their mama. Well, so that's how we were granted our visit. It stretched over two days.

The day when we arrived, and the next day they took us back. And as for Lyubchenko, ... Volodya's mother came to see us outside the zone. She never saw Volodya again. Volodya perished at the front.

CF—So, for these twelve hours, you just sat with your mama on the bed?

IA—Yes.

CF—Or did you chat, did you embrace?

IA—Of course. I fed Mama, Mama fed me. Well, what I had brought with me.

CF—What? Do you remember?

IA—No, I don't remember. Well, there was garlic, butter, lard, these kinds of essential things.

CF—I am trying to imagine the scene. So, you fed her.

IA—Probably. I simply treated her to something like sandwiches. . . .

CF—I have a question related to your mama. Had she changed, that is, when you saw her? . . .

IA—She had changed a great deal. She had aged a great deal. Somewhere I have a photograph of her from 1946, when she returned, she was forty-nine years old. She looked eighty years old. She had aged a great deal, she had changed greatly. . . . A completely old, old woman. Mama had changed terribly. . . .

CF—What, in your opinion, was most difficult for her?

IA—The most difficult thing for her was the absence of her children, this caused her a lot of suffering. . . .

CF—Well, you returned to Moscow. And the war was already going on. . . . What was your experience like during the war? A child of an enemy of the people? What kind of significance did this have?

IA—No, this no longer had any significance. Because I worked at some kind of textile factory. . . . When I got back to Moscow, I went with my school outside Moscow, children were taken out of the city with their schools. I went as a Pioneer leader. . . . I was sixteen years old. I went as a Pioneer leader with the school, and then they brought us back to Moscow just when that panic was happening.[20] Grandmother was no longer there, so I was left alone with two children.

CF—Why was your grandmother no longer there?

IA—She was no longer there, she had been evacuated. . . .

CF—Where to?

IA—She, they went to Fergana.[21] But we stayed in Moscow. So I was left as the oldest. Well, along with my cousin. He was sixteen years old, too. So I was sixteen years old, and here with two little ones.

CF—In that same room?

IA—In that same room, but we were now only four, because everyone had been evacuated. . . . Well, they were constantly bombing Moscow, and we . . . we were on the third floor. In a five-story building. . . . We didn't go to the bomb shelter, we were very courageous, we were very romantic, we decided that, yes, we'll stay put. An acquaintance called, in fact Andrei Vorobyov's aunt. "The Germans are already right at Moscow. You need to . . ." she said. "Well, for you it will be okay," she said. I didn't look like a Jew, but my sister and cousin were such obvious Jews.

CF—You already understood the danger?

IA—I? I didn't understand anything. . . . The nanny Natasha understood. And this acquaintance understood.

CF—Was the nanny also Jewish?

IA—No, she was Russian, she was from the village. But she said that she begged me not to flee anywhere, that she would hide Natalka. And she also begged Igor—Igor was my cousin—not to go anywhere. Don't leave, but when there was a chance to leave, go. So, we went; not I, but Igor went to the Moscow City Council, and he didn't say there that we were children of enemies of the people. He mentioned only one part of it, that we had been left on our own, which was true. And they gave us tickets to leave. . . . We left on December 5. We left on the very day when they drove the Germans back from Moscow. We left Moscow on that day.

20. Inna Aronovna means the panic of October 16, 1941, when the Germans attained their closest proximity to the city.
21. City in the southeast of Uzbekistan in Central Asia.

We left under the most difficult conditions. We squeezed into the train car. Igor stayed with our things on the platform between cars. He was freezing there, so he came and said, "Come, relieve me, I'm completely frozen." He went to the girls, I went to the platform, and our things were already gone. All of our things were already gone. We were left without anything.

We arrived in Sverdlovsk, because our aunt had told us that our uncle would be there. When we got there, it turned out that our uncle was not there. . . . In Sverdlovsk, they told us that there were no spots left and that we had to go to, what was the place called? Irbit. From Sverdlovsk to Irbit, go there, they're accepting evacuees. On the way, we met a girl named Lena Golitsyna, a third-year university student. And so the five of us, including this Lena, who was, thus, the oldest, she was twenty-one. We went to Irbit. When we got to Irbit, they told us there was no place for us in Irbit. But that they were taking people in a village. Horses took us there. Without belongings, without anything. When we arrived in the village, they put us in some kind of peasant cottage. The peasant women said, "What, are you crazy? What are you to do here?" But Lena and I, Lena was in her third year at the Foreign Languages Institute, and even so, we decided to go to the district office of education, maybe she could find some work. Igor and I wanted to go to school, and she wanted to teach a foreign language. When we arrived at this district office, it turned out there was an apparently very wise man, who said, "What are you to do here? Do you want to freeze? Go back immediately."

And so, in the next convoy of evacuees, we rode for three days back to the station. The only thing we could sell was my watch, which my father had given me, and we exchanged it for three loaves of bread with some evacuee—no, with someone. When we got to Sverdlovsk, they told us, "There is nothing for you to do here. So, go to Ufa," because, at the post office, there was a message that they had sent my uncle to Ufa. We arrived in Ufa. In Ufa, in this . . . [evacuation center in the] Andreev Club, in the colossal auditorium. But I don't know how many cots there were, maybe a hundred. And so, they put the four of us on two cots. We got settled on them and the next day they took me away with typhus to the hospital. And the three children were left on their own. And with Lena. And my cousin went to get a job at the cable factory. He hid the fact that he was a son of an enemy of the people, and he got a job. I lay for six weeks in the hospital.

Naturally, I got no parcels, there was nothing. How long—two weeks—I was unconscious.

And then, when I got out—the hospital was on an elevated spot—it was cold there. I sat on my bottom and slid on it all the way to the evacuation center. I remember that as if it were right now. I pushed with my arms and made it. So, and when I got there, the little girls were covered in scabies. I took them somewhere, it was simply terrible there. All of this at one evacuation center. I also went to get a job at this cable factory, where they paid a decent wage. I wrote that my parents had been arrested, and they didn't hire me. They didn't hire me, and I started to search for some place to work, and I found some kind of workers' cooperative (somehow I had to get a worker's card)[22] where they were making buckles for the Red Army soldiers. We made them in the basement. They took me on there. . . . And my aunt came, my uncle's wife. She said they were having difficulties of their own, that they didn't need us, so we should just set ourselves up however we wished. So. They also turned us away. This was the brother who had not been arrested. He worked as the chief engineer at some factory. They had no children. And then we received a walk-through room. That is, the owners had a two-room apartment, and they gave us the room you walked through, and they moved everyone else into the other rooms. We probably should have paid them something, they had been packed into a smaller space, but, my God, how would I have known this? Well, in general, they did everything they could to get us to leave. So, we started to write away to my friend to find out where my grandmother was. We didn't even know where Grandmother was. We corresponded. Grandmother was in Fergana. She sent for us, and we decided to go to Grandmother, it was already spring. And the faster the better.

So, we went to the train station, there were no tickets, there was a line. Just to get away as quickly as possible from the people who owned the apartment, who were abusing us horribly, and my little sister was already seriously ill. She was simply a skeleton from hunger. She was in terrible shape. . . . We started to live on the square, lots of people were living there. So, it was spring 1942, and she had been born in 1936, five, almost six years old.

22. During the war, food rations were distributed only to persons with a worker's card.

And so we were living on this square and, in turns, we would stand in line. . . . And when we went to the police to get passes to go to Fergana, there was a woman from Moscow working there, and she took great pity on us. She arranged the pass, she was very sorry for us. And so, Igor would stand in line, and I would go to relieve him.

They sent our documents to the cashier. I remember this as if it were right now. I had a kind of little cosmetic bag, made of red suede, I put everything in it, so that means our passes were there. . . . The girls were included in my pass, and Igor had his own separate pass. Igor had his and I had mine. In short, when I walked up to the cashier, the bag was gone, someone had stolen it somehow. I ran back with a wild scream, because we couldn't move, Igor had his pass, but we didn't have ours. And sobbing, I went to the police, what could be done? We had already moved out, we had no place to live, we had no pass, we had no money. It was a horrible situation. And she added us onto Igor's pass. This secretary. There were all these forms, and she wrote our names on them. You understand, well, as if we were all minors. "Let's give this a try. Maybe you'll get through." And so, on the basis of this pass, we were simply added on, they gave us tickets and we left. . . .

CF—You are probably trying to get to your own arrest. I wanted to ask when you were yourself repressed?

IA—They repressed me in 1949. The accusation was simple, that I was the daughter of enemies of the people, and it was article 7-35. Prostitutes fell under this article, and we fell under this article. A socially dangerous element. That I was the daughter of enemies of the people. And there it was written Gaister Aron Izrailovich and Kaplan Rakita Izrailovna, about which I said to the prosecutor, "But Mama is not an enemy of the people."[23] Complete demagogy. She said, "And so are you renouncing your parents?" I say, "No, I don't renounce them." "Then sign. Are these your parents? Are you renouncing them?" "But Mama is not an enemy of the people." "But do you renounce your parents?" "No, I am not renouncing them." "Well, then sign." . . . They arrested me in a very interesting way. They arrested me at my thesis defense.

23. Inna's view was that her mother was herself not an enemy of the people, but the *wife* of an enemy of the people.

CF—At your thesis defense?

IA—. . . . So, it was like this. The night before my thesis defense, I didn't sleep at home. I was preparing at a friend's place, with several people who were defending. And they, they came to search. They conducted a search at my grandmother's apartment, where I lived. There was a search, but Grandmother didn't inform me. . . . At four o'clock, I arrived for my thesis defense. I was supposed to be the last to defend, there were five of us. I had signed up to be last. And when we got to the department, someone knocked on the door, and I opened it, and a young man was standing there. He had on a kind of red-checkered scarf. He asked, "Where is the defense?" I said, "There, upstairs in the small Physics auditorium." And when we arrived at the defense, ... he was sitting at the defense.

CF—What institute was this?

IA—Moscow; Moscow State University. The Physics Department. And back then, in that year, I had entered in 1944, the war was still going on, at that time they accepted everyone, both Jews and children of enemies of the people, they admitted everyone. My sister, already [after the war], they did not admit. They still admitted me. The department chair suddenly says, "Gaister will defend." I said, "Fyodor Andreevich, I am last." He says, "No, you present first." . . . Well, I presented, I read through all this, and then this Fyodor turned to me, the department chair, and says, "Go to the personnel department." . . . So. I went to the personnel department, no, to the First Department, and there was this young man. He says, "Come with me, come." And we walked to Kuznetsky Most [Street].

CF—And did you already understand?

IA—I didn't understand a thing. And as we were walking, he was greeting the girls we met along the way. He would say "Hi" to them. So, they *obviously* were running to the university. *Evidently,* he was an evening law student or something. And he was even greeting people. So, when he brought me into the reception, where I had found out information about Papa, then I understood. But while he was escorting me, I didn't understand. He brought me into the reception, he told me to wait, then . . .

CF—To the Lubyanka?

IA—To the Lubyanka, Kuznetsky No. 22—24—now it's No. 22, but back then it was 24. And he summoned some kind of military officer, said, "Here she is." By then I already understood something was wrong. Well, in the first place, they hadn't informed me of anything. And then they took me through a gate. I even saw what time it was, it was six forty p.m. And so I looked at it, it was still interesting for me, this could suddenly be the last time, that's how I looked at the clock. And I went, when we had gone inside already, he presented me with the warrant for my arrest. . . . And that's where he showed me all the belongings I possessed, which had fit in one pillowcase. I understood that they had done a search, because all my belongings were there—two shirts, two pairs of long underwear, stockings, all of these they had brought me from Grandmother. She simply packed everything from my shelf and gave it to them in a pillowcase, they brought everything. . . .

I was in the Lubyanka, then I was in Butyrka. They had arrested eight of us that night, eight children of enemies of the people. They arrested eight of us. So, they arrested me, they arrested Rada Poloz, Artyom Vesyoly's daughters. . . . They arrested Maya Peterson, so we were together. . . . They arrested Zayara's [Artyomovna Vesyoloya] husband, they arrested a certain Erlen Fedin, he is now in Germany. Well, so that was enough. And after that they generally started to arrest children. . . . They arrested my sister in June. Then it was after this they began to arrest children of enemies of the people. . . . I was in the Lubyanka, then we were in the Butyrka.

They then sent me to a wonderful place. I used to say, "I need to go to a resort somewhere, so that people could visit me, either not far, I would say, or I would agree to Komi, so that people could visit me." But they sent me to Kazakhstan. To the city of Kokchetav. When we arrived in Kokchetav, I had traveled for a long time. . . . So, they arrested me and Rada sometime at the end of May already. They announced our sentence. I arrived only at the beginning of August. . . . I told them I would go only to the town of Shchuchinsk, where the Borovoe resort was. And how did I know about it? When I traveled with Mama, the station for the Borovoe resort, it was practically in Akmolinsk. After all, they were obligated to give us work. The man said that he wouldn't get me work there. That my work wouldn't be there, but if I went to the steppe into the collective farm, then I would have work there. But, I, as if I were someone special, said that I would go only to the Borovoe resort. And I really did arrive in this very Shchuchinsk. . . .

CF—You had a choice?

IA—No, there was no choice. It's just that I chose because I knew that there was a Borovoe resort. . . . Otherwise I would simply not have survived. . . . I didn't mention the resort to him, I simply said that I would go to that train stop and that was it. But it's true that it was a good thing that I had defended my degree when I arrived in Kokchetav. . . . I had not passed the graduation exams. Friends sent me a certificate with all of my grades, with all of them, with all of my grades from each year, I had them. So that it was already clear that I had an education. . . . Then there was the fact that my profession didn't have an ideological component, you understand, mathematics, physics. I went to the public education department, and the deputy director said that he had a job in the first to third grades in a distant, distant settlement somewhere, they didn't even have electricity there. The settlement was called Dmitrievka, I remember as if it were just now. But I said that I would go there, as long as I had a job. . . . And when I went back to get the assignment, the head of the department was sitting there, may God bless him! A certain Victor Ivanovich Kryuchkov, who said, "Leave for a minute." I went out, and when I went back in, his deputy said, "But would you go to teach with a teaching load of eight hours per week—a full load was eighteen hours—but it would be physics in the upper grades?" I said, "Yes, I would happily do so." And so this was the Borovoe resort. It turned out that there was a woman in the Borovoe resort, a math teacher, not physics, but math, whom they had separated from her husband; her husband was in the Urals. She was a German. An exiled German.[24] And she was waiting for a replacement, they were waiting for a replacement with higher education. . . . And they sent me there. . . .

CF—So this was exile?

24. The woman was probably exiled in 1941, in response to the Nazi invasion, to remote locations as part of the forced resettlement of all Soviet citizens of German background from central Russia.

IA—We were in exile. We had a room for two persons, a history teacher lived with me there. . . . I didn't have the right to go anywhere. I signed a document stating that if I went one kilometer out of this location, then I would be sentenced to hard labor. So many years of hard labor, probably almost twenty-five years of hard labor. I signed such a document, that if I left, I would receive twenty-five years' hard labor. I taught until our dear leader and teacher gave up the ghost. . . .

CF—When did your worldview, your trust in Soviet power begin to weaken?

IA—I don't know.

CF—Were you still a Soviet person?

IA—Well, no, of course, no, after my arrest. In my childhood, I always was.

CF—After your visit with your mama, were you still Soviet?

IA—Who was analyzing back then? Back then, you needed to focus your strength primarily on living. Who could have indulged in analysis? . . . No one was analyzing this. The primary goal was to live, to live. Someone may say, but the primary goal was to live, somehow to survive. . . .

CF—When you were raising your own children, did this evoke any memories about your family, when you were yourself a child and lost your parents?

IA—Yes, certainly. Certainly. Some kinds of habits all the same are established. And you can't get away from this. My children are, well, as they say, "My own chick is the most yellow." . . .

CF—Were there some, did you sometimes fear separation from your children? Because of your past.

IA—. . . Yes, yes. When I gave birth to my older daughter, I simply said to Volodya [her husband] that, "you keep in mind," we married; well, in a year, I had a baby. I said to him, "You'll probably have to raise her. Don't count too much on me. It's simple."

CF—What year was this?

IA—Val'ka was born in 1964, 1965. And he laughed, "Okay, okay! If they exile you, we'll come." So, it was like that. "Don't worry, don't worry! You'll never get away from us, if they exile you, we'll come." And when I got pregnant, I said, "You keep in mind. This will be your responsibility." Moreover, the daughter of mine who emigrated, she emigrated only because she has genetic fear, that maybe it will all happen again. So that not only I have it, but she does, too. By the way, my husband was completely free of this. He feared absolutely nothing. Absolutely, he would poke his nose into any hole. And my older daughter, she also does not have it. But this second daughter, yes, she inherited this genetic fear, and she was afraid. And she was also afraid, then in the 1990s, when things started to get bad for the Jews—for example, the "Pamiat'" society[25]—she was very, very frightened. She said, "I have to leave, it's no good to be here, you can't tell what this will all lead to." And she left, in the end. . . .

CF—Looking back on your life, how strongly did either the years of your exile or the loss of your parents, the loss of your father, influence your development? . . .

IA—. . . I would say this is a primitive question. Because this was a completely different world. I'm telling you that I was terribly lucky in life with my husband, who somehow was able to heal me. Because everything had turned upside down. I was such a girl, a star student, successful, and then I had to . . .

CF—Struggle?

IA—Well, until I met Volodya, I had to struggle all the time. It's what I said. We left as a foursome, I tell you, two of us returned. Only two of us returned. And of the four of us, two did not survive. And always. And in my grandmother's family, things did not go well for me, because I was always standing guard, to make sure they weren't hurt, my sisters and cousin. Somehow, always. My relatives were a little afraid of me, but they weren't afraid of the little ones. I always stood watch over them. Simply all the time. Until, I tell you, until I married, and I could hide behind his powerful back, until then, it was very hard to get through everything. . . .

Well, how can I say this, well, how it affects me. Just to hand over a parcel for Mama in the Butyrka prison, I had to be there at four in the morning. There was only one letter, the letter "K."

25. A virulently anti-Semitic organization that, among other campaigns, distributed the Protocols of the Elders of Zion.

Mama's last name was Kaplan. If I arrived at five in the morning, I might not make it in. The letter "K" came up once a month, if I don't make it in, I won't know anything about Mama. What do you think, did this affect my life? In order to get Mama a parcel when she had already been sent into exile, I had to leave the city of Moscow. They didn't accept parcels from the city of Moscow. We went to the town of Mozhaisk.[26] They accepted a limited number of parcels, and the entire train, which left Moscow at six in the morning or around five thirty, was completely jam-packed with people who were sending parcels. So, you had to climb up to the bridge, then run across it, and go down to get to the post office, and to be in the number of people from whom they were still taking parcels. They took parcels of exactly eight kilograms. An extra ten grams, it wouldn't go. But to pack two hundred grams under the limit was a pity; you could, after all, add two hundred grams. Well, so just consider: did this affect my life or not?

CF—Yes, I understand, but our American students . . .

IA—A normal person won't understand this. And that's as it should be. He has a normal psyche. . . . And I was just a girl having to run around all the time, what do you think? Did this have repercussions on my life? Of course, it left an imprint. How, I don't know. I lived a normal life. I tell you again, this was thanks to my husband and his family. . . . But I will tell you, how many years have already passed? You rang today via the intercom, you know? Well, once at night, this same intercom signal rang. We both jumped up, my granddaughter who lives with me. So she took the phone and asked, "Who's there?" They answered, "The police." She pressed the button to let them in. No one came up to our apartment. They were hooligans. But even so, I trembled until the morning; I thought, why had the police come? I understood that this was not an arrest, I understood all of this. But there are still some subconscious things.

CF—When was this?

IA—Well, this was, probably, a year ago. Someone was just playing around. . . .

26. Mozhaisk is one hundred ten kilometers (sixty-eight miles) from Moscow.

CF—To what extent do you consider the repressions to be the most significant era which illustrated everything or almost everything about the Soviet Union's history, about the Soviet system? This was only a part. Is this an important part? An insignificant part?

IA—Well, understand, there were always repressions. In 1929, 1930—dekulakization. This was repression after all. And then the trials of the Trotskyists were already going on. And then the repressions that began in 1937, mass repressions with torture. There were repressions in 1949. There was no period without repressions. So, the period between 1937 and 1939, there was the war, yes. But for me . . . well, recently Aleksei German spoke on television. He said, "I always feel like a prisoner and a participant in the war." That's what it is like for me, in my life the two most important points were the repressions and the war. . . . But, in my opinion, there are two watershed moments in the Soviet Union, the repressions and the war. Without a doubt, war, this was something that you can't imagine. . . .

CF—I have one last question. If you can say, what are you most proud of in your life?

IA—What am I proud of? My children. The children. I believe, well Volodya left this life, I believe that he left behind a very good memory in his children and grandchildren. His grandchildren. And there's nothing else I'm proud of. I don't have any kind of these degrees. I have nothing of that sort. My children do. I don't.

CF—Thank you very much for your interview.

IA—You're welcome, you're welcome.

Inna Aronovna Gaister died in 2009, when she slipped and fell under a Moscow city bus.

CHAPTER THREE

"I, you understand, for my generation, . . . we have the psychology of persons devoted to society. We can't separate ourselves from society"

ANDREI IVANOVICH VOROBYOV

Moscow

May 4, 2005

Transcribed by Elena Vetrova

Introduction

Andrei Ivanovich Vorobyov was born in Moscow on New Year's Day, 1928, to parents who already understood they were likely to become victims of Stalin's rise to power. Ivan Ivanovich Vorobyov and Maria (Mirra) Samuilovna Kizelshtein were Old Bolsheviks who "were always in the opposition" to Stalin, and totally committed to Vladimir Lenin and Leon Trotsky. Both were prominent in their fields. Ivan Vorobyov was a professor at the First Medical Institute of Moscow, and Kizelshtein was a prominent research scientist specializing in endocrinology. As soon as Trotsky lost out to Stalin in the struggle to succeed Lenin as leader of the Communist Party, they knew they might be arrested. Despite this reality, their young son, Andrei Ivanovich, continued to enjoy some privileges of his parents'

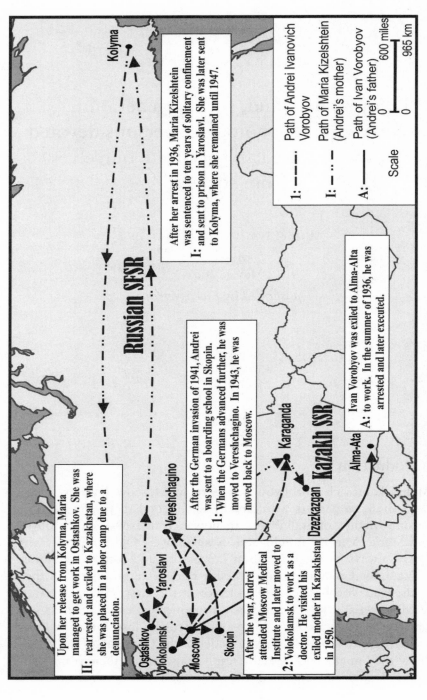

Upon her release from Kolyma, Maria managed to get work in Ostashkov. She was rearrested and exiled to Kazakhstan, where she was placed in a labor camp due to a denunciation.
II:

After the German invasion of 1941, Andrei was sent to a boarding school in Skopin.
1: When the Germans advanced further, he was moved to Vereshchagino. In 1943, he was moved back to Moscow.

After the war, Andrei attended Moscow Medical Institute and later moved to Volokolamsk to work as a doctor. He visited his exiled mother in Kazakhstan in 1950.
2:

After her arrest in 1936, Maria Kizelshtein was sentenced to ten years of solitary confinement and sent to prison in Yaroslavl. She was later sent to Kolyma, where she remained until 1947.
I:

Ivan Vorobyov was exiled to Alma-Alta to work. In the summer of 1936, he was arrested and later executed.
A:

Russian SFSR

Kolyma

Ostashkov
Yaroslavl
Volokolamsk
Moscow
Skopin
Vereshchagino
Karaganda
Dzezkazgan
Kazakh SSR
Alma-Ata

1: ------- Path of Andrei Ivanovich Vorobyov

I: --··-- Path of Maria Kizelshtein (Andrei's mother)

A: ——— Path of Ivan Vorobyov (Andrei's father)

Scale

| 0 | 600 miles |
| 0 | 965 km |

The journeys of Andrei Ivanovich Vorobyov, his mother, and his father, 1936–1950 (Map by Eric Pugliano) professional status and Party associations until he was eight years old, despite his recollection that they rarely had butter to eat. He and his sister had a nanny; they lived in a desirable district close to the Kremlin; they summered with their parents in the elite vacation community of Nikolina Gora. His parents were arrested in 1936. Ivan Vorobyov was executed. Kizelshtein was sentenced to ten years in the forced labor camps, ultimately in Kolyma. The Vorobyov children avoided Soviet orphanages, staying with family members in Moscow. After enduring wartime separation and starvation in the postwar famine years, Andrei Ivanovich struggled to hold on to his schooling, even as he had to work full-time as a laborer. He eventually was able to continue his education. He followed in his parents' footsteps, becoming a physician. In the post-Soviet era, he served as Minister of Health of the Russian Federation under President Boris Yeltsin and directed the Institute of Hematology of the Russian Academy of Sciences in Moscow.

Andrei Ivanovich's interview introduces a lifelong Leninist's reflections on Stalinism and Soviet power. He adds more names to the pantheon of teacher-Samaritans whose intervention contributed to the survival of orphans of political repression. He also provides an evocative recollection of joy among children of the Gulag at the news of Stalin's death. Readers will recognize that however anti-Stalinist Andrei Ivanovich was, he remained a thoroughly Soviet person in his high valuation of collectivism, internationalism, service to society, and orientation by political events as the road markers of his life.

I interviewed Andrei Ivanovich in his office at the Institute of Hematology. I noticed that he kept photos of his parents in his office. As any person in his professional position would be, Andrei Ivanovich was conscious of the time he was giving me in his overscheduled day. Only his sense of responsibility to history made this interview possible.

CF—. . . . How old were you when you became a so-called child of the Gulag?

AI—. . . . I was not yet eight years old when Papa was arrested. And Mama was arrested about three months later. They arrested Mama on December 20, 1936. . . . And fifty years later, we learned that, precisely on that day, Papa was shot dead. I don't know the exact date of Papa's arrest, since he was arrested in Alma-Ata, where he had been exiled. Both Mama and Papa were longtime Bolsheviks from before the revolution. They formally entered the Party right after the February Revolution. De facto, of course, they were in the Party earlier. But since it was illegal, it wasn't recorded anywhere. But as soon as the February Revolution happened, they were officially registered as members of the Party, the Russian Social Democratic Party-Bolshevik.

CF—In what city was this?

AI—Moscow. They lived in Moscow. My parents were born in Moscow. And both of them were in the opposition to Stalin, from the very beginning, since 1923. For that reason, they were expelled from the Party in 1927. After that, Mama did not apply for reinstatement in the Party. They readmitted Papa to the Party, he remained in the opposition, but by then it was underground. . . . But my parents were scientists. They spent most of their time, of course, in scientific work. Papa taught physiology at the First Moscow Medical Institute. He was a doctor by training. Mama was a biologist by training. . . . She was an endocrinologist, her works were published at that time primarily in German, because the working language in science was German, not English. Well, Mama was constantly losing her job because of her past. And she, even so, continued to do experiments with the endocrine glands. . . .

CF—Where did you live?

AI—We lived in Moscow, in Zamoskvorechye, on Malaya Ordynka, in this original, ancient part of Moscow. And my childhood was impoverished, everyone had an impoverished childhood; after all, the entire country was poor. Even scientific workers did not eat butter. They eliminated ration cards only in 1934.

CF—And you yourself were born in what year?

AI—I was born January 1, 1928. So, at the time of Papa's arrest, I was seven, and when Mama was arrested—eight years old. But I must say that I had a happy childhood. Of course they told me a lot of stories and read to me a lot. Mama read out loud to me, she understood that they would be arrested, and that is probably why she found time for raising her son.

CF—When do you believe they understood they would be arrested?

AI—In 1927, in 1928, no doubt remained that there would be arrests—no doubts. Therefore, I can't say that they didn't know what was happening in the country.[1] . . . Two parties made the Revolution, the October Revolution. The first and strongest was the Socialist Revolutionary Party [SRs], the left SRs led by Maria Spiridonova. And the second was the Bolsheviks, with Lenin at the head. Trotsky made the overthrow happen; Lenin came later. Naturally Lenin had tremendous authority. Why is it important to remember this? Because there is the tyrant's responsibility, and then there is the amorphous responsibility of some people whose identity is not clear. Blame the Bolsheviks? Well, this is also without naming anyone in particular. It's the same as blaming an earthquake, blaming bad weather. You can do it, but it's senseless. No, the Revolution is one thing, while a tyrannical regime is another.

CF—I should say that my interest in this book is not as an indictment of the Bolsheviks. . . . I am interested more in the experience of persons like you, and how you constructed your life. . . . That's why my questions are more personal. If you don't object, there will be questions of this kind.

AI—I, you understand, and for my generation, for Inka Gaister,[2] we have the psychology of persons devoted to society. We can't separate ourselves from society. . . . [He asks his assistant to bring him a photo from his files and shows it to me.]

I see this picture before my very eyes. Papa and I . . . I'm seven years old. And I asked him—where did I come up with questions like this? From the questions posed by my parents, things talked about in the family—"Papa, why are they always talking about Stalin? Is he a tsar or something?" I'll remember this my whole life. He smiled, he was a very kind person, he stroked my head. And he said, "You shouldn't talk about this," or something vague. He knew that they might have been listening in on us. Even if they weren't listening in, they could still eavesdrop, and he understood what might await his son if his son figured out what his father knew. . . .

So, Papa knew that he would be arrested. And his son, that is—I—am lucky in this, that I had at least some time with my

1. Andrei Ivanovich here spoke for several minutes to provide a history of the revolution and civil war, 1917–1921.
2. Inka is a diminutive of Inna, a sign of endearment.

Andrei Ivanovich Vorobyov with his father on the eve
of his arrest (Private collection of A. I. Vorobyov)

father. My father was exiled, he was home for short periods of
time. This is my entire family history. . . .

CF—What were the chief goals, the main ideas, the main
Communist ethics that your parents taught you?

AI—Well, first of all, they never called this communism. They
didn't use such words. I know that the first condition is democratic behavior and collective leadership. Indeed, the October
overthrow was achieved collectively. Lenin was the spiritual
leader. But it was really Trotsky who did it all, Krylenko[3] did it,
Dybenko[4] also was part of it. Lenin could not command Trotsky,

3. Nikolai Krylenko was an Old Bolshevik who rose to prominence in the
Soviet judicial system, becoming Commissar of Justice in 1936, only to be purged
and executed himself in 1938.
4. Pavel Dybenko was an Old Bolshevik; a key leader of the revolution among
sailors, he was purged and shot in 1938.

who was then the leader of the army, only the Politburo could. This collegiality, this prevention of a cult of personality lay in the very foundation. [. . . further disquisition about collective leadership during the revolution and during New Economic Policy] Well, of course, my childhood was full of books, books that Mama read, well, and the stories that she told. . . . Yershov, "The Hunch-Backed Horse,"[5] of course, all of Seton-Thompson,[6] the marvelous Seton-Thompson, well, and "The Song of Hiawatha" of Longfellow. Well, and then of course there were Pushkin's fairy tales.[7] That was my alphabet book. We didn't even have enough money for an ABC book. Papa drew me an alphabet book. He drew little pictures, and under the pictures he wrote block letters, what they signified. He drew well. . . .

CF—When you said that Papa had already been exiled to Alma-Ata, that means you said good-bye to him, not knowing that this was the last farewell, not having any notion that this was forever?

AI—Yes.

CF—Were there searches after his arrest?

AI—No. After his arrest, there was no search at our place. They arrested him in the city of Alma-Ata, where he had been sent to work. He was expelled from the Party and sent to work in Alma-Ata. He directed the department of physiology and medicine in an institute. . . . But Mama stayed in Moscow. Papa came here for the summer. This was the summer of 1936. . . . The first show trial of Zinoviev and Kamenev had already happened.[8] They were shot, and everyone already understood everything. I can see before my eyes the conversation between my parents when Gorky died.[9] We were living at the dacha at Nikolina

5. Russian fairy tale in verse.
6. Ernest Thompson Seton, was a naturalist, a founder of the Boy Scout movement, and an author of many illustrated works about the natural world.
7. Aleksandr Pushkin, Russia's most beloved national author, was a key figure of the Russian "golden age" of literature in the first quarter of the nineteenth century.
8. Grigory Zinoviev and Lev Kamenev, Bolsheviks who contributed to the movement since before the October revolution of 1917, were the central defendants of the 1936 show trial.
9. Maxim Gorky, prominent Soviet writer, died under mysterious circumstances in 1936.

Gora.[10] And Gorky lived right next door. I remember the day when he died well, on June 18, 1936. Papa said, "It's all over," when Gorky died. They understood that he had been removed. And right after this was the show trial. And so someone called us and told us that they had come to our apartment. Therefore, Papa did not return to the apartment from the dacha. He went back to Alma-Ata. They arrested him there in Alma-Ata. . . . At that point, this was 1936, they were arresting the opposition. But when they arrested Mama, there *was* a search. But I slept through it, and through Mama's arrest, too. Mama asked them not to wake the child, and in the morning I found out that Mama had left on a business trip. And that was it. Well, that's how it was. After a few months, they kicked us out of the apartment, sealed it and seized all our property. . . .

At first, we stayed in that apartment with our nanny. Our nanny did not abandon us. . . . We had, it was a communal apartment, we had two rooms. Then they were sealed, and they put us out in the hallway. With two bundles of children's things. We went to live at my Grandmother's place, to my father's mama, Evgenia Yosifovna Vorobyova. She took us in. Well, and the family supported us, of course, we were our family's children. They didn't let us fade away. . . . Our nanny didn't live with us then. She got a job at a factory and didn't live with us. It was very crowded at Grandmother's. I slept on chairs in the hallway. . . . Then I went to live with my aunt, Mama's sister, whose husband had also been arrested and shot, but she had been left behind with two children. . . .

CF—What happened with school?

AI—Nothing. I went to school and at first had to take two trams . . . . to my school on Ordynka. I really didn't want to transfer. . . . But in the third and fourth grade, I lived with my aunt Zinaida Samuilovna Kizelshtein. And I went to this School No. 43 on Prechistenka. So that was another school. I finished the fifth grade, and the war started. Well, they suggested that I go to a children's home. Of course, we weren't about to go to any such place, that was clear. But when the war started, then I was sent to a boarding school. My sister was studying at the medical

10. Nikolina Gora was a summer cottage community outside Moscow for members of the Soviet elite.

institute. The boarding school—this is a type of children's home, and I was there for two years.

CF—You said, "Of course, they suggested a children's home." Who suggested this and why?

AI—The KGB. When they took our home away from us. Yes, they suggested I go to a children's home, they really tried to tempt me, they told all kinds of stories. I refused even to talk to them. . . . I was eight years old; they suggested this to me. But that these were enemies I had no doubt, not for even a second. It was Grandmother, though, who sent me to the boarding school. It was just that Moscow was to be evacuated, I needed to go somewhere. Everyone understood that there would be famine. People understood everything. They sent me away. So we went to the boarding school. . . . At first this was in the city of Skopin in Riazan district. Then the Germans started to advance in that direction, and they transferred us to the Urals. There's a station there, Vereshchagino, thirty-five kilometers from the station. This is Perm district. . . . I had friends, well, a few. The war scattered us. But, a few years ago, I attended the funerals for two of my friends from before the war. From the boarding school, there is one friend left, and we get together from time to time.

CF—Did you conceal your parents' fate?

AI—Never. *Never,* never under any circumstances. I did not hide the fact that I was a son of enemies of the people. Never. I didn't write the words "enemies of the people." I had to write in all my forms, I had to write in all my biographical materials that my parents were arrested in 1936. My mother was convicted, sentenced to ten years, my father to ten years without right of correspondence. I didn't know, of course, that he had been shot. But Mama received ten years in solitary confinement. But the prisons were already overloaded, so she was paired with another. She was in the Yaroslavl central prison. From there, they were transferred to Kolyma. . . . All of the Bolshevik women, Old Bolshevik women, were arrested, whether they were in the opposition or not. All of them. Those who were in the opposition were mostly shot. They didn't shoot Mama, she was lucky. She had already been expelled long before from the Party, so they didn't execute her—although she was arrested in connection with my father's case, but that's how it was. Besides, there was something

curious about my mama's arrest, well nothing especially puz-
zling—before an arrest, they had to procure some kind of special
sanction in the Party organization. Prior to her arrest, Mama had
been working on very important research on the endocrinology
of cancer. And after she had returned from her term in Kolyma,
she was told that that when they came from the KGB to the institute of nutrition, the Party organization there requested that
they postpone her arrest for a few weeks. She was supposed to
submit her report on her work to date, a very important report.
Later, the report was defended as a doctoral dissertation, but
not by Mama of course. They told her about this later. She said,
"I have no claims of any kind. It's laughable." And the Party
organization postponed her arrest. And she was arrested when
Papa and the other persons in his case had been shot that day.
So, that's the story. Stalin arrested anyone he concluded needed
to be arrested.

CF—How did your teachers treat you?

AI—They always treated me well. And, moreover, I sensed
implicitly a certain special attention. A special attention, kind
attention. Only once was there this kind of episode at the boarding school, when a group of children was leaving for Moscow,
and I was also supposed to go with them, but they didn't take
me. I started to become indignant. And the boarding school's
director said, "But you, Vorobyov, really should know your
place . . ." And I swore at her in front of the whole administration. I had a good command of curses back then. And I swore
at her, and that was it. But, I repeat, neither in the early grades,
nor later.

And then later, already, when I was in the ninth and tenth
grades, I was surrounded by such care, because I had nothing
to eat. After I came back from the boarding school, I started to
work. I worked as a house painter, then as a lab assistant. You
had to get a worker's ration card, otherwise you would starve to
death. And to eat, who was going to get food for me? So I went
to night school. . . . This was during the war, this was 1943. . . . I
returned in 1943, I entered the eighth grade in a school for working youth, and I worked as a painter on construction sites. And
a year later, I turned sixteen, and that meant that my workday
was supposed to be eight hours long. I worked a six-hour day
up to age sixteen—well, of course, nobody ever worked just six,

a bit more, and but just a *bit* more. But I wasn't strong enough
for an eight-hour day. That is, I could get through the workday,
but after this, I couldn't go to school. I didn't have the physical
strength. So I quit school.

And then a year later, in 1945, the war ended, my cousin returned from the army and said that he would earn the money,
but Andrei [I] should study. And I started a normal high school.
. . . Immediately, I was somehow surrounded by an unspoken,
invisible solicitude. No one said any word of any kind, but during the breaks, during the lunch breaks, they would call me over
to eat with them. They gave me something to eat, they saw that
I was as skinny as a skeleton. They would give me something
to eat. Then they laid their hands on some kind of order form,
they dressed me. Because I had nothing, only a dirty padded
jacket. And then my marvelous teacher Varvara Aleksandrovna
Tsareva, I owe her everything. She was the literature teacher, I
will remember her for my entire life. She organized classes in
literature for me to teach to younger school children. I had excellent language skills; I, of course, was a good student. Because,
people held onto this school with their teeth. It was my entire
future. I already knew that my cousin had been arrested, this had
happened right before my eyes. I understood that I could also be
arrested at any moment.

CF—Tell me about his arrest. . . .

AI—It happened at home. We were sleeping, in the room,
there was a knock on the door, "Document check." Three men
in uniform entered, showed him the warrant for his arrest. And
well, the search started, everything was turned upside down. One
KGB guy, a good guy, said, "Are these your felt boots?" I said,
"No, they are his." "I *told* you that these are *your* boots." I gathered as many things as I could, because they sealed the room.
Everything had to be removed.

CF—Was this in 1945?

AI—This was 1944. Yes. I was working. . . . That's why we
studied hard. Varvara Aleksandrovna Tsareva organized a group
of schoolchildren, whom I tutored in Russian language. I was in
the tenth grade; they were in the seventh. She received the money
from parents and gave it to me. Therefore, I can't say that I had
to encounter the consequences of my parents' arrest in society.

Society, the cultured part of society, did not accept the regime. It's also clear that everyone was afraid. *Horror, of course, seized everyone. We didn't talk about politics, this was understood. But we helped each other a great, great deal.*

CF—And did you correspond with your mother while she was in the Gulag? . . . .

AI—There were different systems. When she was in Yaroslavl Central Prison, she wrote rarely, I have forgotten now, but rarely. But in Kolyma, more often, but, I think, no more than once a month. We sent her packages all the time. These were the most simple parcels, onions, bread husks, sometimes lard—well, whatever we could get. And I should say that all the parcels reached her. And during the war, when I was in the boarding school, which was basically a children's home, I exchanged a piece of bread, back then they gave out portions of bread, a piece was two hundred grams. I would exchange bread with the collective farmers for onions, or something else, and I would send it to Mama from Perm district to Kolyma. And she received it all. She used to say, "Andryusha, I owe you my life, because there was scurvy there, teeth fell out, but here I was with onions." Onions, of course, saved her from scurvy. We wrote each other all the time. Mama and I were generally very close before and afterward. . . . Mama came back in 1947, she completed her sentence in 1946. She just managed to leave. In 1947 already a decree came out ordering that prisoners not be released from the camps. In 1936, these arrests were relatively rare. Primarily they shot people arrested in 1936. But she ended up being arrested at the very end of the year, she was not shot even in 1936. When 1947 arrived, an order came from Moscow to Kolyma and to all camps. "Release from the convoy, do not release prisoners, hire them as freed laborers, but don't release them from the camp zone."

Mama managed to get out, and she even told how she arrived in Magadan.[11] She lived beyond Kolyma, there at Yagodnoe, on the Elgen collective farm . . . . she arrived in Magadan when she had served her full sentence. She said, "You understand, I went to Dal'stroi.[12] I went and arrived at the director's office of Dal'stroi

11. A town in the far northeastern part of Siberia, founded in 1929 as a port city. It was the transit point for prisoners being sent to Kolyma.

12. An NKVD-run Northern Construction Trust for mining in Kolyma region, it was a network of forced labor camps.

and simply walked past the secretary into his office. She rushed after me into the office. I handed in my application and said only one thing, 'I have children there.' He looked me over silently." He wrote, "To the mainland." And she left on the last steamer out of Kolyma. Well, here she found work in the town of Ostashkov, she had one really bad minus: the hundred-and-one-kilometer limitation. She could not live in any district centers. I would go there to visit her. But later they arrested her again and that time gave her permanent exile to Kazakhstan. In Kazakhstan, she fell prey to a provocateur; there was a provocateur among the exiles. I saw him and told Mama. This is a very strange phenomenon, that I figured it out better than she did. Because she had lived for ten years among persons like herself, people whom she more or less trusted. But I lived in this world, where every other person was a provocateur or informer. Of course, I was on guard, and I always feared them. I was afraid, I kept my distance from them. And when I saw this person, I said, "Mama, he's a provocateur." "Andryusha, what are you saying!" One day, he said something really good about Stalin. Mama sighed and said, "How can you say kind words about this bloody tyrant!?" . . . But someone was listening and informing on her, and this person came out in the open at the public trial as a witness. And she received ten years hard labor, with a number in front and a number on her back. Without a name, ten years of hard labor. But that was already, I think, in 1950. Mama was sent to Kengir. This is in Karaganda District, Dzhezkazgan, I think. I'm afraid I might be wrong about the geography. . . . Khrushchev began to free people in 1954.[13] At first they just freed old people. At that time, Mama was fifty-five years old, but she was an old woman without teeth, they transferred these people to being "on record." Being "on record" meant that the person is an invalid, unsuitable for work. If he's unsuitable for work, he was thrown out of the camp. And from the moment she was liberated, I categorically forbade her to work. Well, so . . . . because by that time, my older son was born—"Take care of him." It's interesting that she always called

13. Nikita Khrushchev assumed leadership in the Communist Party after Stalin's death, initially in close cooperation with Georgi M. Malenkov. From 1953 to 1956, they quietly released many Old Bolshevik political prisoners in a process Kathleen Smith describes as "silent de-Stalinization." See Kathleen E. Smith, *Remembering Stalin's Victims. Popular Memory and the End of the USSR* (Ithaca, New York: Cornell University Press, 1996), 21.

my son Andryusha, although I had named him Vanya in honor of my father. . . .

CF—What was your conception of Soviet power during all of this time when your mother was in the Gulag? That is, was this simply a question of Stalin, did you consider yourself to be a Soviet person? That's one question. And the second question is, to what extent do you believe that your dossier or biography as a child of an enemy of the people influenced your studies?

AI—I can say, of course, that I was a good student. And I graduated from high school with a gold medal, but my teachers helped me with this, or I might not have received the medal. And I graduated from the institute with honors. I had help there also. But as for what the arrest of my parents did to me—I wanted to enter only the Physics Department of Moscow State University after I finished school, but they laughed at me and explained that I was simply a fool. With my dossier, I was not even to approach the Physics Department. And so I didn't approach it, I went to the Medical Institute from which my father had graduated. They really loved Papa in this institute—I repeat, he was a very kind, jovial person—and this extended to me. People helped me. There was one son of a bitch or maybe more who acted just the opposite. You see, they did not take me into the army, they did not take me into military training at the institute. Of course they didn't place me in either the internship program or graduate school, naturally. And I went to work in Volokolamsk[14] after I graduated from the institute. I thank fate that I worked in Volokolamsk. I saw normal life, I worked twenty hours a day as a doctor. I got to know this life. This is a good, not a bad, thing.

Of course, I was never in the Party, I wasn't even in the Komsomol. I never took one step in this direction. If I had had a different biography, perhaps I would have joined, and later I would have been ashamed. But I had no contact with them, I knew that this was a Party of degenerates, that this was in no way the Communist, but the Stalinist, Party. That's what we said in our family; it was never a subject of doubt. We knew who the revolutionaries were, I knew many of them personally. Well, I knew

14. Volokolamsk was a provincial town one hundred twenty-nine kilometers northwest of Moscow. As in the case of Irina Dubrovina, Vorobyov's excellent academic record did not earn him a job in Moscow, much less admission to graduate school, because of his status.

Inka Gaister, I knew her father, her mother Khilya, I knew their circle. These were the purest of people. Self-sacrificing people, who gave their lives to the people. Really, you mustn't forget that many came to Moscow from the provinces, from oppressed Jewish places, from pogroms. The tsarist regime really was horrifying. . . . And that's why it came to Soviet power. I can even say that we knew that there was no such Soviet power. And when our circle got together—Inna Gaister, my sister Irina, Nina Gigichkori (her father was also shot), and many others—we would often drink a toast, so it would sound good (and we knew that they were listening), "to Soviet power." Because we said that the Soviet power that existed for that short period after 1920–1922, that was democratic power, elected by the people. Then it was liquidated. So we were drinking to democracy, and that was all. We, of course, understood that this disfigured power of the Lubyanka,[15] the power of Old Square,[16] of the Party apparatus, that these were our enemies. And they called themselves Soviet power. But this was their affair. We didn't consider them as such. Neither I, nor my sister, nor my cousins—categorically they all refused to enter the Party.

CF—Where were you and how did you react to Stalin's death?

AI—[Laughs out loud] I reacted with joy, immediately, and nothing else. I did not know where to hide. It was March 5th, it was a sunny, clear day in Moscow. To begin with, it [his death] lasted for three to four days after we were told that he had developed Cheyne-Stokes respiration. We thanked the great Cheyne-Stokes. I knew that all evil was in him. It would be better or worse, but I instinctively sensed that it could get no worse. After all, we understood; the Doctors' Plot was going on at that time.[17] I was graduating from the First Medical Institute at that time. I

15. Headquarters of the security services, then known as the NKVD, later the KGB, now the FSB.

16. Staraya Ploshad' was the location of the headquarters of the Communist Party.

17. The Doctors' Plot was a fabricated conspiracy that led to the arrest of Jewish doctors who allegedly had plotted to kill Soviet leaders. Announced publicly in January 1953, the Plot signified a major feature of accelerating official anti-Semitism. On the "Doctors' Plot" see Jonathan Brent and Vladimir Naumov, *Stalin's Last Crime: The Plot Against the Jewish Doctors, 1948–1953* (New York: Harper Perennial, 2004).

was around many of the doctors who were arrested. And arrests
were happening everywhere. I didn't know that they were about
to deport the Jews, to send them to the north, but we sensed
that it could go no further, that the terror which the crazy tyrant
had let loose, that it had reached its apogee. And we all understood when the new government was formed, with Malenkov at
the head and Khrushchev as first secretary. . . . We understood
from the very first day that indisputable change for the better had
happened, because anti-Semitic leaflets suddenly disappeared. In
Pravda [the central Communist Party newspaper] they weren't
writing against the evildoers-Jews. And that was an indicator.
We knew how to read between the lines like no one else. And we
understood that, no, no, no, something was changing for the better. . . . There was no public anti-Semitism. And after a month,
they freed the doctors. That was such a celebration that you could
have lost your mind. Well, you needed to see it to believe it.

Then there was the fact of where I lived. When I married,
the father of my deceased wife, Inna Pavlovna Kolomoitsevaya,
had also been shot, her mother also was imprisoned, and their
apartment had also been taken away. They were given a place
on Kuznetsky Most [Street], a long hallway, they had one room.
And every night—that was in 1952 or '51, and we got married
in '49—I heard a nightly stream of cars below us on Kuznetsky
Most. And I understood that they were transporting arrested persons. They would shift gears right there, crossing Rozhdestvenka,
it was called Zhdanov Street then. It's a horror to be present
during arrests every night. Stalin croaked—and then silence.
No cars at night, immediately. We all immediately understood.
Everyone. . . .

In general, I have the impression that all our stories about the
past can't be understood by people today. . . . You understand,
the whole issue is the tyrannical regime. If there is no such regime,
you have one kind of country. If there is a tyrannical regime, then
it drags terror in with it. A tyrant can't exist without terror. It's
not feasible. . . . A tyrannical regime is short-lived. What are
thirty years in history, this is not much. Nothing remained from
it. From Stalin, nothing remained except rivers of blood. . . .

This generation needs to know the history of Stalinist repression. They need to know the history of Hitler's repression. This is
one and the *same mechanism*, after all, and *one* and the same *ter-*

Andrei Ivanovich Vorobyov with his son Ivan Andreevich
Vorobyov, 2012 (Photograph by Cathy A. Frierson)

rible consequences for one's own people. I would not want at all
to forget the victims of repression. . . . Tyranny destroys the roots
of culture. It appears that Hitler's tyranny was directed against
Jews, Poles, and the complete destruction of gypsies. . . . It would
seem that this was against other peoples. Others, but out of their
blood rose Israel, rose Poland, while Germany fell from the apex
of culture and science. Perhaps no one understands this as we
do, because our medicine is very close to German medicine, and
spiritually—well, forgive me, may English-speaking peoples forgive me—but of course, German culture is closest to me in spirit,
we have common roots. We have many German roots and many
scholars . . . . studied in Germany. . . . This is the tragedy of a
destroyed culture, it is nevertheless the result of this tyranny and
terror, directed ostensibly against another people. . . .

But, of course, the collapse of 1991—this was the payback for the tyrannical regime, for the destruction, so to say, not only of cadres, but of this spiritual, explosive beginning that was born during the revolution. And even so, the art of the Soviet Union, its physicists, mathematicians, doctors, biologists—its biologists were geniuses. . . . And, of course, I believe that our collapse, this is the collapse of Stalin's tyranny, then of Brezhnev's[18] tyranny—liberal, well, half-liberal, but rotten. A rotten, senseless tyranny, where a disintegrating tyrant did nothing, but he was a tyrant. He was the sole ruler.

CF—I am very grateful to you. Thank you for your time. Would you like to add something before we conclude?

AI—No. Well, people need to know, do whatever you want, but never the absolute power of one person. That is the *death of the nation,* and even if it appears that he has positive features. No. *Never. Never.*

18. Leonid Brezhnev succeeded Nikita Khrushchev as Soviet leader for the years 1964–1982.

CHAPTER FOUR

"I would ride as far as Karabas Station, but then, I don't recall, I had to go about fifty–sixty kilometers on foot"

VALENTIN TIKHONOVICH MURAVSKY

First interview in Saint Petersburg, February 2006
Second interview in the United States, October 2007

Transcribed by Natalya Maeden

Introduction

Valentin Tikhonovich Muravsky was born in 1928 in Leningrad. His mother was a medic and a member of the Communist Party. His father, a radio engineer, was not a member of the Party. The family lived prosperously until the Great Terror. As a "child of the Gulag," young Valentin Tikhonovich endured a life of exceptional displacement, family loss and separation, and imprisonment. He lost his father to arrest as an enemy of the people in 1937. The Soviet government then exiled him and his mother and older sister to Central Asia for being relatives of an enemy of the people. In 1941 the Soviet state informed his mother that their exile had been a "mistake" and returned them to Leningrad on the eve of the German invasion in World War II. Evacuated from the Leningrad Blockade in 1942, young Valentin Tikhonovich was seized in the North Caucasus by the invading German forces

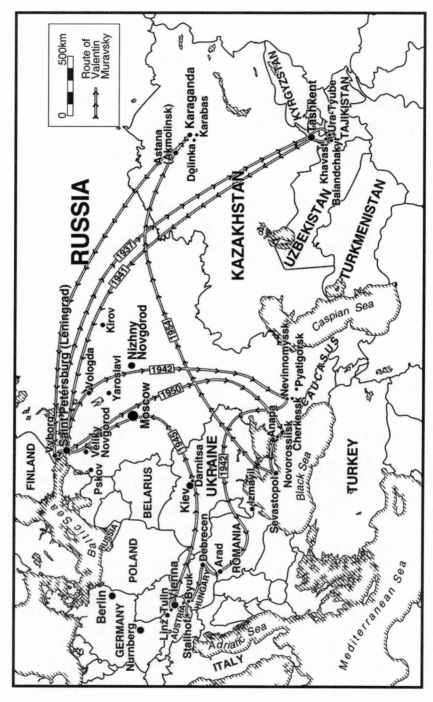

The journeys of Valentin Tikhonovich Muravsky, 1937–1957 (Map by Darya Oreshkina)

and taken as a slave laborer to work in Romania, Hungary, and Austria. He escaped to join the Red Army in Austria in March 1945.

Upon his return to the USSR at the end of the war, Valentin Tikhonovich was soon arrested in connection with his sister's decision not to return from Germany, where she had also been a slave laborer. She went instead to the United States with an American soldier she met and married in Germany. Officially, Valentin Tikhonovich was charged with possession of equipment related to his work in mine demolition, but he remained convinced that his sister's situation and his refusal to summon her back to the Soviet Union were the true deciding factors in his arrest. His mother was also arrested because of her daughter's decision and exiled to the prison camp for wives of traitors to the motherland in Kazakhstan. Upon release from prison, Valentin Tikhonovich was drafted into the navy. When he completed his military service, he moved to Kazakhstan to be within visiting distance of his mother in the camps. After her release in 1956 and death in 1957, Valentin Tikhonovich returned to Leningrad, his hometown. That is where I interviewed him the first time in 2006 in the offices of Memorial. I interviewed him a second time in 2007 in the United States during a visit to his son at his home in New Jersey. In June 2010, Valentin Tikhonovich traveled to a conference in Kazakhstan on the history of political repressions. This was his first return to the region since 1957. He continued to be active in Memorial activities in Saint Petersburg into 2013.

Valentin Tikhonovich's interview is exceptional in the panoramic portrait it provides of one boy's, and then man's, experiences as a victim of multiple forms of political repression in the Soviet Union and as a teenage slave laborer in Nazi-occupied Eastern Europe. His experiences illustrate how Soviet policies truncated and divided families, displaced adults and children, jeopardized educational opportunities, and imposed political stigma across three generations. Valentin Tikhonovich's interviews also reveal how hunger, illness, and frequent sighting of corpses were constant features of this young Soviet citizen's life, as they were of so many Soviet citizens' lives in the 1930s–1950s.

CF—How old were you when you became a so-called child of enemies of the people?

VT—The beginning of the terror, the repression, that was 1937, and at that time, I was nine years old, I think, or eight years old.

Valentin Tikhonovich Muravsky in Saint Petersburg,
2012 (Photograph by Cathy A. Frierson)

CF—Can you describe your family before . . .

VT—Before the arrest? We had a fine, large family. We had
everything we needed. Both Mama and my father worked. My
father was a radio engineer. I remember—this is from memory,
that he had radio instruments at home. He was making new instruments, and in fact it was then, when I was still a child, that
something extraordinary happened. At New Year's, there was a
New Year's tree, a special dinner and so on. And suddenly my
father . . . the guests started to raise their glasses for toasts and
so on, and Galina Ivanovna was not raising her glass, and on
the radio, a voice said, "The time has come, Comrades, to make
a toast. Galina Ivanovna, why aren't you raising your glass?"
This was so unexpected, this was 1937, 1935, or 1936, I don't
remember anymore. This was so unexpected. My father had set
up a microphone at home. He had gone into his room and done
this over the radio! This would be nothing at all now, but back
then. . . . This was his joke. . . . So, we were from this kind of
family. At home we had a piano, as you would expect.

CF—And where did you live, in what city?

VT—I both grew up, and was born here, in Leningrad. . . .
We were Papa; me; my older sister, Dina; and Mama. But Papa
worked as an engineer, with equipment and so forth. . . . I'm
from this kind of family. . . . When I was a child, that is, before

our exile, before my father's arrest, I . . . . attended a little group where I studied the violin, but this was my, so to speak, past. . . . There was a large kitchen, then a dining room, Papa's bedroom, and the children's room. So that we had one, two, three, four—four rooms and a kitchen.

CF—Was your father a Party member?

VT—No, no.

CF—And even so he received such a fine apartment?

VT—Perhaps it was because Mama was a Party member. I never gave it much thought for some reason. But I remember that Mama used to say that she was—just a minute, I'll think of it and I'll tell you—a deputy of the Petrograd, not the Leningrad, but the Petrograd City Soviet of the First Session.[1] What that was, I have no idea, it probably was when the first elections happened—she was a real activist and so forth. She was a medic, very active, she spoke and wrote very well. But my father, he wasn't even in the Party, and I don't know why. . . .

The reason I noticed after all of this was over, they had already returned us to Leningrad, home, and when this rehabilitation started . . . , what year this was, there's no way I can remember—and when they permitted me to see my father's case file, that's where I read it, what he was arrested for, that was already after he had been rehabilitated. There were a total of three pages, three or four pages, and there, the first question, well, there were these statements. "So," he says, "you served in the White Army." And Father answered, "I did not serve in the White Army, there was only one army." And from conversations, I recall, Mama told me that he, during the World War I, that was in 1914, he was seventeen years old, he wasn't even of military age, he went as a volunteer to fight for Russia, for the motherland, to defend it. And he answered, back then there was neither a White nor a Red Army: "I went to war as a volunteer." That was his first answer. . . . During World War I, so, in 1916, there was this river—it's called the Iprit, and he was poisoned in a gas attack at the Iprit. And after that, he no longer saw combat, that is, he'd been poisoned and he constantly had trouble with his lungs. . . .

1. The capital of the Russian Empire, Saint Petersburg, was renamed Petrograd during World War I, and then renamed Leningrad after Vladimir Lenin's death in 1924.

As for Party membership, that is, was he in the Party? One of the questions to him was, "Do you have ties with Rykov?"[2] And Rykov, he was a Party member, I don't remember anymore, was he right or left, I'm not a Party member. My father answered that, "I am not a member of the Bolshevik Party," or something of the sort. As for ties with Rykov, it was just that Rykov before this was the People's Commissar of Communications, and Father worked on the radio, that is, at some point, he was the director of the Short Wave Institute for correspondence students. So, through his work, because of the radio, while Rykov was the minister or People's Commissar for Communications, and for that reason, he contacted him, he had some kind of contact with him, but not because he was some kind of Party member, left or right. . . . And then there were some other kinds of questions. "Are you an English spy, a Polish, a Japanese spy, and such like." He said, "I have no such connections of any kind." This was during something like the second or third interrogation. But at the fourth interrogation, it's like this: "So, you served in the White Army?" "Yes, I served." "You," he says, "had some kinds of ties with Rykov?" "Yes, I had such ties." "You're some kind of Polish or English spy?" "Yes, I am a spy for Poland." So, they—excuse me, I won't tell you what I really call these scum— . . . they beat this testimony out of him.

I read this. And how do I feel about all of this? . . . I won't read it a second time. That is, I know the essentials, how this is all done, how all of this is extracted through beatings. Now, I'm a grown man, on the downhill side of my life. It doesn't so much upset me as stun and oppress me, how it could be at that time that someone was speaking—who was in charge here then? Vyshinsky,[3] and then there was Yezhov,[4] and when he spoke, so, "enemies of the people," and everyone applauded! I say, My God, how many people are there saying "Death to these spies, these enemies of the people!" and so forth? When Stalin and who

2. Aleksei Rykov was an Old Bolshevik who held a series of major posts. He was purged and executed in 1938. The most relevant of his positions for Muravsky's fate was Commissar of Post and Communications.

3. Andrei Vyshinsky was Prosecutor General during the terror years; he oversaw and played an active part in the show trials.

4. Nikolai Yezhov was head of security forces during the most notorious terror years, 1936–1938.

else—Beria[5]—made speeches, and how everyone there . . . Are we really such cattle, such a herd?" . . .

CF—You said that you studied violin. Was this considered typical for engineers' sons, or do you think that you were exceptional?

VT—Well, to some extent. First of all, in our home, well, not every household had all of these things—well, what I had before the arrest, before the exile. I remember that we had a very large library. Enormous. At home. It had everything: Schiller, and Shakespeare, and Leo Tolstoy, all ninety volumes, and his correspondence, everything, everything. They were enormous walls, there was a Great Soviet Encyclopedia, I remember all of this. And I read all of it. This was everything for me, I lived on it. I don't know how it was in other families, but our circle, that is Mama's and Papa's circle, was like that. . . .

CF—Did you have close friends?

VT—Why, but of course! . . . We had one game—stickball [*lapta*]. We played. This, I think is like baseball or something like that, yes, that was our game. We played in the courtyard, we ran, we jumped, when it was winter, then we skated. Back then we used to tie them onto our felt boots somehow. We also would go into the woods, we would catch tadpoles. . . . We would swim in this pond where there were tadpoles. We would catch them and sometimes we would throw them at the girls. [Laughs] You asked what we did, this was my circle, this was youth, this was childhood. . . .

CF—Did you have any pets at home?

VT—A cat, I think, but we, I think, ate her during the blockade. I don't remember. . . .

CF—Can you recall your father's arrest? . . .

VT—I have a very vague memory of it. I recall for some reason, that our apartment was fine, very orderly, with a piano, . . . But then all of this was thrown about, the radio equipment was on the floor . . . I remember that there was a desk with all kinds of drawers . . . Either this was after the search, or after something

5. Lavrenty Beria was head of security forces 1938–1956.

else that I can't remember, but for what reason, how, I can't imagine.

CF—Were you home when your father was arrested? Did they arrest your father at home or at work?

VT—No, it happened like this. This is from Mama's words, she told me, I wasn't present, it happened like this. In Russia, it is the custom in every family to call home to let the family know, "I'm going to be a little delayed, or I'll be an hour late. You go ahead and eat," and so forth. . . . One hour passed, two hours passed, even longer—this is what Mama told me—it was eleven o'clock, and he still wasn't home, and that was the end of it. And we never saw him again, and we didn't know, and so on. And after this, when they came and destroyed all of this, they were looking for something, I don't even know what . . .

CF—You didn't say good-bye.

VT—No, no. But in my memory, I remember him.

CF—Did you understand immediately that he had been arrested? Did your mama explain and did you understand where he had gone? Was there any kind of explanation?

VT—No. No explanation of any kind. Either she believed that I was too little, but I was already not that little, but she . . . I did not know that it was an arrest and all the rest. I remember that we began to pack. . . . And I remember this: first there was a train, our belongings, we rode and rode, we rode for seven days. This I also remember. And then from conversations, from Mama's stories, too, how it was for us. We went to Tashkent, in Central Asia. . . .

CF—How much older was Dina?

VT—She was two years older than me.

CF—So, she was eleven years old. And seven days by train.

VT—Yes, but the thing was that, so we arrived in Tashkent, Mama told me this, she went to register there or somewhere else, and they said to her, "Tashkent does not answer to Leningrad." And they sent us somewhere to a village, it was in the steppe. But it was a good thing that Mama was a medic, she had a lot of work. There was a clinic of some kind there, to treat people. Or she set it up herself. And I remember how she would go, say someone got sick there, and there was a cart, it was called an *arba,* with great big wheels, not like our wheels, big wheels like they have in Central Asia, it would take her there. And then, someplace else, and someplace else. . . . The first place we lived was the Khavast Region, Ursatyevsk Station. There was some kind of small center there. But they would send Mama all over the place. To practice medicine. There were inoculations to do, and epidemics. For some reason, I remember two or three places: Balanchikir, some other place, and Ura-Tyube, I think. But the thing is, now I'm already an adult, but Ura-Tyube—this is Tadzhikistan. We went all over Central Asia, mountains and so forth, I never gave it much thought, this was not only Uzbekistan, but they sent her all around.

CF—You went with her?

VT—Yes, naturally, of course. . . .

CF—And what kind of housing were you given there? . . .

VT—Well, as it is called, *saman. Saman*—it's clay, straw, manure, all of this is mixed together and applied to the cottage . . . The floor was clay, the walls were clay. . . .

CF—If I may ask, how did you understand your situation? . . . At what age did you understand that your father was gone, that this had been an arrest, and he had disappeared. When did you understand that this was forever?

VT—So, at first, when they arrested my father in Leningrad, before we left, when we were still going to school and so forth, I truly do not recall how this affected me. I was in the first—in the second—grade at that time. But my sister, my sister came home from school, I could see that she had been crying. Because someone had said to her, "You're the daughter of an enemy of the people." I didn't really understand this, but then it was already palpable that there was a certain attitude toward us. Even our neighbors. . . . Many of them had sympathy for us, they were sorry for us, we were a normal family, and even, "We feel for you," but there was a kind of fear that, "Won't they arrest a neighbor, someone else?" and so on. That kind of situation. . . .

CF—And when did you begin to think that this, perhaps, was forever, that your father was gone?

VT—For some reason, I never thought that. That is, after many, many years, I wrote both to the prosecutor's office and someplace else. . . . I was always searching everywhere for my father. I wrote to the prosecutor's office, I wrote to the Minister of Internal Affairs. . . . But I received acknowledgments of receipt, but not a single answer: about where, how, what had happened to him and so forth, I did not receive that. . . .

CF—How many years did you live with your mama and sister in Central Asia, in exile?

VT—We didn't live there very long, four years; we left in 1937 and they sent us back in 1941.

CF—When? During the war already or before the war?[6]

VT—No, the war started in June, and they sent us back, . . . when? . . . This is how it happened. You know that when you lived there, you had to go to register. Mama would do that . . . So, on one of her regular visits to the police, to the NKVD, and they say to her: this and that, there was a mistake, and you're going back. You see? And they sent us back, we packed up and came here. . . . They sent us back to Leningrad. . . . We lived at Auntie Dusya's place, she was Mama's friend. . . . And so we began to live for the time being with her, but later they gave us a room, not an apartment, but a room. There was one room, it was on Serdobolskaya Street. And so we lived there. . . . But my father was gone. . . .

CF—Can you describe the start of the war? Do you have any memories of that day?

VT—Well, the first thing is that the war, June 22, found me—how was that? It was summer, June, warm, good weather, I was at camp, outside the city in a small village—well, not a village, at a camp there called Tokshevo. And so I was in this Tokshevo, and for some reason they announced there that the war had started. . . . And we all looked to see what was happening over Leningrad, but nothing was visible. Then—what next? Then we arrived at Finland Station[7] . . . . and then, on September 8 already, the blockade began. . . .

6. World War II began for the Soviet Union on June 22, 1941, when Germany invaded.
7. One of the major railroad stations in Leningrad/Saint Petersburg.

CF—Did you live through the Leningrad Blockade together?

VT—Not the entire blockade. . . . We count the blockade from September 8 when the heavy bombings began and food vanished. We lived through all this. At that time, we lived on Serdobolskaya Street. That is, I recall when they took me on a sled, well, already half-dead to some kind of little hospital . . . But before that, when there were still those ration cards, the worst time would be the end of the month. . . . They would give you one hundred twenty-five grams of bread, this was very inadequate, very difficult. But by the end of the month, around the twentieth of the month, but the ration coupons, they hadn't been exchanged, they were just as they had been distributed on the first of the month, the one for cereals was not torn off, there weren't any cereals, nor—what else did they give coupons for—sugar? I don't recall what was there, but it was all very difficult. That is, really, how did we manage to survive? People were dying there and everywhere. Yes, and something else happened: one of the bombs landed on some part of our building, and people began to loot it. And we moved from Serdobolskaya Street . . . You know Bolshaya Spasskaya . . . And right there is The Prospect of the Undefeated, there, where the Piskaryovskoye Cemetery is. . . . And we lived there. But, as fate would have it, when we began to live with Mama's friend, they began to dismantle the house for firewood, it was half-destroyed. We arrived there, this was a wooden house, there was a wood-stove, it was heated and the like. But in front of the windows, through the window, was Bolshaya Spasskaya Street, The Prospect of the Undefeated, and there was the Piskaryovskoye cemetery, Bogoslovskoe cemetery and Piskaryovskoye cemetery, and all the sleds, all, all of this was right in front of us.[8] But, again, this was an ordinary phenomenon. And they didn't even get all the way there. They would abandon the sleds, and they would themselves fall down. So, when you came out for water, for snow to make into water, you would look—sleds and people were lying here and lying there, but this was ordinary.

And that's not all. Where we lived at first, at 36 Serdobolskaya Street, not far from there was the Kalinin Tram Depot. There was no electricity. The trams were standing empty. You would

8. During the Leningrad Blockade, mass death resulting from famine overwhelmed the city. No public transportation existed, so citizens pulled the corpses of dead relatives to mass burial sites on sleds.

walk along the street and the tram would be standing there, the doors open, and the entire tram—corpses, the deceased were lying in it. We would walk past, and all that. I am not a harsh person, but this was what it was like. I was a boy. . . . So this is what I remember. I was at the banya[9]—the hot steam baths. This was on Serdobolskaya Street, there was Yazykov Alley. And there was a banya there. I would go to the banya. It was customary to go to the banya. . . . So they would say: "men in one section; women in another section." And there would be these enormous, fat legs, all swollen. That's in my memory to this day. I don't recall whether it was cold or not, usually there was a basin there and people washed each other's backs, rub . . . fat, swollen legs. These are fragments of the blockade period.

What else is still with me—this was still in the good times, well, not *good* times, in October, November: when we, Mama, my sister, and I went, by the way by foot, there was nothing, no trams, no transport running any longer, to the Musical Comedy Theater. Why? First of all, because I heard all the operettas there, "The Merry Widow," to this day I remember. . . .

CF—Your mother must have been an extraordinary woman, if she took you to the opera even in such times. And on foot!

VT—Yes, that was during the blockade. But, in the first place, why? Because Mama was a medic, and she worked in some kind of hospital, somewhere, well, in the city center, I don't know, or in the Hotel Europa,[10] and she would come to the Musical Comedy Theater, they would take our sugar coupons there and give us little sweet cookies. . . . Then, there was something else interesting. Somehow they distributed, somewhere, soy milk. And I had to walk with the little can, for some reason this was far away, for some reason in the bitter cold, it was cold, this was at the Finland Station, but we lived on Serdobolskaya. And so they would pour the milk into it for me and I would walk back. And so, on the way I put my finger into it, and when I got close to home, I looked—it was frozen.

9. Public bathhouse, similar to a sauna.

10. Hotel Europa—one of the grandest hotels of the imperial era, and now again one of the grandest hotels of the post-Soviet era in Russia—was used for various purposes during the Soviet era, from children's home to hospital during the war, to hotel again after the war.

CF—But you say, "We survived."

VT—We were evacuated. . . . When they breached the block-ade, this was 1942, I don't remember whether it was March or April. But when they started to take people across Lake Ladoga, and for some reason I ended up, I remember they carried me to some kind of little hospital. And then again on a sled they brought me to the train, boarded from Finland Station by steam engine, and took us to the shore of Lake Ladoga. On trucks there, I re-member all of this very hazily, I was sick. . . . All of us, my sister was there, and Mama was there, and I was there. I don't know in what capacity she was there, as a medic or an evacuee. I was half-dead, they'd taken me on a sled, and we went together. But then, not that this was the worst. This was a bit of fate. While we were crossing through the blockade, they were shooting at us, bombing. . . . But when we arrived on the other side, they loaded us in a convoy, this was in cattle cars, and there was already food there, there was everything, everything, I couldn't think straight. Those who overate, they died. But I was fine, I stayed alive.

But the worst thing was, most of the convoys, the majority of convoys were being taken somewhere beyond the Urals, or to Central Asia, where we had been in exile. Everything was normal there. There, everything was already over. But our convoy ended up in the North Caucasus. We arrived there, Nevinnomyssk Sta-tion, this is between Pyatigorsk and some other place. . . . When they brought us there, they sent us to different places there, but I remember this: somewhere in the mountains to different houses, apartments, Collective Farm No. 4, and we were recovering there. Some time passed, and the Germans arrived there. And for us everything began not exactly all over again, but in any case. . . . I was on Collective Farm No. 4, we cut hay for the col-lective farm and for something else there. But I didn't cut, since I was so thin, probably. I sharpened sickles. I turned the device and sharpened sickles on a stone. That was so tedious, all day long, sit and around and around. . . . The Germans rounded us up, and since my sister was older than I was, some time passed, and they gathered those of her age and sent them to Germany. . . . There is a city called Nuremburg, she wound up there. I did later, but, I, actually, did not wind up in Nuremburg, but in Austria, at first in Arad. This is a city somewhere between Romania and Hungary, no, it was Debrecen. . . .

CF—How old were you?

VT—I was fourteen. . . .

CF—If it is not difficult to describe, how did the Germans treat you? What was your status?

VT—We were simply abducted to labor for Germany. And sometimes, I can't understand, because we weren't in a ghetto there. . . . I'm not Jewish, I stayed alive and so on, but they brought an enormous number of us to work. They would choose in Arad whether to send you to Hungary or Romania. There were enormous fields there. And we lived—enormous barns, to-bacco grows there, and when they harvest the tobacco, they hang it in these barns. And these barns, they don't have closed walls, but there are spaces between the planks. . . . We lived in this kind of barn. And it wasn't bad there, nothing drips on you from above, but when it rained it would be wet, and the wind came in terribly. . . .

CF—How did they feed you?

VT—Turnips, a bit of blue soup. When they drove us some-where else, yet again, when they gave us a place to sleep—well, in Russian it's called a barn, where cows and horses—it was splendid there, it was warm there. Now *there* it was so splendid. And how did they feed us? A sort of bread made from turnips which we would pull off, we would tie them into bunches and then carry them. Then they moved us, to this station, Byuk, I think it's called. There were all kinds, Arad I remember, Debre-cen, Byuk Station. Then they loaded us up in a convoy and took us to Shtalhof. That's somewhere outside Vienna. . . .

CF—Boys, all of your age? . . .

VT—There were older ones, too, in Shtalhof, there were adults there, too. Some of them wore the badge OST, light blue letters on a white background.[11] . . . And then they took us to all kinds of jobs. If something was bombed, then we would clean it up, and so on. For the most part, they took us to some kind of factory where they made storage batteries. They weren't big, but they were so heavy! We had to carry these storage batteries, some kind of lead plates. But on top of that, they would take us

---

11. Slave laborers from the East wore a badge that spelled "East" in Ger-man: OST.

somewhere, then to another place, for a week or a month they would deliver us to one place, and then, I don't know why, they delivered us to some kind of hospital, to be furnace stokers. For some reason, I always ended up at train stations, or loading at stations. . . . I was always hauling something. And the last thing was that they brought me to be some kind of furnace stoker, from there they no longer took me anywhere. They brought four or five other persons with me, it turned out to be a hospital. I worked there as a stoker. . . .

On March 4 there was shooting, rat-a-tat-tat, the Russians are coming, the Soviet troops. We got up and fled, this Alyoskha and I. We went to an attic, and from the attic we watched. [. . .] We were watching through one window, some people were on the roof, and then we would look, two Germans with machine guns had hidden, so, we could have run into them, it seemed . . . But this didn't happen. And so, when we saw that there was an exchange of fire, the Germans there, and here—our, Soviet soldiers, BTRs,[12] the tank men and so on, we jumped out, and we joined them. The BTRs, I don't recall what they are really called, back then we called them "Farewell, Motherland," and so I was on this "Farewell, Motherland" through Vienna, this was all in Vienna, I knew a little bit about it, from when they had moved me about there. There were two train stations: the Westbahnhof and the Franz Josef Bahnhof. And so he asks me, the captain, or major, "Where is the Franz Josef Bahnhof?" I said, "I know." And I was on this BTR until the end of the war. And so when we would be taking some building, I now have come to understand, I was a boy, I had a machine gun, I remember the Franz Josef Bahnhof, we would take the first floor, then go up, there would be shooting, I always went first for some reason, he was always behind me [laughs]. And so I think, "What's the matter with you, such a skunk!" But this is what I think now. I was a boy, without a uniform, well, not a little boy, but a grown youth.

CF—How did you locate your mama and sister after the war?

VT—I knew practically nothing about my sister for a very long time. She found us through the Red Cross. . . . When the war ended, I was the first to return. Let me explain this in chronological order. . . . I wound up—what is that station called, I don't

12. Armored personnel carriers.

remember, Darnitsa. . . . All the troop trains went there. I wound up in this Darnitsa. . . . And then they lined us up and said, "Those born in 1928 and 1929, two steps forward!" We stepped forward. "It's over, guys, you are still young, you are minors, you need to study, and so, go ahead, go home." Someone among us said, "Let us serve to the end, since we've already been fighting." "No, no, you're still young" or something in that line. . . . Then I came here, home, to Leningrad, and I found Aunt Anya, that's Mama's sister. I also found Katya, Lyonya—he's my cousin, but we are only one year apart, so he's like a brother, while Katya, she's his mother. And then Mama showed up. She also arrived, they had also been in some kind of camps. But Dina, my sister, she stayed there. The Americans liberated her in Nuremburg. She was young, she married and stayed there.

CF—As I understood, after you were already an adult, your mama was in exile again. . . .

VT—The thing is that I returned, Mama returned, but Dina didn't return. And so they started to question me: "Why did that sister of yours stay there? Write her, tell her to return!" . . . Let me give you a bit of an introduction to this letter. Earlier the situation was this. You get yourself a job, it's over, the war is over, there's no place to live. I had a lot of cousins, and I found Aunt Anya, that's Mama's sister, she was a medic. . . . And she lived in the outskirts of Leningrad, toward Vyborg. She had a first-aid station there, a clinic. . . . I began to live with her. Then, some time passed, Mama was found, she also returned. . . . And then they started to bring Russians in, our Russians, from Novogorsk, from Kirov region, from Yaroslavl, to settle this territory. Since the war had just ended, there were land mines there, shells, trenches, entrenchments. And this was right next to the Gulf [of Finland]. And they decided to set up a kind of fishing collective. So they brought two boats, big boats, they transported the fish. But when there was some kind of choppiness, a small storm, land mines tore loose. And in the morning, they arrive, and see their two boats sitting there, and there were two mines floating. Well, what should we do? . . . There was a commotion. They began to call for mine experts to take them away, to explode them. A whole day passed—no one came. And the second day passed. And my cousin, Lyonya, arrived. I say to him, "What are they waiting for?" We took a little boat, we put a chain on the mines, dragged

them two hundred meters out into the Gulf, we suspended a blasting cartridge of TNT and somehow exploded it. . . . But by then
I was already becoming an adult, and I had to go to register for
military service. And this was in Koivisto, eleven kilometers away.
I arrived there, handed in my documents, and he said, "You're
Muravsky? There's something familiar about your name. Was it
you," he said, "who exploded mines there?" Where could I hide?
I said, "Yes, it was I, it turned out that way." He said, "And what
made you decide to do it?" Well, I had been in the war after all,
this wasn't new to me. "Well, and fine, you'll work in de-mining."
And from that point, I became sort of the director of the detach-
ment working on de-mining. This is a small introduction.

So then I worked there a year or so. Well, what was the work
like? Not only looking for mines. There were entrenchments,
trenches, dugouts stuffed with shells in boxes, machine guns, au-
tomatics, cartridges in boxes. We would gather this all in a pile,
a blasting cartridge of TNT—we exploded it all. We cleared the
territory, it was nothing very difficult. But of course, I had a pistol, that is, they were all over the place, and a blasting cartridge
of TNT. . . . And when I was done there, I came to Leningrad.
To see people and so forth. And I had all this equipment with
me. And so they summoned me again, "And why are you here,
and your mama returned, and why didn't your sister return? So,
well, write your sister a letter, tell her to come back." And I, out
of stupidity, wrote, "Dina, they are demanding that you return."
She wrote me back, "How are things there?" There was nothing good, but this was the war and so on. And I didn't summon
her back, and I even wrote, "At least *you* should live," and she
was there in the American zone. And so they came to search my
place and found what I had with me: a pistol, and a blasting
cartridge, but I needed all this for my work, when I came here, I
had brought it with me. . . .

And there still another stupid thing happened. I remember that
in the room where I was living, there was an electric hot plate.
It was on, either I was cooking something or it was to warm
up the room. And back then, they had these red coils. When
the two policemen came in, one was a policeman, the other one
wasn't in a uniform, and, they, the dogs, knew everything. They
opened my little suitcase, and there was all I had with me. I was
like a terrorist, but that word didn't exist back then. I said that
this is my work, that I was leaving from there to go back to the

division. And he still took out this blasting cartridge of TNT, it wasn't large, a hundred grams, and he put it on the hot plate. "What are you doing?! It will explode!" It would never have exploded, there was a capsule. He put it on the plate, having no idea what it would do, and it started to burn, dripped on the floor, and a terrible smoke rose from it; we had to break open a window to breathe. So that made it public. And this one himself got frightened that there would be a fire, or not a fire, but that the cartridge might explode. Of course they took me in. And when the investigation took place, it was ostensibly about this, but the main thing was my sister. I was sentenced to three years for this. Possession of firearms and so on. . . .

CF—Where did they take you?

VT—They arrested me, they convicted me for weapons possession. Not for a political crime, there wasn't a word about my sister, about my correspondence with her, they didn't bring my phrase "At least you should live there" into the trial. They gave me three years, I was in the camps for three years. I had already been with Mama. Someone came to visit me, then they took me away. But from Mama, no one knew anything, nothing, and suddenly I received the letter that I told you about, "Farewell—farewell, forever, farewell!"

CF—Please describe where you were when you received this letter.

VT—This was in the zone, this was in the camp. I can't even remember right now where this was: either near Podporozhe or near Toksovo. Because this was a temporary facility, while they gathered the convicts for further transport. . . . I remember the name of the director of the KVCh [Cultural Education Section (CES)], she was either a captain or a lieutenant, her name was Zoya Ivanovna. This I remember, it is with me for the rest of my life. . . . And so she summoned me to the KVCh, gave me this letter. It wasn't just that this touched me—I looked, she was somehow unusual, usually they were rather stern. But I was no longer a little boy, I was seventeen or eighteen years old. . . . And she said to me, "Here, a letter came for you." And she gave it to me—I don't even recall, either she read it herself first and then gave it to me. But this was the first letter I had gotten from Mama. They had convicted her, because Dina had remained

there, my sister, that's really why! . . . And I read it. . . . The epi-
graph was from Byron. "Farewell, farewell, if it is forever, then
forever farewell!" Something like that stays with you for your
whole life. . . . The officer didn't say that Mama had also been
arrested and was in the Dolinka camp. Just "a letter has come for
you from there." Later, more came.[13] But this was the first letter
from Mama. . . . The other guards there weren't just strict, they
were simply like wild beasts. This was in March, I remember. It
was cold. And it was a holiday, your Women's Day, March 8. Or
just a day off, we weren't working. And so we were sitting, and
there was still snow, it was cold, but the sun was already out. We
sat on a bench at work, in the zone, and someone started to take
his clothes off. So that his body would get some sun and so on.
And from the lookouts, they started to shout, and most of the
guards were women, saying, well, "Put your clothes on." And
they were malicious. But that one gave me the letter to read. And
to this day, I have kept a feeling toward her—I'm not a person
who holds a grudge. I won't ever forgive those who tortured my
father, or didn't torture—after all, I didn't see it myself. But at
the fourth interrogation, he signed. . . .

CF—How many years was your mother's sentence? Her exile?
After she was convicted because of your sister?

VT—I really don't know and didn't ask about these details.
. . . When they released me . . . Let me say a bit about something
else, so that I won't have to return to it. When I was released, that
was it, completely, I was free. I knew that Mama was out there
somewhere, at some address or other, or a third one. I thought,
"What am I to do?" There's no one at home, I didn't go to Aunt
Anya. I had another aunt, Dusya, Papa's sister, who had been exiled, and I decided to go to her. . . . I was here [in Leningrad] for
a week or two, then I went to her. And she lived in the Caucasus,
in Anap. . . . And so it happened that I arrived there one day, two
or three days, everything was fine, they had food there, their own
little house, right next to the sea, but a person had to work. And
so I got a job. There were cement factories there, Novorossiisk,
Tonnelnaya, big cement factories there. And I went to work at

13. Some of Muravsky's correspondence with his mother from these years is
available in English translation in Jehanne Gheith and Katherine Jolluck, eds., *Gulag Voices: Oral Histories of Soviet Incarceration and Exile* (Palgrave-Macmillan,
2001), 219–222.

these cement factories. . . . But I worked there for literally one month total, . . . and then suddenly I received a military call-up paper. Their view was, "You didn't serve in the army, go serve in the army." So they took me again, to the navy, and Sevastapol was right there, and I served there, slaved five years there. But this was the law, five years in the navy.

CF—Where was your mama all this time?

VT—Mama was in Akmolinsk, it's called ALZhIR. It was for wives of traitors, enemies of the people, something like that. And then they transferred her to Dolinka, and I corresponded with her in Dolinka . . . . and then she wrote me from there at that time. And what happened next? Oh! Then my sister found me again. And once again it was through the Red Cross, when I was already in the navy. . . . And when my service was coming to an end—I thought, that's it, it's tedious, four years have passed, I'm finishing my service, what next? And when I corresponded, called—well, corresponded actually with Katya, Lyonya, with my cousins, they said, "Well, what, Valya, such is fate. Your Papa is gone, and he's disappeared, don't say they lost him. Your Mama, such is her fate, that she is there, you can't do anything about it, come here to Leningrad, study." But I thought, "Well, how could I? After all, she's also in the camps for no reason! Isn't that true?" I decided to go there, otherwise what else could I have done? I went there. . . . I'm demobilized, I order a ticket, I receive a free ticket. I arrive, and the place was Karaganda—not far from Karaganda.[14] I arrive in Karaganda. I went somewhere, I found work. At the Kirov Mine. Kirov Mine No. 3. I started to work there. . . . I got out in 1954 or '55.

[Describes his marriage during the last year of his naval service to a girl he met on the beach. The marriage endured.]

CF—So, you were still in the navy when Stalin died? Do you remember his death?

VT—I remember. And again, this was not in Sevastopol, March 5. I think, in Izmail. This was the fourth division of armored cutters. That was my service, that's where they tossed me. And so Mama would write me letters. . . . And she wrote this

14. In Kazakhstan.

and that, "Valya, in Izmail lives the daughter of someone with me here in the camp, her mama is in the camp." They became friends, they shared a bunk, and so on, but I don't remember why she was in the camp, for religion or something like that. I'm not very, I'm not a historian. And she gave me the address of where the daughter lived. I had a day off, the weather was fine, so I go over there. . . . And so, well, so this was on the eve of Stalin's death. And we were sitting there, maybe he wasn't the commander of the entire Danube, but he was some kind of commander there. . . . And at that time, March 5, Stalin was dying. And we all sighed with relief. I remember that moment. And even though some may have cried, something extraordinary, we felt, I personally, we felt . . . . relief, and the fact that he was older than me, maybe smarter, more experienced, and we felt a kind of relief. I didn't know what the future held for us, but that was great. . . . After that, I got married on August 9, 1953. . . . Mama wrote that, "So, Stalin is gone, they'll either issue an amnesty or rehabilitate us," something like that. They had already started to release a lot of people. I said to my wife, "Tonya, you know, you shouldn't go for now." After all, our daughter, Nina, had been born. "Stay here, I'll go [to Dolinka], I'll find out what's what, I'll figure it out, and then we can decide, how it is there and so on." I arrived there, for a while everything was fine, I went to work, I began to study, I was an operator on a coal combine. . . . I arrived, I worked, and lived in a dormitory. . . .

CF—And did you see your mama often?

VT—Again, I don't even remember. Not every day off, but, let's say, that I would finish work at six, I would ride there that night—I just now looked at the map, where this place was. . . . And there was a station there called Karabas. And when you write a letter: Karabas Station, P.O. Dolinka. But Dolinka, this was an enormous camp, something like fifty thousand inmates, where there were these barracks, barbed wire and so on. I would ride as far as Karabas Station, but then, I don't recall, I had to go about fifty–sixty kilometers on foot.

CF—Fifty kilometers on foot.

VT—Yes. . . . By then it was morning. I would leave at night, arrive in the morning, early in the morning, and I would start walking. But I couldn't get there in one day. I would walk and

walk, walk and walk, and once more, walk and walk. A haystack, I would find myself a haystack. . . . At night, I would sleep
there, sometimes it would be fine. But sometimes, it always happens that way when you are asleep, toward morning, the jackals would start howling, but it turned out that these were not
jackals, but wolves all around. . . . I walked, I walked to this
haystack, and then in the morning, I would wake up, everything
was okay, no one had eaten me, and I would walk further. And
this is interesting: so I walk and walk, and by afternoon, I'm
already there. But there, you walk, to the right is the road, then
the camp already, to the right barbed wire and to the left barbed
wire. And what really shocked me, not that I was a little boy, but
there was a whole line of women standing there, young and old,
at the barbed wire, on the right side. On the left side were the
little houses, the houses for visits.[15] They would stand there at
the barbed wire, and I was a sailor, after all, I had a striped vest
and a pea jacket, and they would say to me, "Sailor, love me!" It
made me crazy. I thought, "What do you mean, 'love you?' I've
come to see my dear Mama!" The women were young, after all.
And this phrase, back then, I didn't understand what it was, now
I understand, what it means, but so these phrases . . . I walked on,
I walked past, then I came to the turn, and what was there, they
had guard posts, I presented my documents. And then they gave
us . . . I saw my mother for the first time, God knows through
what kind of procedures. . . . Then they gave us a little house for
the meeting. I was there all day, and then I walked back.

CF—And what did you and your mama do? Did you simply
sit together or talk, or read?

VT—I don't even remember, what we talked about there, what
we did there. This was Mama, there were tears.

CF—How long did this last?

VT—. . . . This was 1954, and she was released in 1956. Two
years. But the thing is . . . She died after she was free. . . . In
1957. In August. She was . . . she was older than Papa, Papa
was born in 1896, she was born in 1894. . . . She was freed in
1956. I go to meet her. Tonya arrived with Ninochka, I have a
photograph. That was it, she was free. And, since I was a young

15. The House of Meetings was the facility where family members could visit
their relatives in the camps.

specialist, they gave me an apartment. But Tonya just could not stand it anymore, and she just picked up and came. . . . I was young, energetic. . . . I had a good job. Mama was free. Tonya's there, they give me an apartment, this was generally somehow unusual, don't you think? Then I requested to be transferred to Russia. Now, we are free, but this is a long story already. But Mama. . . . it was terrible, a skinny little thing, in a cheap quilted jacket. . . .

CF—And now to the final questions. How strong was the influence of terror during Stalin's rule on the history of the USSR?

VT—This is the way I would put it. Not only I, but also my friends who were older than me. We were so beaten down! I raise my hat to young people, before the dissidents: They were the first to see this difference, that we were being such idiots then. . . . And the propaganda was so strong! Although we saw the terror, they were grabbing people for no reason—and they're all signing their names, so, well, yes. Zinoviev,[16] Kamenev,[17] and my father signed. He was no politician. That's how they instilled it in us, propaganda, movies. Now I get indignant. And we used to say, "On whom does this depend? On only one person." These, what do you call it?—lickspittle—it's always around. It was like that before, and they surrounded Khrushchev, as well[18] . . .

CF—Please tell me . . . what is your attitude toward Khrushchev?

VT—My attitude. They say, but this is nothing new, that his hands were covered in blood, that's for the famine in Ukraine, but the fact that he took the first step away from tyranny, toward something new, this thaw, that was wonderful. . . . Whenever I am in Moscow, on business or something else, I buy flowers and go to the Novodevichy Cemetery. And, although my friends—for instance, when we were at a Memorial conference—they say, "What are you doing going there!" I answer, "No, I am going." So, I go there, put flowers on his grave, and this is wonderful. And

16. Grigory Zinoviev, an Old Bolshevik, was a key defendant in first major show trial of Bolshevik leaders, 1936.

17. Lev Kamenev, an Old Bolshevik, was a key defendant in first major show trial of Bolshevik leaders, 1936.

18. Nikita Sergeevich Khrushchev, General Secretary of the Communist Party and leader of the Soviet Union 1953–1964.

the second step, although he made mistakes, was Gorbachev's.[19]
He took the second step. . . .

CF—Well, and the last question. Looking back on your entire
long, complicated life, what are you most proud of?

VT—Proud of? I don't even know. I had, this is why, I had this
goal, well, such a distant goal, sort of. First of all, I completed
practically no education. Except for the technical school, I don't
remember, a vocational school of some sort . . . technical school.
I became a coal combine operator. That was the highest I could
accomplish. But when I returned here, I would go to the university and sit in, as an auditor. . . . My goal was that my children
not live in a time like mine. And therefore, I have three children,
I already have seven grandchildren and one great-granddaughter
now. And I am proud of this. All of my children, my daughter
and two sons, they all finished kindergarten, school, and institute. Now they all say, "Papa, why did you make us study?"
Now they are all working. In a different specialization, they all
studied in energy engineering. Misha became a computer pro-
grammer, Vova works in something else, and so on. So, this was
my goal. I am proud of the fact, I don't know, that I have friends,
that I believe in good. For myself, what I did for my children,
that's my legacy.

CF—And how did you preserve this capacity?

VT—Probably, Mama taught me, my father taught me
this . . . And then, so I don't know this, I went through a lot,
these camps and those, and those. And what I did have was the
classics. True—Russian, from the Russian tradition, but not only
Russian, because Goethe, he's not a Russian. But the best stayed
with me, and that's what I passed along to my children. And
grandchildren. . . .

CF—You said that one inheritance from your parents is this
love of reading and literature. What other legacies were there?

VT—There was a legacy, one that, it seems to me, may have
been bad for me to some extent. Because I was raised to be decent, not to be a slimeball. This is my faith in the good, faith in
people, I always try—so, I am happy when I do something good,

19. Mikhail Sergeevich Gorbachev, General Secretary of the Communist Party
and leader of the Soviet Union 1985–1991.

and this, in our day and time, this is both dangerous and difficult. It is not justified. So this remained with me from my parents, from my parents and their milieu. So, that's what I think. I don't know, perhaps I'm really mistaken? But I can't be a hypocrite, I can't say I'll do something and not do it, that is, I'm principled in everything I do. . . . The most important thing is a person's principled core. That comes from my parents. The second thing, well, I could choose from other things. People know me, they respect me, too, for other things. I searched for my father, I was the leader of the group "The Search" [*Poisk*] in Levashovo.[20] I got the entire city moving, I got the entire country going, I wrote, and so on. And many people are grateful to me for that. But it's good when people can associate this with a particular person, then it is even better for you. . . .

Second Interview
Short Hills, New Jersey, at home of son, Mikhail Valentinovich
October 2007
Interview conducted by Cathy Frierson
Transcribed by Natalya Maeden

After explaining that I would like to revisit some of the points in our earlier interview, I turned to the first questions on my list.

CF—When people started to die because they had eaten too much (on the evacuation trains out of besieged Leningrad), you said yourself that you were barely conscious because of your condition. Do you have any memories of the people around you?

VT—In the first place, these were big train cars, freight cars —for goods—there were wooden plank beds, we slept there. And we rode for a long, long time. It wasn't like a day or two or three

---

20. In the late 1980s, when Mikhail Gorbachev permitted Soviet citizens to revisit the Stalinist past through his policy of glasnost (openness, or transparency), Valentin Muravsky published a query in a Leningrad newspaper in search of information about his father. His gesture inspired others; eventually a non-governmental organization called "The Search" formed, comprising citizens in search of their relatives lost during the Stalinist repressions. They took up the task of searching for mass graves and the killing grounds from the terror years outside of Leningrad/Saint Petersburg. They located one of the largest, Levashovo, which is now a commemorative site for the terror victims.

and "That's it!"; we rode for around two weeks from Leningrad to Vologda. . . . I don't know whether this was our first stop or not. This was a long stop, where they unloaded those who had died while we were en route, the corpses, they had died, they lay where they had died—where could they be put? . . . I don't remember how long the stop was, two or three days, or a week, I don't recall. I just lay there, and that was it. . . . But as for those who overate, maybe they were dying anyway. And there were a lot of children. There were a lot—grown-ups, and children, that's how they threw us into the train cars. And I remember that when we stopped in Vologda, this was a big station, after all, they fed us, and I think they even washed us, and there were fights of some kind. The reason for the first incident, I remember, was that someone made off with someone else's piece of bread or some kind of canned foods, and so it seems they were arguing, they were cursing each other and so on. . . .

CF—And when you reached the station [in the North Caucasus]?

VT—When we were unloaded, some people were unloaded earlier, because this was a big troop train. At first there was this group, three or four or five people, a group, they delivered us to houses. These were villages, in the mountains, and they gave us to families of local residents. We lived there, they made our meals, we ate . . . Well, since we were in communities, it was like being on vacation. Can you imagine? It wasn't like being in a big orphanage or a dormitory. . . . Then they started to take us to work. At first we cut hay, then we did something else—where, I also don't recall. But it was for some period of time, after some time they sent us, in a group, to this Farm No. 4. This was either some kind of collective farm or state farm . . . And we mowed hay there. I was too weak or something, I sharpened the scythes. . . .

CF—When you were there, did you know where your mama and sister were?

VT—That's the thing, I didn't know at first, we were all in different places somehow. Then we would run into each other, because after some time, we went to town, to the town of Cherchessk, and also to Nevinnomyssk, and we would get our mail there, and some kinds of food. . . . I would go as a sort of escort, together, an older one would go and one or two, well, children. As a person with a trade, a student. . . . And the last time when we made a trip to town, we went on horses, without a saddle or anything. And after all, I was a city boy, I didn't know how or what. And it was a long way to ride, everything was rubbed sore. So, we come at our usual time to this town, and you could feel there, everything was clear to us: people were lugging some sacks, well, I don't know, with flour or something else. . . . "What's happening?" "What do you mean? The Germans are in town." And that's how we somehow didn't know what was going on with the war, that is, we were somewhere in the mountains, in the fields, where the hay was. And then we—I don't recall, either we'd come back to get money, or our mail, and there was panic, everyone was fleeing. And we went back, a group of people gathered, and we went to Pyatigorsk, on the road to Pyatigorsk. So we walked and walked, and then a column of people was coming toward us. Negotiations. Who are we? We were still young boys. "Where are you going?" "The Germans are already there, we're getting away from them. And where are you going?" "The Germans are there, we're coming to you." Like that, you understand. And then everyone ran off. But we remained in a group as we were. But when we arrived in this little town, in Cherkessk, . . . And then where we lived, I also don't recall, somewhere in a school. I remember that there was some building, a three- or four-story school, so we lived there for some time. Then—it was all over, the Germans arrived, they were riding on motorcycles and so on. And we also worked somehow. I remember, once the Germans came, we were constantly loading on the railroad: we loaded coal, and metal, we were always doing some kind of work, we didn't loiter, it was all the same in some kind of group. But after that, I've remembered something else, either they had a labor market, or they wanted to set up some kind of system, and they took us to work. And for some time I worked where they repaired motors, I . . . . was like a mechanic. For three months, I didn't know how to do anything, I was learning. Then, Mama and Dina were there someplace, but we didn't see each other, we didn't know who was where. You would find out from someone that there was some kind of group there, that Mama was there someplace, Dina was there someplace, and so it was after this that Dina, she was older than me, and Mama, probably, they were loaded up and sent directly to Germany, or someplace in Austria. . . . People talked about this. They would say, They're collecting young people and sending them to Germany. . . .

CF—That is in fact one of my questions. Did you consider yourself back then to be a boy or an adult? This is a specific time in a person's life, fourteen years old. How did you view yourself?

VT—You know, now I look back—well, I'm analyzing. So sometimes people ask, they pose the question, "The war, there was shooting, were you afraid or not?" And you know, amazingly, I know that everyone was afraid—that is, there were a few fools there or someone else, but my answer is: the children were not afraid, they didn't think about that when there was shooting; we, the guys, went right into the inferno. And this happened. Why, because so, the elder among us, we were mowing hay there, drying it and so on, and somehow to participate or to be, if not on Russia's side, at least against the Germans, we started to burn the very haystacks that we had built. We began to think, what is this for? We set fire to them. And then . . . . this was also part of the war, I wasn't afraid of this. And then we piled them all up and dried them and all of it . . . We tried to pull off some kind of tricks, and there was no fear at all. But now when I think about it, the children weren't afraid of anything, they weren't afraid of death. I could say this already after I had been in Germany already, in Austria, and when I had fought with a machine gun and took part in street battles. . . .

CF—Can you describe your feelings when you were taken from the collective farm to be sent to Romania?

VT—No feelings whatsoever. We were loading something all the time—coal, boards, something else, we did what we were told—followed orders, followed orders. Still more interesting, there were moments, there were horrible Germans, and there were decent Germans, but there was a period, I don't recall, who they were, either guards, but these were young Germans. These were either Hitler Youth or something else, but they were boys, and we were boys, we almost got into a fight with them. . . . But right now I don't recall how they fed us. Either they brought something, or some other way . . . But, even worse, this was already later, two or three days I had—this was Arad, Debrecen, and Byuk station, this is on the Hungarian border, but when

there was a big transfer—we were going as a convoy, we walked
under guard, and they fed us in the evening. There was some sort
of carriage with us, or there was some kind of food there, I don't
recall whether it was hot or not, I think it wasn't, but they gave
us bread or something. And so it was already nine or ten o'clock,
we needed to go to sleep, and we slept right on the ground, on a
tussock somewhere. And they're still not feeding us. And no one
said anything. And it would happen that they wouldn't feed us
for two or three days. But they're supposed to give us food, but
still they are not giving us anything. And I went, well, this was
like a reconnaissance mission. It turned out that the person who
was senior, the German, in a uniform, but he was somewhere
in some house carousing, and I made my way there, and there
they were drinking and so on, talking, but they weren't giving
us food. I didn't come up with anything clever, but walked into
this house and started—well, not exactly cursing, "We want to
eat, we need to sleep, and it's already nighttime—isn't it?" And
they started chasing me, shooting, through the gardens. This
happened. This was savagery, but it happened. I went to sort
out the situation. And it wasn't so much that he didn't manage
to shoot me. I ran away, even though he was shooting, but when
I ran back to our camp—I don't even remember if it was fenced
in or not—I hid. . . . It was a childish thing to do—well, I was
only fourteen or fifteen years old; that's not such a little boy, but
I did it. . . .

CF—Before you were already in Romania, on what kind of
transport did they take you?

VT—Mostly on trains. . . . But in some places we went on
foot. Under guard, we walked on foot and so on. And also, so
you were asking about the attitudes of those who had been repressed, at that time, no one talked about it or thought about it,
we had one goal—sometime this would end. In Romania and in
Hungary, everyone had the dream, especially the guys, the kids:
to walk away, across the Danube, and that would be Yugoslavia
already. And we had this idea, there were partisans there and
everything. And we tried to run away there. I made two such
attempts. Unsuccessful. . . . We didn't even make it to the Danube, they already caught us. We had worked out this strategy, we
would be spending the night somewhere, but we would have a
few things with us, a little sack, a backpack . . . And so when we

all decided to make a run for it, we would be sleeping, we would have hidden our knapsacks somewhere, and then we would be walking with the column somewhere. And then you would walk and walk, ten or twenty kilometers, and then all of a sudden you would run away into the bushes somewhere. And then when they had left, we would come back, take our knapsacks. But—they caught me the first time and caught us the second time.

CF—And what were the consequences?

VT—Well, they would really give it to us. And what was most interesting, I don't remember if it was the last time they caught us, when they caught me, there were, I think two or three, and they caught us on a motorcycle. He rode around and saw us, and where were we to hide? . . . So at first he said, "This is a foreign country, you don't know the language," and then he really gave it to us. . . . He took my knapsack away from me (there were three of us), and he put two of them in the motorcycle. "And you'll walk back on your own!" And what was I to do? And I ran behind them. I was by myself, I didn't know anyone, I didn't know the language. And so that's what happened. . . .

CF—And were there workers around you whom they killed, in your group?

VT—You know, before my very eyes . . . there were. They shot one or two, they fell, and that was it—quiet—peaceful.

CF—Who shot whom? Why?

VT—You know, all it took was for us to talk to each other there, and so there would be this guard, and it was very easy, so he would stand there, and with his automatic: he'd shoot someone just like that. He would fall, and that was it. And that would be the end of it. Why did they do it? This was before my eyes, this was as if it were right now, I saw it myself. At times, I even thought, "So, he doesn't have to go to work, everything's over for him, these boils won't hurt." Was I crazy or like some kind of machine? . . . But this happened, I saw it, they shot them. Why they shot them, I don't know. . . .

CF—When these things happened, when they beat you or they beat the person next to you, did you still have the capacity for sympathy?

VT—I did. . . . And that's not all. Other people covered their faces as if they just didn't see anything. But I wasn't like that. I don't know why. I even tried to intervene . . . . there was nothing to lose. . . .

CF—How do you think that seeing so many corpses in your life affected you? The ones you saw as a youth, beginning with the blockade.

VT—This is also complicated. I've never thought about it. I saw a lot of corpses. A lot. And during the blockade, for some reason, I was astonished . . . We lived not far from a tram depot. Where trams stood. . . . And the trams were stuffed with corpses: they were piled up there, people gathered them from the street. And piled them in the tram. . . . That's hideous. You can never forget this. This was the war. Then, I also saw a lot of corpses . . . a lot . . . This is really a horrible question. When a person is alive, is talking and so on—like this?—they kill him, and that's it, he no longer exists. Idiotic thoughts came to me, "Well, so, lucky for him, he doesn't have to think about anything, he doesn't have to go to work." This was stupidity, but that's how we thought about this. Then there was also the feeling of terror. I wasn't afraid, maybe out of stupidity, but I was afraid when airplanes were chasing you. I was afraid of low-flying aircraft, and then everyone ran in different directions. Whose airplanes were these? We were walking in columns. I don't think that these were Germans, or were they English? They began to shoot at the column, we ran in different directions, and someone is lying here, and someone is lying here . . . A young girl, or a woman, this was the feeling of terror. But when you were fighting out in the open, it is not frightening. But when you are going along chatting as I am with you—knock on wood, of course, and then just like that, I'm alive and you are gone. Somehow feelings are dulled. . . .

CF—Did you have the sensation that you bore a stigma because of your father?

VT—I felt this everywhere at work; I could not get a good job. And that's not all. Even my children, they—they all graduated from the institute, the Physical-Technological Institute, but they had limitations. That is, they could not be admitted to departments, where there was Physics-Mathematics, where there was a military section and so on, they would not be accepted there. . . .

CF—As grandchildren of an enemy of the people! Was this in the 1980s? Before Gorbachev?

VT—This was before Gorbachev. Sometime in the 1970s. . . .

CF—How do you compare the repressions and the war? In your life and in the life of the country?

VT—I believe . . . I consider myself to be one among those who were repressed. But during the war, I did not feel this. We had one goal. This was to finish the war, liberation, to remain alive, that was our goal. . . . And then, somehow it turned out that when we were in the platoon, among our own, half of us were of the repressed, children of enemies of the people and so on, but all the same, we had one goal: this was victory, to end the war. . . . In the life of the country? That's a different matter. So, when we first began to gather, when Khrushchev was in power. When Mama was in the House of Meetings, and I was in Karaganda, when Khrushchev gave his first speech, this was joy![21] . . . I worship him as a god.

21. In 1956, Nikita Khrushchev delivered a major speech denouncing Stalin and Stalinism at the Twentieth Congress of the Communist Party. One of his declarations was that the term "enemy of the people" was sheer Stalinist invention and led to unwarranted political repression.

CHAPTER FIVE

"Silence was salvation. That's what I knew"

IRINA ANDREEVNA DUBROVINA

Kotlas

July 9, 2005

Transcribed by Elena Vetrova

Introduction

Irina Andreevna Dubrovina was born in 1928 in Tsaritsyn (also known as Stalingrad and Volgograd). Her father, Andrei Matveev, had been an elected delegate of the Socialist Revolutionary (SR) Party to the Constituent Assembly in January 1918. He left the SR Party and withdrew from all political activity after Lenin's Soviet government shut the Constituent Assembly down through a military show of force on what would have been its second day in session. Irina Andreevna's mother was an educated young woman who was not a member of the Communist Party, and she was working in library development in Smolensk when she met Andrei Matveev. Despite their efforts to live inconspicuously, far from Moscow, Irina's father was arrested in 1938 in what by then had been renamed Stalingrad. Her mother was not arrested. This enabled Irina Andreevna, her mother, and her sister to remain together in Stalingrad until German forces approached the city in August 1942, at which time the family was exiled for being untrustworthy relatives of an enemy of the people. Three years later, the exiled Matveev women received a letter from Irina Andreevna's father, who had been unable to send letters during

117

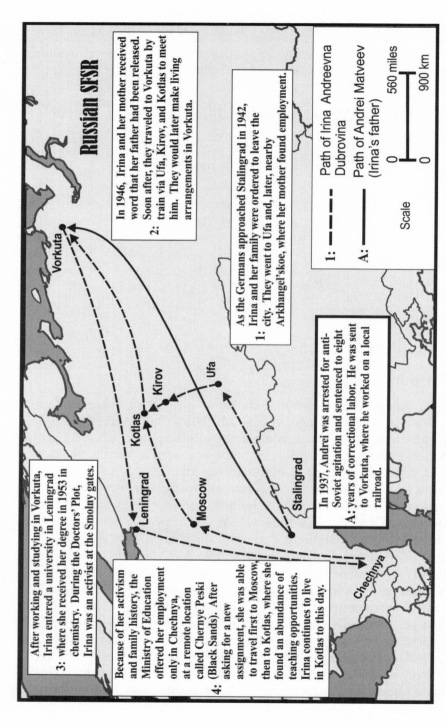

Russian SFSR

In 1946, Irina and her mother received word that her father had been released. Soon after, they traveled to Vorkuta by train via Ufa, Kirov, and Kotlas to meet him. They would later make living arrangements in Vorkuta.

2:

As the Germans approached Stalingrad in 1942, Irina and her family were ordered to leave the city. They went to Ufa and, later, nearby Arkhangel'skoe, where her mother found employment.

1:

In 1937, Andrei was arrested for anti-Soviet agitation and sentenced to eight years of correctional labor. He was sent to Vorkuta, where he worked on a local railroad.

A:

After working and studying in Vorkuta, Irina entered a university in Leningrad where she received her degree in 1953 in chemistry. During the Doctors' Plot, Irina was an activist at the Smolny gates.

3:

Because of her activism and family history, the Ministry of Education offered her employment only in Chechnya, at a remote location called Chernye Peski (Black Sands). After asking for a new assignment, she was able to travel first to Moscow, then to Kotlas, where she found an abundance of teaching opportunities. Irina continues to live in Kotlas to this day.

4:

Vorkuta

Leningrad

Kotlas

Kirov

Ufa

Moscow

Stalingrad

Chechnya

Scale

Path of Irina Andreevna Dubrovina

Path of Andrei Matveev (Irina's father)

1:

A:

0   560 miles

0   900 km

The journeys of Irina Andreevna Dubrovina and her father, Andrei Matveev, 1937–1955   (Map by Eric Pugliano) the war (all correspondence with camp inmates had been banned), explaining where he had been incarcerated. Upon Andrei Matveev's release from the Gulag installation in Vorkuta, Irina Andreevna and her mother joined him there, where he had decided to remain as a contract laborer. Irina Andreevna eventually made her way to Leningrad State University to study chemistry. When she graduated, she ultimately received a job placement in Kotlas as a chemistry teacher, a career path she followed for the rest of her working life. After she retired, she joined the Memorial movement, becoming one of its most persistent and creatively active leaders in a regional organization. As of 2012, she was still making regular trips to Moscow to assist Gulag survivors in Kotlas with their rehabilitation cases.

Irina Andreevna's interview illustrates how Soviet political repression shaped the full span of a former Socialist Revolutionary's family, from 1918 through the end of the Soviet era, and into the post-Soviet era. Andrei Matveev was a member of the Socialist Revolutionary Party for a mere few months, from spring 1917 to January 1918; nearly a century later, Irina Andreevna's daily life continues to be defined by the Russian Federation's reckoning with Soviet repression. Her recollections reveal how her family, like so many families of enemies of the people, tried to evade the Soviet government's scrutiny or found itself under its direct surveillance. They also convey the widespread poverty experienced by Soviet citizens outside Moscow in the 1930s–1950s. Irina Andreevna remembers teachers and school directors as generous individuals who helped preserve her truncated family after her father's arrest. Her descriptions of her own studied silence and the conscious lies she sometimes told to escape stigma offer vivid examples of some of the survival strategies Soviet citizens adopted. The interview reveals how even a strong-minded woman like Irina Andreevna could feel profoundly isolated within the Soviet collective, due to the stigma she experienced as a result of her father's arrest. It also provides snapshots of the journeys children of the Gulag took as involuntary travelers across Soviet space. Their geography lessons were lived experiences.

I located Irina Andreevna through the Memorial organization in Moscow. I interviewed her in her apartment in Kotlas and stayed with her for a week. During that time, I interviewed other child survivors in Kotlas whom she knew through her advocacy work. Irina Andreevna also guided me through mass graves in Kotlas in a neglected spot on the outskirts of town. She was then mobilizing the local community and government to establish a memorial site at the site for victims of

Irina Andreevna Dubrovina, 2012 (Photograph by Cathy A. Frierson)

Soviet repression. We became intimates through the daily rituals of
stoking the wood-burning hot water heater in the bathroom, doing
aerobics under her instruction to a vinyl recording of 1980s disco
music, buying groceries at the market and corner store, and eating
together at her three-person kitchen table. We sat down to conduct
the interview late in the week. A short, vigorous woman, Irina Andreevna impressed me with her intellectual and physical energy, confidence, and shrewdness. We have since met four more times during
my subsequent research trips. In this interview, you will see evidence
of Irina Andreevna's long career as a high school teacher, her tenure
as a leader in the Memorial movement, and her own decadelong experience interviewing victims of political repression for the Memorial
archives.

   IA—My father was from a very remote agricultural village, a
member of the Veps ethnic group, who were peasants. His family
was large. His parents had seven sons and one daughter. At first,
my father went to the local parish school, then he finished a four-
year school in Vinnitsa. And then he went to Petrozavodsk and
entered a teacher's seminary, which he completed in 1911. I have

a document. Then he taught in a rural school. The First World War began, but at first they didn't take teachers into the army. He was drafted at the end of 1915. He was a rank and file soldier, but not in the usual ranks, he wound up in the ambulance corps because he was extremely nearsighted, and he wore glasses. He couldn't shoot. So he was in the war as a medic, carrying out the wounded. In 1917, after Nicholas II abdicated, the army started to scatter. And my father, using the excuse that he had lost his glasses, whether that was true or not I don't know, he also was demobilized, because of his eyesight. He came to Petersburg and there he witnessed this entire revolutionary history with his own eyes. He was there the entire summer. He went from rally to rally, he heard all kinds of speakers, including Lenin, and decided which group to join. Because he was young and very active. He joined the Socialist Revolutionaries [SRs]. And he thought that the SRs represented the peasantry's interests. He became a Party member, and in the fall he went back home, to Petrozavodsk. And there, the preparations were already, the preparations for the elections to the Constituent Assembly were under way. And he actively participated, and became a candidate of the SR for the Constituent Assembly. . . . And he went to Peter[1] when the opening of the Constituent Assembly was announced. It's well known that it sat for one day, and then they wouldn't let them back into the building. My father understood he could not overcome violence through a parliamentary path. Some people proposed that they gather in another location. He refused. He said, "If there's violence—that's it. There is no more democracy." The Bolsheviks were using violent methods, so he renounced the political struggle and any kind of political work. He was not a proponent of violent actions. So that's the prehistory. . . . After that, he immersed himself in working with cooperatives. At that time, . . . consumer and credit cooperatives were developing. He became interested in this work, which was very useful for peasants, because the model had been taken from Western cooperatives.

CF—Did he still consider himself to be a peasant?

IA—Yes, he came from a peasant family, and he decided that he was obliged to help the same social group from which his family had come, as a member of the intelligentsia who had emerged

---

1. A popular nickname for Saint Petersburg to this day.

from this milieu. He took courses at the Central Union in Moscow, where the central agency for this work was, and became an instructor. He traveled around different provinces, he gave lectures on advanced agriculture. . . . So he became a lecturer. He was in Smolensk on an assignment. And that's where he met Mama, who was also there on assignment, but in library work. She was setting up public libraries. In Smolensk there was a depository of books from the libraries that had been confiscated from gentry estates in 1917, 1918, 1919. . . . They would bring her mountains of books. She was a specialist on Russian literature. She would put together small libraries and send them to rural locations for the peasants. . . . So they became acquainted there. And their wedding was in July 1919. After this, they lived in Moscow, because they were expecting a child. They were given a room, but it was a very small, cramped room without windows. In some kind of big apartment, taken from some rich person, where there were several families. It was hard to live there. Furthermore, there was famine in 1920, it got worse in 1921, and Mama gave birth in 1921.[2] Mama gave birth, and my father said, "Why should we starve here? I'll take you to my parents in the countryside. They have livestock there, they have grain. They have a cow. Those are the right conditions to raise a child." So, they went there. My father transferred his work from the Moscow organization to the Saint Petersburg organization. And he began to operate from Saint Petersburg. Also in rural locales. And Mama lived in the village with his parents and with his brothers' families in one house with all the children. Mama used to talk about how twenty-one people sat down at the table. It was that kind of large peasant family. Mama didn't know how to do anything in the peasant way. Not a single thing. And when the daughters-in-law realized this, they said, "Masha, you sit with our children, we'll have peace of mind, and we will do your fieldwork for you." And she, having gathered these children, and there were seven or eight of them, all under school age, she did all the pedagogical work with them. . . . They depended on her. Her child was part of this group. Up to age three. In 1923, the child suddenly died. Some

---

2. The famine of 1921–1922 led to an estimated five million deaths. For a compelling account, see Bernard Patenaude, *The Big Show in Bololand: The American Relief Expedition to Soviet Russia in the Famine of 1921* (Stanford University Press, 2002).

kind of fulminant disease, apparently of the brain. And after this, Mama could not remain in the village. She had a very hard time getting over it. She went into shock, she was shaken to the point of losing her mind. And my father took her away from there. That was in 1924. January. They buried the child in the autumn of 1923. And by January 1924, they were already in Moscow. Lenin's funeral. They saw this. . . . Father received an assignment to Orel Province, to the city of Yelets. And they went there. The year 1925 found them there. And 1925, this was the beginning of the New Economic Policy.[3] It got easier with food, everything showed up at the market. They rented a room there. And they started to live there. A second child appeared. Another girl. This was my older sister, their second child, Lidia. So, what happened in Orel, that is in Yelets, Orel Province, I don't know, but Father tried to get farther still from the capital. Farther, even farther. I think that he was apprehensive that they would persecute SRs. And they were already persecuting them, trials were already going on.[4] He evidently was trying to disguise himself, because he didn't want his family to suffer such a fate. They move to Tsaritsyn. They leave Yelets, they move to Tsaritsyn. In Tsaritsyn, he again got a job teaching in a cooperative technical school. . . . They joined the housing cooperative and received two rooms in this housing cooperative. So, in 1928, I was born there. We two girls survived. The first child perished in the village. And we're living there, a happy, very successful family. Because Papa never drank, he never put a drop of spirits in his mouth. He never smoked. He was physically very strong. He worked a lot. He told Mama, "You look after the children while they grow a bit. I'll work two shifts." And he worked from morning till night. And on top of that, he became a correspondence student in the Economics Department of the Moscow Institute of Economics, with a specialization in teaching.

CF—Please describe this apartment in Tsaritsyn in the 1920s and the beginning of the 1930s.

3. The New Economic Policy had been introduced by Lenin at the 10th Party Congress in 1921. It was a form of mixed economy, permitting small-scale trade while the major industries and banks, the so-called commanding heights, remained under the state's control.

4. The first major trials of members of the Socialist Revolutionaries took place in Moscow in 1922, resulting in executions or exile for the accused.

IA—I see this apartment before my eyes right now like a photograph. Because childhood memories are so strong. First of all,
it was a two-story mansion, evidently confiscated from someone,
from rich people. It was the only brick house on the street. The
rest were small, wooden, private houses. So, this cooperative was
organized in this mansion. They divided the big spaces into separate rooms, and people moved in. One family might have one
room, another two. We had two. It was heated by a stove, there
was a shared kitchen on each floor. A shared toilet on each floor.
. . . Let me count, on the top floor, there were one, two, three,
four—four families on the top floor, and probably the same number on the first floor. I didn't have much to do with the first floor.
There was a big yard. In this yard there was another separate toilet, masonry, because earlier there hadn't been any water closets,
because this house had been refitted for that, as I now recall. Of
course, there was no tub. There was no shower. But there was a
water closet. There was a stove. We heated with the stove. . . . So
these were the conditions we lived in. We had a big veranda running along the back side of the house. This veranda was divided
into two parts, one family used one part, and we used the other.
This was very good, because in the hot weather it was hard on
the children. But the veranda had a big roof, there was a lot of
room. And we played. I remember my childhood as very happy,
despite the fact that I didn't have much in the way of clothes. I
wore my sister's hand-me-down dresses, and her shoes, too. For
the most part, I went barefoot. Here is a photograph from Stalingrad, where I am in the last group in kindergarten. . . . Where am
I here? Here I am. . . . They shaved our heads so we wouldn't get
lice. For some reason, lice were very widespread at that time. My
sandals have holes in them. And I'm wearing only underpants and
nothing else. The situation with clothes was rather bad.

CF—Almost all the other children are barefoot.

IA—Yes, they're barefoot. It was difficult to get clothes. Even
though my father earned money, there was nothing to buy. There
was nothing in the stores.

CF—And did all of these children live with their families?

IA—All these children had families. They took them to kindergarten when their parents were at work. . . . I started school.
By the way, they accepted me in a school that was called a dem-

Irina Andreevna Dubrovina's kindergarten class in Stalingrad, ca. 1934; she is the first child on the left in the first row (Private collection of I. A. Dubrovina)

onstration school. Why did they admit me? They accepted only select children who would study well. But my sister was already a student there. And she proved herself to be an A student. Therefore, when my father arrived with me at the director's office, he said, "And is this child from the Matveev family? Yes, we'll take this one." They admitted me. But I had a hard time in the first grade. Home schooling had left its mark. At lessons, I did well, I knew everything. I was already reading big books. I didn't need the first grade curriculum. Recesses were hard for me. I was shy, I hugged the wall and even, I recall, sometimes I cried during breaks. It was difficult for me. The teacher was very good. Very. She was quite young, she was still a student herself. And she was very well disposed to us. Like a big sister. I was fine in class, but she left during breaks, and it was sad for me with the other children. I remember something else about her, about the teacher. Since she was herself a student, and she also had her own assignments. And so she needed to read *Dead Souls*.[5] She

5. Nikolai Gogol's masterpiece, published in 1842. Decidedly an adult novel, it is characterized by his inventive use of the grotesque.

proposed, "Anyone who wants to listen while I read *Dead Souls,*
stay after classes." I was such a book lover, I loved to listen and
to read. I stayed. About five of us stayed. We sat around her. And
Zinaida Sergeevna, I remember her name and patronymic, she
read *Dead Souls* to us. This to children eight years old! We understood everything beautifully. . . . So that's the kind of teacher
she was. Very lovely.

From our grade, I remember the daughter of the tractor factory's director. Because elite families sent their children to this
school. So the daughter of the director of the Stalingrad tractor
factory came to school in a car, because where they lived near
the tractor factory was far away. The father's driver delivered her
in the car. . . . From those kinds of elite families, because it was
considered a demonstration school. My sister told me that at the
school the teachers in the upper grade were from the pedagogical
institute itself. . . . The music teacher was marvelous. This I remember. She would sit at the piano and teach us to sing, then she
would stand up, lead us into the ballroom, and on the parquet
floor, show us dances. And we would dance in pairs those dances
we could manage, the polka, the Cracovienne, and so on. Like
that. This was very good for us, we were happy to dance after
sitting behind our desks. . . . The physical education teacher was
also good. Also. It's a pleasure for me to remember school. . . .
But, alas, this childhood came to an end. In 1938.

In 1938, in August, on the thirty-first, they came for my father
at night. They got us all up, made us stand up against the wall,
and while we were standing there, they carried out the search.
They seized the photographs, documents, savings account book,
bonds, all the money in the house, and took it all away and they
took our father away. Mother was in such shock, so stunned,
that she couldn't do anything. She couldn't find anything out,
she simply lay prostrate. My sister was fourteen years old, and
she took it upon herself to do all of this—to find out, to try to
make arrangements, to go here and there, to hire a lawyer. And
my father was locked up while under interrogation until April.
We didn't see him. They didn't grant anything, neither a visit,
nor parcels, *nothing!* And we were only invited to the trial on
April 11, 1939, but not into the courtroom. We stood behind
the doors. It was a closed trial. They let us into the courtroom
only when they read the sentence. Article 58, chapter 10, anti-
Soviet agitation. Eight years of corrective labor and five years'

deprivation of civil rights. So that was that. They didn't give my father his glasses. He was terribly nearsighted. He was standing far away from us. We stood at one end of the room by the doors, he was over where the judges were. He didn't see us without his glasses. I did not see him, because I was also very nearsighted. . . . I saw only a pale spot instead of a face. And they took us away, they took him away, they took us away, they led us out of the courtroom.

CF—How did your classmates receive this news?

IA—Mama told us, "You must not talk with anyone about this. Because if you say even one word about this, then they will arrest me and take me away. You'll be left on your own. Therefore, no one must know anything." Many years later, Mama told me, "Among your classmates, half of the fathers were arrested." And we kept going to school. We said nothing to anyone.

CF—No one knew.

IA—No. Not a single word. Parents didn't permit us to talk about it, because there were instances when they arrested the father, and later the mother. Therefore, we were afraid. Children would *vanish!* One of the first to vanish was the daughter of the director of the tractor factory. She *vanished,* and that was it. No one said where she went, why she wasn't at school, not a word.

CF—How did your teacher treat you?

IA—She treated us, as before, very well. As before. She evidently really loved children. But she also did not say a word. She must have known that they had taken our parents. But she didn't say a word.

CF—And was it hard for you, as a child, to keep silent?

IA—It was not difficult for me to keep silent. I was a very taciturn child. I resemble my father. My aunt later even nicknamed me "the pensive girl." I would just go into the corner and think about how it could be that my papa, who was so good, could wind up in jail. I looked for answers in books. I found one book about Hitler's Germany. And there it was written how the Fascists arrested the father of one boy or girl, I don't recall which now. I was stunned that my experiences were very similar. . . . I was just surprised that there were also such experiences in Germany. . . . The book by the American author Beecher-Stowe,

Uncle Tom's Cabin, made a very strong impression on me. I really worried about the negroes. For the separation of the family. When I read this, I also felt something like an echo of my own pain. But I couldn't imagine that such a thing could happen in our country, and for that reason, I sat in the corner and kept thinking, "But why did they take Papa? Our papa is so good." Mama said, "Just keep quiet. Our papa is good. But you must remain silent." Nothing else.

CF—And after that?

IA—After that. By that time, Mama was working, because she and my father had agreed earlier that she would go to work as soon as her last daughter entered school. And when I started first grade, she went to work. She worked in a school on the outskirts of the city. She was a teacher in the early grades. When my father was arrested, she expected that they would fire her. But the director, a woman, came up to her herself and said, "Don't you worry, I won't fire you." And she used the informal "you" form![6] Even though she was a Party member, she was a very decent woman. She said, "Don't be afraid." In the informal "you" form. Mama told us about this. "Don't be afraid, I won't fire you." In general, she also acted as if she knew nothing, and Mama stayed on. This is how this director would help Mama: as soon as one of the teachers got sick, Mama immediately became the substitute. She received pay for this. Because her salary was very low. And she, Mama, had to feed, educate, and dress two girls. So that was the director, Anna Ivanovna was her name. To this day I remember her, how Mama always thanked her in front of us, "How good she was. She was a Party member, she was a school director, she could have gotten into trouble for this, but she said to me, 'Don't you worry, I won't fire you.' Even addressing me in the informal 'you' form."

CF—Yesterday, you told me that when you had your last visit with your father, you were able to speak to each other.

IA—Yes, after the trial, a visit was granted. There were a lot of prisoners, there weren't enough jails. So they cordoned off an

6. In Russian, as in French and German, there are two forms of addressing another person. The "Vy" form is a sign of respect, used in addressing social superiors or older persons, as well as persons who are not one's close friends or relatives. The "Ty" form is used to address intimate friends, relatives, and children.

area not far from our house. The railroad bed ran by there. Residential buildings were on this side of the railroad bed, and along that side they cordoned off the zone with barbed wire. They put up some kind of temporary wooden barracks, and they put all those who were convicted there, as their living arrangements in the summer. So we would run along the rail bed, we would wave, but you couldn't hear much. They granted a visit in this camp, yes. There were gates where relatives gathered at an appointed time. At the appointed time, they let us through these gates, we went into this barrack. There was a very long table inside, along both sides of which there were very long benches. The prisoners sat on one side, the families along the other. We could talk to each other across this table. I recall from my mother's conversation with my father that he was constantly giving her instructions on how to live from then on. "Sell our belongings, feed the children. Do not ever give this apartment up. Under no circumstances. We have a good apartment. Raise the children there."

CF—And when the war began?

IA—At first we corresponded with our father, he was in the Far East at a timber operation. He was building this road, BAM.[7] It was just being started back then. They had already started it in 1939. . . . We corresponded in 1939–1940, but when the war began in 1941, correspondence was halted. They didn't grant them permission to write, and we received no answer to our letters. Afterward, we learned that they had moved them to Vorkuta.[8] To build the railroad that ran from Konosha to Kotlas to Vorkuta. . . . In the camp barracks, he lived with regular criminals. And in order to survive, he would take time at work to recall the adventure novels he had read as a youth, by Collins, Dumas, Mayne Reid.[9] Everything that he remembered, he would recall during the day while he was working, he had a good memory. And in the evening, when he came back, he would tell the stories to these criminals, "to be continued." For that reason, they didn't touch him; after all, there was no radio, no newspapers, no kind of information. This was entertainment. He told these novels to

7. A railroad line running across eastern Siberia, north of the Trans-Siberian Railroad.
8. A major coal mining operation in the north of European Russia, which was also one of the largest forced-labor camps in the Gulag.
9. The three were adventure novelists of the nineteenth century.

them, and they didn't steal his bread, they did not force him to
sleep in a bad spot where it was cold. They protected him as a
good storyteller. So that's how he survived. Only this enabled
him to survive.

CF—Well, you were in a famous city in the war. Tsaritsyn had
become Stalingrad.

IA—It had become Stalingrad in 1929, soon after I was born.
And by 1942, this city was at risk of invasion by the Germans. By
that time, my sister had completed tenth grade and was studying
in the first year at a medical institute. She graduated from school
in 1941, and in 1941 she began to work in a hospital at the
same time. She studied at the institute and worked in a hospital.
They were bringing in the wounded. All the schools were turned
into hospitals. So this is how I went to school in the fifth grade.
A group of five to seven children would gather at the homes of
classmates who had bigger apartments. The teachers would go
from apartment to apartment, giving one and the same lesson
several times in a row. There simply were no larger spaces. . . . We
immediately lost German as a language, they ceased to teach it.
Because, as I now know, they immediately removed our teacher,
a Volga German, a lovely woman, she worked very well with us.
She taught us for only one year, and then immediately she was
gone. Well, that's how we studied. In 1942, when the Germans
took Rostov for the second time already, there were no obstacles
of any kind between Rostov and Stalingrad. The naked steppe,
flat as a table, you could go in any direction without any road.
In war, this is very advantageous for attack. But not for defense.
And so the Germans overcame this distance very quickly. My
mama's daughter, my older sister, came home from the hospital
and said, "Mama, the wounded are arriving by foot." Mama
said, "So what?" "The thing is, do you know what Germans
do to young girls? And you have two daughters. Let's leave."
Mama said, "But no one else is leaving. And also Papa said that
we should hold on to the apartment. Where will you find such a
big apartment? I won't leave for anything." The next day my sister came in and said, "Nothing is having any effect on Mama."
Mama said, "I should sit tight where your father said." And so,
in the end, an official document came to us, ordering us as the
family of an enemy of the people to leave the city of Stalingrad
within forty-eight hours. . . . As the family of an enemy of the

people to leave Stalingrad in forty-eight hours. It didn't say where to go, how to pay for it, on what kind of transport, *nothing!* Get out, and that was it.

So my sister was very happy that she could get Mama . . . out. She herself ran to the market and began to sell all our remaining belongings. The only thing Mama held on to was the sewing machine. . . . My sister was able to sell the rest, even books, this was in August! Of 1942. The Germans were already somewhere in the outskirts. She was able to sell the books, no one in the population was leaving, everyone was sure that they wouldn't surrender Stalin's city, there was no need to spread panic among us. But there were rumors going around the city that the NKVD was burning its archives and evacuating some things. The NKVD was saving all its property, but the population was left to the whim of fate. Like that. We sat on the embankment for entire days on our bundles, having left the apartment open, we abandoned the apartment and bought tickets within twenty-four hours. On an ordinary steamer on the deck, because there weren't any seats inside. On the deck, having bought tickets, we left. This was practically one of the last boats to run. Our steamer no longer went during the daytime, it went only at night. During the day, it stopped next to the bank, hid in the bushes, and waited, because there were air raids. So that's how we landed in Bashkiria.

Why Bashkiria? Because Mama was a very well-read person. She said, "We don't have any relatives in the east, but I know that Aksakov wrote beautiful things about nature in Bashkiria, so we'll go there."[10] . . . At first Mama tried to find a position in Biisk. There were no positions in Biisk for teachers. We went to Ufa. There was a huge flood of evacuees in Ufa. Everything was arranged to receive them, job placements, but we had no documents of any kind. We couldn't show this shameful order. So Mama told them we were from Stalingrad, that we hadn't managed to receive anything. And they took her at her word. And they gave us evacuees' documents. Mama was given a job in Arkhangelskoe, this is around thirty to forty kilometers from the Ufa-Sterlitomakh railroad. . . . We lived there four years.

10. Sergei Aksakov, Slavophile author of a lightly fictionalized family memoir written a century earlier, in which the lead character was based on his grandfather, who moved out to Bashkiria during the reign of Catherine the Great.

CF—And in all this time, you didn't receive a single word from your father?

IA—Not a single word from my father. For the entire war. . . . We decided that our correspondence had ceased precisely because he had perished. We didn't know that it had been forbidden. . . . And the way they treated the dead in the camps was, "Someone dies, fine." They didn't inform anyone. This we knew. That they never informed anyone about someone's death.

CF—And did no one in the village know about . . .

IA—In the village, they knew. Mama had to write this in official documents. Because if she had not written this, they would have considered her an enemy, because she was hiding her biography from the Party and the government. That she was some kind of suspicious person. . . . Therefore, she received no bonuses of any kind, no promotions of any kind, nothing, nothing. Everything just depended on the kindness of the people with whom she worked.

CF—How did you eat? How did you feed yourselves in this village? And where was your older sister?

IA—My older sister stayed in Ufa, because she said she wanted to continue her studies in a medical institute. . . . She was admitted to an institute, but at night she had to work in a hospital to get enough to eat. On top of that, she gave blood for the wounded, for which she also received a special ration and some money. She gave blood and worked nights in a hospital. But she was also hungry. Because those nurses who worked in the daytime could eat in the kitchen. But at night the kitchen had already been shut down, they didn't feed anyone. So the wounded themselves would give her some food, those who had a bad appetite and had something left over, they would give her something to eat. Later she married one of the wounded soldiers she cared for.

CF—While she was working there, you and your mama lived in the village.

IA—At first Mama and I lived in the village. Then in the town, where I completed a ten-grade school. They did not admit me into the Komsomol because of that stigma. I was in tears, I was the best student in the grade, a straight-A student, the only student in the grade to be left out of the Komsomol.

Irina Andreevna Dubrovina's high school graduating class, ca. 1947; she is the first student on the left in the front row (Private collection of I. A. Dubrovina)

CF—Before that, did you feel alone?

IA—Before then, I didn't feel different from the others. But when they all entered the Komsomol, they started to have all sorts of Komsomol meetings, and they would ask me to leave. So this was very humiliating for me. . . . I tried not to discuss this with Mama. I knew that this would traumatize Mama badly. I simply said nothing. I just had to tell her that they hadn't admitted me to the Komsomol. I told her, but that was all. Mama took this as to be expected. They didn't admit me, so they didn't admit me. But that I was suffering this exclusion in my grade, that she didn't know. I hid it from her.

CF—Well, how did you feed yourselves?

IA—We fed ourselves like this—at first, in the settlement during the first year, we had absolutely nothing. We arrived in late autumn. We couldn't plant anything. The collective farm gave us a bucket of potatoes. That was all that they could spare us. The collective farm couldn't help us either, it was also very poor. They settled us with a peasant family, a grandmother, grandfather, their son was at the front, their daughter-in-law lived with them with her two small children. We lived in one room with them. We slept in the loft, they had lofts there, some on the stove.[11] The old folks would sleep on the stove, but we were on the loft with these little children also. And the daughter-in-law slept on the only bed below. Because she had to get up early to tend to the cow, to the livestock. And we slept up there. As a rule, we simply went hungry. . . . This first year was terrible.

The second year was a bit easier, because they gave us some land. We planted potatoes, so it was much easier. The government distributed five hundred grams of oats, ground with the hulls, per month to evacuees. Not even sifted. And so, Mama and I received one kilogram of these oats per month, and that was all. . . . So, we sifted these oats, from the hulls we made oat pudding; from this flour mixed with potatoes, I made bread. Just a tiny bit of the flour; the rest, mashed potatoes. I learned how to work with a Russian stove. Mama couldn't master anything you do in a village. Nothing. I mastered the Russian stove, I baked bread, it was enough for us. . . . Half-starving, we lived half-starving. In the summer, I planted gardens. When I had more or less mastered farming, I started to grow tomatoes to sell. I would sell tomatoes, and use the money to buy milk. Bread was beyond reach, but milk, dairy products, I could buy these. Sometimes a small piece of village butter, sometimes farmer's cheese. Sometimes milk, that was still something I could afford, but bread wasn't affordable. A loaf of bread cost as much as Mama's monthly salary. Bread was absolutely out of reach. . . .

CF—Where were you when the war ended?

IA—The war ended in 1945, I was in the eighth grade then. Well, of course, everyone was very happy. But no one shouted, "Victory!" So I used to ask people, "And so what do you think we shouted when the war ended?" "Victory," they say. But no one shouted "Victory!" We didn't think about victory. We shouted "The war is over!" Now that was joy. No one even pronounced the word "victory." The most important thing was that

11. In peasant households, the stove for heating and cooking was a large structure that occupied a quarter to a third of the floor space. Covered with plaster or adobe, it had sleeping shelves on its top and sides, which were considered the most desirable sleeping spaces in the home.

this horrible time was over, this bloodletting. People would come home. That's what mattered.

CF—Well, you weren't expecting your father to return.

IA—We were not expecting him. We knew that he had been in the camp during the entire war, or that he had perished there at the beginning of the war. We didn't know. And suddenly we received a letter from my father. This was the happiest day of my life. To this day it is. The happiest day! And how did my father find us? He wrote to Buguruslan, where there was an information bureau about the evacuees. And there was information there about my sister, who was working and studying in Ufa. . . . She received the letter. She told him what our address was. He wrote us, too. So after this, we began to write back and forth. He was released only in 1946. When he was freed, we waited for him to come to us. He refused. As a rational person, he calculated that it would be better for us to come to him.

We were preparing to leave as soon as I was finished with school. We sold everything we had, including the sewing machine, because it was the most valuable thing we had. . . . We sold the sewing machine, bought the tickets, some bread, and departed. At first we took the train to Ufa, then to Ruzayevka, then to Kirov. Then to Kotlas, with a transfer. There were no direct routes. . . . We traveled for a long time. Probably an entire week. . . . We sat up the whole way, squeezed right up against each other, these were third-class cars. There was no place to lie down. . . . We were robbed during the trip. Yes. Our bundle was down below, and the planks for shelves were in the open. . . . Someone slipped in under there and I was dozing, and somehow I heard our bag shuffling. I said, "Mama, a mouse, a mouse!" I slapped the bag, and there was a bad man there. He cut our bag from the bottom, and took out our bread and Mama's jacket. It's a good thing that this happened not far from Papa. This happened when we were already between Kotlas and Vorkuta. The last leg of the trip. The jacket was valuable, the jacket had come from American humanitarian aid. . . . It was an American jacket. It was the first time we ever saw a zipper. The jacket was warm, wool. . . . I had received clothes from English workers. A children's coat, a pretty light blue color with beige lining, very warm, and there in the pocket was a little piece of cardboard that said, "To Russian children from English Workers." So Mama's

Irina Andreevna Dubrovina as a young teacher at her desk,
ca. 1947 (Private collection of I. A. Dubrovina)

American jacket was stolen, but I had my coat with me, but I
outgrew it in 1950. . . . Mama then made me a jacket out of it.
I still wore it as a jacket, and she made a beret to go with it. . . .
My father met us at the train. The meeting was, of course, dra-
matic. I did not remember my father well. My sister was not with
us. She had married before my father's release and had moved to
be with her husband.

CF—Was there an opportunity to work there?

IA—In a new school. The school had just been constructed, a
pretty wooden building. It had a lot of air and light. There were
rooms for two classrooms, a gym, a teacher's room, and two
apartments. So, the school director took one of the apartments.
That was my mama. And the cleaning woman and her children
took the other apartment. The apartments were small, only one
room apiece. So, they set me up in the teacher's lounge. . . . I
was very happy there, I felt so happy! I turned nineteen there in
November.

But I hadn't received any word about my university studies in
Leningrad. I had submitted the documents from Bashkiria already. I was a gold medalist, they were supposed to admit me
without any entrance exams. But for some reason, there was no
answer from the university. So I decided I would study by correspondence. And I concluded that they hadn't admitted me simply because I had the biography I had. That my father had been

imprisoned. I sent my documents to the correspondence section, also for the Chemistry Department. Why did I choose chemistry? While I was still in school, I had consulted with my father in our letters. I said that I really liked history, literature, and journalism. He answered, "The path is closed to all of these specializations for you, because you have such a blot on your biography. Therefore, choose an exact science." He believed that math and physics were too complex for women. Chemistry was a newly evolving science and would be sufficiently exact and sufficiently in demand. So, he recommended chemistry. So, I followed my father's advice. . . . So that's how I came to apply to chemistry. Well, and having received no answer from the university, I asked them, I sent a letter, to transfer my documents to the correspondence division. I worked and studied. They would send my exams, I would complete them and send them back. . . . At the end of the academic year, I went to Leningrad to take the final exams. I had four exams; I received two fours and two fives [with five being the highest possible grade]. I did all of the lab assignments, satisfied the lab requirements, and was promoted to the second year. After that, I went to the rector's office and asked, "I just finished the first year by correspondence. But I was admitted as a residential student, but they didn't inform me, and I didn't come. So, is it possible to transfer me to residential status now?" He refused. "It is possible to transfer from residential to correspondence, but not from correspondence to residential." I was very, very upset. But even so, I had a triumph of sorts, I had completed the first year. I decided that I would work a bit longer, and I went home. The second year, I was teaching the second and fourth grades already. My students were graduating from elementary school. My fourth-graders were to take exams at that time. It was very strict. In Vorkuta. They didn't trust the elementary school to do the examinations. They had to go to the middle school, the teachers there examined my children. We arranged a place for them to spend the night there and we took two exams: in Russian language and literature, and in mathematics. My little ones did very well.

CF—Congratulations!

IA—I was very pleased. Mama was pleased. So. But I was still intent on getting to Leningrad, to continue my studies as a residential student. . . . I decided that I was willing to lose a year, as long as they admitted me for the second year as a residential student. And I decided to make such an attempt. At the end of the second year, I went to Leningrad and went around to many offices, I wrote, I asked for my documents, I tried to prove my case, and all to no effect. I went to the very top, no effect whatsoever. And one day, as I was walking along Nevsky Prospekt, I saw a sign, "Legal Consultation." I went in. And there was a man who was unusually attentive for some reason. Now I understand that this was an experienced, older lawyer who decided to help a young girl. And when he began to question me so attentively, so considerately, I burst into sobs. He became even more sympathetic, apparently, as if he were dealing with his own daughter. And he gave me this advice: "You need to write to Moscow, to the Ministry of Education, but you won't get anything accomplished here." So that's when I understood that I needed to write to the Ministry. And he helped me compose an appeal to the Ministry with a description of all of my obstacles. And this appeal worked. It was successful.

CF—And in these documents, which you sent to Leningrad and Moscow, did you include the fact that your father had been in the camps?

IA—Just this, as it happens, I did not include, not the first time I sent my documents, not the second time when I wrote about transferring to residential student status. I did not write it. I understood perfectly that this was something that would prevent me from studying in an institution of higher education. Therefore, I decided on a conscious lie. Conscious. I decided that this was not some closed institution, but an open institution of learning, and that I had the right to study there. Therefore, I decided on a conscious lie, knowing how my biography would be an obstacle. Well, so I entered the second year. My classmates welcomed me. Very well. They admitted me to the Komsomol without any problem. Even though I confessed to them. I quietly told the Komsomol organizer for the second year that I was not so good, that I was such a person. He said, "A lot of us are. We admit everyone." . . . I absolutely never felt guilty. I felt no guilt on my part of any kind. I had always worked to the full extent of my abilities both in my studies and in supporting myself. So that I felt no guilt about myself at all, I lied consciously, but I was not guilty before my government or my people or my comrades in *any way.* . . .

CF—When did you complete your studies? . . .

IA—In my diploma, it is written that I studied from 1948. In fact, I started in 1949. . . . Exactly at this time, as I later found out, was the Leningrad Affair. Mass arrests of Leningrad leaders were organized. But in the family where I was living, I lived with the family of my father's brother. Of course, they didn't talk about this, no one said anything about this. My uncle was a very wonderful person, but as silent a man as my father. He would come home from work and read newspapers. In *Leningradskaya Pravda,* he would mark something, he would mark something, I recall he read with a pencil in his hand. And one day, I got up the courage all the same and asked him, "Uncle Yosha—his name was Georgy—tell me, please, what you are marking." "I'm checking off how many times in one issue of *Leningradskaya Pravda* the words Stalin, Stalinist, about Stalin, and so on appear." I was so surprised. "And, so, how many?" "In one issue, I counted two hundred times." So this was all he ever said to me about politics. But that made me reflect, of course. I then began to think about the fact that Stalin had taken too much power. Coming in from work, my uncle would sometimes say, "So and so was arrested." But for me, this was not very terrible, because I didn't know these people. But I always remembered that this was like my father. And this was the reality for me that nourished my silence, so as not to harm anyone, including myself. Silence was salvation. That's what I knew. . . .

I completed the university in '53, in 1953. But by the fall of 1952, the situation was still very difficult. Because of the case of the Jewish doctors. I don't remember in what month, we were sitting in the lab, several of us, we were discussing work of some kind. There were a lot of Jews among us, and suddenly we hear on the radio that Jews wanted to murder our leaders. We all froze. We simply froze. Everyone held their breath; we listened. And we thought, "Have we not gone crazy? Haven't we gone crazy?" Because we had been raised at a time when all nationalities were the same, that all nationalities were the same, that we were internationalists, that we welcome everyone. And all of a sudden, something like this, in the Soviet Union. It was very difficult for us and incomprehensible. And I was sorry for my comrades whom this was soiling. And in the fifth year, I had already gradually become the Komsomol organizer—KOMSORG. . . . The KOMSORG for each year was on the Komsomol bureau for each year's class in each department, and the Komsomol bureau for the department had representation on the Komsomol bureau for the entire university. . . . So, I was among those at the *very top* of the Komsomol organization. And I, having heard such a thing, considered myself obligated to stand up for my comrades. So, we organized a kind of committee to do something against any unjust treatment of our comrades. So. The committee chose an activist group. I was on it, and we went to Smolny[12]—to find out what was going on and to say we didn't want this.

CF—You were brave to go to Smolny.

IA—It was a brave and completely foolish step. We should have already understood by then that this was senseless. But we were still naïve, and I especially so. . . . I was twenty-four years old. By then I should have already been wiser. I was so indignant that I didn't consider this. So, I led this group, and we went. When we got to Smolny, we came to Smolny; there was a pass system there. In the vestibule, there were telephones. "So, please, call the person you need." We called, and the answer we heard was, "We cannot admit you. Go home." "What do you mean you can't?" "Just that, we can't. Go home." Already more harshly. And that was it. They didn't want to talk to us, we left.

And our job placement process began that February, even before the final state exams, approximately then the placement process began, who would go where. Where they would work. And so the commission would call each person at a time and offer a position. And they kept not calling me in and not calling me in until the very end. I was one of the last, two or three persons were left after me. So, they called me among the last. And they offered me a spot in this scientific institution called AZChERNIRO, which studied the Azov-Black Sea basin, on research vessels, on which they needed a chemist. "You will spend your whole life on the sea making analyses on those bodies of water where the boat goes." Well, for a young girl to be among

12. Communist Party headquarters in Leningrad.

male sailors, this wasn't very appealing. But, I decided all the same to write there, this time I wrote openly that there was this issue in my biography, that my father had served a prison term as a political prisoner. And they wrote back that they couldn't take me on. I wasn't offered any other position. And I began to take the state exams. First I finished my senior thesis, then I took the state exams. . . . And only after I was a fully graduated specialist, they called me again to the commission and offered me a position as a chemistry teacher in Chechnya, to be assigned by the Chechnya regional department of education. "And what else is there?" So that there would be a choice. "There is nothing else for you." That was it. Categorically.

CF—Do you think that this was the result of your biography or because of your, how to say . . .

IA—Activism?

CF—Activism at the Smolny gates.

IA—It could very well have been both the one and the other. Because all of these things converged in one place, in the KGB. Everything wound up there. And when I graduated, when I filled out my job assignment dossier, I wrote the truth, after all. At first I went to my uncle, with whom I was living, and began to consult with him, "What do you think? Should I write the truth or lie, as I lied when I was entering the university?" He said, "Don't lie! Maybe there will be a major background check, and then you will really suffer." And I wrote the truth. I was afraid to consult with my father about this. I didn't want to. . . . I consulted only with my uncle. So the commission looked me over. From two sides. In the first place, daughter of an enemy of the people; in the second place, actively defending Jews, who deserve to be driven out as wreckers. Okay. Chechnya. And I had to go to Chechnya.

Of course there was a graduation dance. I went to this dance. But I was very unhappy there. Not all of our classmates shared my view, and few people had anything to do with us. And in general, people began to be afraid of me, to distance themselves from me. So, I was left alone in this misfortune. So, I can't even recall how my closest girlfriend behaved, the one who is now in Moscow. She disappeared from my line of vision, that is, she also distanced herself. So, that's how I was left by myself.

I walked around Peter like a castaway, because, as one of the best graduates with an Honors degree (a red diploma), I had to go to Chechnya. There was nothing I could do. It was a state law that you had to work for three years in the place where the commission sent you. I spent the summer with my parents in Dnepropetrovsk,[13] and then I went to Chechnya. . . . I arrived in Chechnya and was assured in the regional department of education that there were no positions in my specialization in the towns. And they offered me a job in a remote area, called Chernye Peski [Black Sands], which I could reach only by plane. A place where a non-Russian population herded livestock. And it would be a seven-year school, teaching two hours of chemistry per week. I refused this assignment. I asked, I demanded, I begged them to give me any other assignment. I agreed to teach physics, math, but they were implacable. So then I went to the local trade union committee, which said that there were no jobs in my specialization here. "Give me the document that states that is the case." They prepared this document and gave it to me. So, in this the trade union helped me.

With this document, I flew to Moscow for a new assignment. I showed up on Chistye Prudy, where the Ministry of Education for the Russian Federation was . . . . and said I wanted a new assignment. "Fine," they said, "wait two days and we'll find you something." I had an aunt in Moscow. I stayed with my aunt for two days, and they offered me Kotlas. And they looked at me to see how I would react. First we offered you the south, and now the north. But I was thinking, "How lucky! My parents are in Vorkuta, and I'll be in Kotlas, halfway between Moscow and Vorkuta. So, they'll visit me, I'll see them, I'll be able to visit them." I agreed. In Kotlas, the director of the municipal department of public education met me immediately. She took me to her home to spend the night. She gave me a choice of schools and said that I would have a lot of work. Because the Arkhangelsk Pedagogical Institute did not produce graduates in chemistry. And so I stayed in Kotlas. They gave me housing in the former Pioneer room at the school along with another young teacher who had just arrived, and we began to work. I worked the first shift in the school, and I worked with evening students during the second and third shifts. There was a lot of work. So that's

13. Her sister lived there with her husband.

how I remained in Kotlas. Since 1953, so I have lived here more than fifty years already. . . .

Here Irina Andreevna describes her life as a Memorial activist after 1989.

CF—May I ask you, to what extent do you believe that your status as a daughter of an enemy of the people influenced your life? What were the most important consequences?

IA—The things I lived through in my childhood were difficult, being left an orphan, losing my loving and beloved father, such a good parent, this was very hard. The lack of any information about him during the war led us to the overall conclusion that we had lost Father forever. The fact that he returned after the camp was a miracle for us. The happiest moment of my life. And so this, of course, left its mark. All my student life I had support from my father. He was already free at that time, but he couldn't leave the location where he had served his sentence. But he was already working as a hired laborer, he earned some kind of extra pay there for working in the north. He also educated me, because he sent me money. My student stipend was small, but he wanted me to make use of all the cultural benefits of the city. I would go to theaters, to exhibitions, to the libraries, to concerts. In general, my father supported me financially. I didn't work while I was a student, because my father believed that I should work on self-cultivation in addition to my university studies. And he didn't mind sending money for this. So my father played a positive role in this, very much so. If he hadn't wound up in the camp—this is a paradox—he would not have survived. If he had been sent to the front, he would have perished there. He was forty-six years old, but he was still eligible for the draft. But he was in the camp for the entire duration of the war. He got out only in 1946. And so, strangely, this had a positive influence on my life after that. He could provide me support during my studies.

CHAPTER SIX

"I was so overjoyed that I had found you"

VERA MIKHAILOVNA KOSTINA/VERA YULYANOVNA SKIBA
Kotlas
July 7, 2005
Transcribed by Elena Vetrova

Introduction

When Vera Mikhailovna filled out an information form I had given her at the beginning of our interview, she filled in the lines for "Family Name," "First Name and Patronymic" thus: Kostina (maiden family names: Skiba and Teplukhina) Vera Mikhailovna. During her interview, she explained that her birth father's name was Yulian. Thus, she was named Vera Yulyanovna Skiba when she was born in western Belorussia to parents of Polish background in 1940. Coming to understand her various names and choosing the names by which to identify herself became steps in her childhood survival and construction of her adult self. Although my own preference would be to honor Vera's birth father by referring to her as Vera Yulyanovna, I have chosen instead to use her name and patronymic as she, herself, listed them: Vera Mikhailovna.

International political developments threw infant Vera Yulyanovna Skiba into this confusion of names and identities. The signing of the Molotov-Ribbentrop Pact in August 1939 and the subsequent Soviet invasion of Poland on September 17, 1939, set the stage for deportations of Polish families from western Belorussia. Still in diapers, baby

144

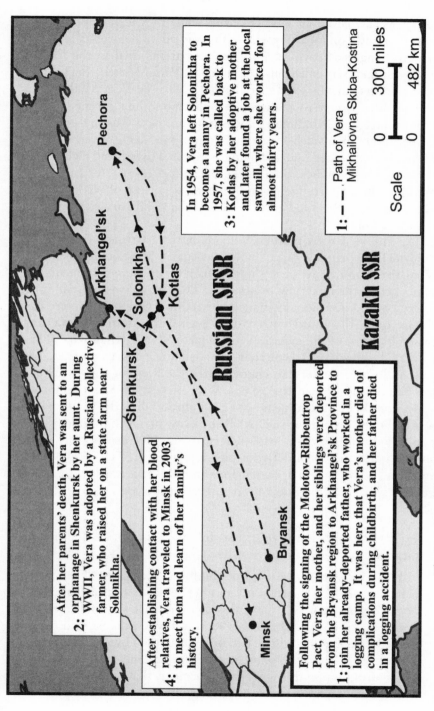

After her parents' death, Vera was sent to an orphanage in Shenkursk by her aunt. During WWII, Vera was adopted by a Russian collective farmer, who raised her on a state farm near Solonikha.

After establishing contact with her blood relatives, Vera traveled to Minsk in 2003 to meet them and learn of her family's history.

In 1954, Vera left Solonikha to become a nanny in Pechora. In 1957, she was called back to Kotlas by her adoptive mother and later found a job at the local sawmill, where she worked for almost thirty years.

Following the signing of the Molotov–Ribbentrop Pact, Vera, her mother, and her siblings were deported from the Bryansk region to Arkhangel'sk Province to join her already-deported father, who worked in a logging camp. It was here that Vera's mother died of complications during childbirth, and her father died in a logging accident.

Pechora

Arkhangel'sk

Solonikha

Kotlas

Shenkursk

Russian SFSR

Bryansk

Minsk

Kazakh SSR

1: — — · Path of Vera Mikhailovna Skiba-Kostina

Scale
0   300 miles
0   482 km

The journeys of Vera Mikhailovna Skiba-Kostina, 1939–2003 (Map by Eric Pugliano)

Vera was carried in her mother's arms when they were deported and forced to travel on foot for much of the way out of Belorussia to northern Arkhangelsk Province. Both of her parents died in the logging camp's special settlement in 1942. One of Vera Mikhailovna's aunts, who also lived in the special settlement, delivered Vera Mikhailovna and her sister, Irena, to a Soviet orphanage after their parents' deaths. From there, Vera Mikhailovna was adopted by a Russian collective farmer, who changed her patronymic and last name. Even so, Vera Mikhailovna's sister and surviving aunts in Poland and Belarus always searched for her, finally locating her in 2002. Her case is remarkable in its narrative of family separation, loss of birth identity, and reunion with blood relatives when the child survivor was over sixty years old.

The interview took place in Vologda in the apartment of Irina Andreevna Dubrovina. Vera Mikhailovna began talking as soon as she entered the room. Some of my questions refer to these comments she made before the interview began. Irina Dubrovina was present at the interview and occasionally made interjections. One of the interesting things about this interview was that even Irina Andreevna was surprised by some of the material hardships of Vera Mikhailovna's life.

Vera Mikhailovna's interview revealed the poverty, hunger, and lack of durable shelter that characterized the Russian north well into the Khrushchev era in the 1950s. With only seven years of formal education, Vera Mikhailovna spoke simply and directly. She provided a straightforward narrative of what she knew of her childhood, young adulthood, and reunion with her relatives. Her use of verb tense shifted back and forth between past and present. This verbal habit suited a life history that moved forward and backward in time and centered on family fragmentation and reconstitution.

CF—Please describe your first childhood memories, and from there, we can move on to your history.

VM—Let's see, what kind of childhood memories? I remember only when . . . . when my mother took me out of that, out of the orphanage. So, I have this memory that she took me by horse, in a cart. And that I was so afraid when she walked over to the horse that I would be left alone. And then I was afraid that I would fall right off. No one would ever find me, so that's what I was afraid of. So this is what I remember, that I was scared to death. But then later, somehow, things went on, they brought me here. My mother, as they say, gave me a new start in life, because I was very sick. I was covered with scabs. I couldn't walk well at first, although I was three years old. Later, she managed to cure me. . . . And so, and I started to run. Well, and when I began to grow, I would walk everywhere, people would tell me that I wasn't her real daughter. We lived on a state collective farm. "You're not her real daughter." So I go to her, I ask, "What do they mean, that I'm not your real daughter?" "Well, don't listen to them. Let them talk. So-and-so was brought here, another one was brought here. They brought you here from Solonikha." "And those, my friends who were brought here, so where were they brought from?" Well, she would tell me later, this and that. So that's how it was with her.

CF—Where did you grow up after age three?

VM—Krasnoborsk region, the Bereznauvsk rural soviet, there was this state farm near Solonikhi, I've forgotten everything . . . "The Spark," "The Spark." We also lived on the state farm, then it became a resin factory when they combined all the state farms.[1]

CF—And where did you live with your mama, in a cottage?

VM—Yes, we had a house, we always had a cow, there was always a cow, sometimes we kept a sheep, and pigs—once a year, no matter what, my mother raised a pig. Well, so. We had our own garden, ... it was a big garden.

CF—And where did your mother find you? And why did she take such a step?

VM—Well, during the war, when everyone was forced to do some kind of defense work, she didn't have any children of her own, she had to take care of her farming, so she decided to take me out of an orphanage. . . . This was in 1943. . . . They brought us to Solonikha from Arkhangelsk. . . . We were brought by steamboat, along a river, and so, we were really hungry. Basically, it was starvation. On the whole, all the children were sick. So, that's when she took me. When she took me, she asked, "Why is she all covered with scabs?" "They are supposed to be fed," someone told her, "a hundred grams of bread and a

---

1. She may be referring to the amalgamation of collective farms under Nikita Khrushchev.

glass of milk. And do they actually get it? They don't get even that." . . . .

CF—When did your mama first tell you that you were indeed adopted?

VM—She told me straight out later that I was adopted. After all, everyone in the village, everyone knows everyone else. As soon as I started to walk, that's when I found out that she was not my real mother, everyone was already saying that.

CF—Can you explain it to me again? Earlier you told me that she took on a child to save herself. Well, to save herself from what?

VM—. . . . During the war, after all, they were at war until 1945. They drove many people out of the village [to labor or some kind of work for the war effort], and she would have been one of them if she hadn't had any children. But they never forced people to leave who had children. . . . Or else to timber felling. That's right. To the one or the other. And she had a farm, she needed to leave it with someone. But there was nobody. Her husband was at the front, she didn't have any of her own children. That's all.

CF—And how was your relationship with your mother?

VM—Well, it was something a bit peculiar. A little bit of everything. Sometimes she would lose her temper and beat me, and anything could happen. I had to live through everything, in short.

CF—Were there moments when it seemed to you that she regretted her decision or not?

VM—Yes, there were, she did all sorts of things to me. And I grew up a bit, I began to grow, and we started to have shortages. "Why on earth did I take you in?" she would say. "I shouldn't have. I don't need you now." And what am I to do? I would leave, I burst into tears, and come back. Right away, where would I go? I had to start working early. She would go out to work early in the morning, my job was to saw firewood, to split it, to haul water, since you have to do everything on a farm. In short, as soon as I started to walk, I started to do everything.

CF—And you of course went to school? Was the school right on the collective farm?

VM—Yes, at first it was on the farm, until fourth grade, the school was practically next door. Well, in short, the school was across the field. But then, from the fourth grade to the fifth grade, I walked seven kilometers to get to school.

CF—How many children were there in your school, in your class usually?

VM—Well, there were probably twelve or thirteen children, no more. . . . But when we went to fifth grade, there were already as many as thirty, twenty or twenty-five, well, let's say twenty-seven.

CF—And were there any other adopted children in the group?

VM—No, not at that time. Not with me. I was the only one like that.

CF—And did you ever feel different?

VM—No, no one ever offended me. I didn't experience that. People, I lived on friendly terms with everyone. No one offended me. On the contrary, everyone felt sorry for me.

CF—Well, in the end, after seventh grade, you left the village already?

VM—Yes, I left, I left to go to Pechora. To be a nanny.

CF—Please explain how you went there.

VM—How I got there? My aunt took me to Kotlas. They put me on a train there, and so I was so frightened—in short, I hadn't seen trains or cars, or anything. We didn't have anything yet in the village, no tractors, nothing, well, so, no lights. That is, no electricity, all kerosene lamps. So, I lay twenty-four hours on the upper berth, without getting down. . . . This was in 1954, well, so, I arrived, I got off the train. They told me, "This is Pechora, get off."

CF—And whose nanny were you?

VM—A girl, too, Rita. . . . She was a little girl . . . . my mother's sister's daughter. . . .

CF—As I understand it, you didn't have a passport?

VM—We didn't. People tried to get one any way they could think of. To get someone in the state farm to give a certificate.

Some people gave bribes, others came up with other ways, any way they could they got out. But, as for me, I left, at that time, they didn't make you stay after you finished school. I was still a minor, fourteen years old, at that time no one tried to make me stay. . . .

CF—Did you know your real name?

VM—Yes, I knew that I was Skiba, Vera Yulyanovna. . . . But when she adopted me, I received all her names, I became Teplukhina, Vera Mikhailovna, well, they didn't change my first name. She gave me her husband's name as my patronymic. . . .

CF—Please describe what kind of place Pechora was at that time.

VM—Well, there wasn't anything there. No industry of any kind. Only a market, and the railroad, and that was it.

CF—And that was it. And did you live in an apartment or in a house?

VM—We lived, at first after I arrived, we lived in a dugout, a zemlianka. . . .

CF—Please describe it.

VM—Basically, you dig out a ditch in the ground. Generally, a pit as they say, a kind of big trench. Well, and it's covered.

CF—With what?

VM—Boards, whatever you could find. And that's all, and inside it was plastered, and it was finished.

CF—And what did you sleep on?

VM— On beds. There were beds. The only thing was that you went down into a cellar, in short. That's how we lived.

CF—Were there any lights?

VM—Yes. They had lights there already. There was electricity. They worked at the electrical station. . . . Both of them.

CF—But of course there was no plumbing of any kind.

VM—No, we had to carry water. We still carried it from a stream. . . . We heated with coal, there was a small stove, a burner, and that's all.

CF—Did it seem strange to you to live in the ground?

VM—No, no. I didn't feel anything in particular. After my collective farm, I thought, well, it's not so bad here. [*Chuckles at the memory*]

IA [Dubrovina]—There was electricity, at least.

VM—Yes, electricity was the most important thing. . . . And later we moved into a house. My uncle built a house out of railroad ties.

IA—Out of railroad ties?

VM—From railroad ties.

IA—Railroad ties—these are what they put on the railroad, they were made of wood.

VM—Yes, but my uncle plastered it, he did everything. The house was not bad, well it was fine, it was all right.

IA—This is the first time I've heard of a house built from railroad ties.

VM—From railroad ties, he built it himself out of railroad ties. . . . There were railroad ties around, the railroad, the station was right there in Pechora. . . . Worn out railroad ties, the railroad ties they had discarded. . . . Almost all of the houses were built out of these railroad ties.

I worked as a nanny for a year and a half. I received a passport. As soon as I succeeded in getting it, I immediately looked for a real job. Once I had a passport, why should I work as a nanny? . . . I went to the post office. They promised me that someone would be leaving in two weeks, she was quitting, so, "You should come back in two weeks." . . . Then, after I had been on the job for four days, they bring me a telegram one night from my mother. "Leave immediately." Well, I didn't know what to think, they delivered the telegram at night. "Immediately!" Who knows, maybe she had fallen ill, maybe something had happened. Just before that, she had written a letter, everything was fine. I received it from her. "Leave immediately." Well, what was I to do? In the morning I got up with Marusya, the wife. She also didn't know anything. "Look, Vera. Maybe she's fallen ill. Something could have happened. Who knows, maybe she's in a bad way." So, that was that. We decided that I had to go. . . . After all, it was my mother who sent it. "Leave immediately. Mama." So, I arrived here in Kotlas just before New Year's. This was already 1957. Well, I arrived here, but it was sixty kilometers more to get to our place, and entirely through forest, well, you had to go by foot. Well, she came for me herself on a horse, she took a horse from the state farm and came. . . . She arrived, and I said, "Why did you come? What has happened? Why did you call for me to come like that?" She says, "But you'll forget me!" I immediately started sobbing. . . . "Well, so I was afraid that you would forget me." I started to cry, I said, "What are you saying? I can forget you here just as easily." Well, what was I to do? I had a cry, but there was nothing to be done but to go home. So, I arrived in the winter. I worked there with her on the state farm through the winter.

Vera Mikhailovna then described other manual labor jobs she took on outside the state farm, including clearing brush along riverbanks and working in the forest industry until she injured her shoulder and couldn't lift her arm. She decided to leave the village again.

VM—Well, I told my mother, that I was leaving the state farm, yes. . . . She thought I was joking. Well, later she told her brother, "No matter how much you feed a wolf, it will still have its eye on the forest." . . . Well in the end, I left.

Vera Mikhailovna found a job near Kotlas in a sawmill, where she worked for almost thirty years. During the Gorbachev era, the mill closed, but she found another job, which lasted until she retired eight years later.

CF—How did you find out more about your family background?

VM—All of this was in 2002 when I found out. Kreider comes to me and says—

CF—Who's Kreider?

IA—He's our director of the pension division of the welfare department of the local government.

VM—He comes to me and says, "Your sister is looking for you. Do you have a sister who lives abroad?" I told him frankly, "I don't know." I had lived an entire life, but I didn't know of anyone. But that I was from an orphanage. So he says, "How should I answer your sister?" "How should you answer? Tell her my address, and that's all." "You're not opposed?" "How could I be opposed?" "Of course not." I was really happy that I had someone, even if I found them only in my old age. Well, this department informed her, and a letter arrived soon from my sister. She sent photographs of everyone with it, all our relatives, cousins—photocopies, of course.

CF—How did she find you?

VM—She said, "I've been searching for you for fifty years."

CF—She was older than you?

VM—She was older than me. And it was our aunt who gave us to the orphanage, a distant relative of my father's. She had kept an eye on us all the time there in Shenkursk. . . . It was this aunt, but me, well, they had already given us over to the orphanage. My sister was a bit older, so she went to the one for kindergarten-age children.

They separated us from each other, and moreover, since I was sick, they sent me away, I wound up separated in Arkhangelsk someplace.

CF—Did you find out where you were born?

VM—In Belorussia, in the Briansk area. . . .

CF—And what did you find out about your parents?

VM—I found out that three of my aunts were still alive, my mother' sisters. None of my father's brothers were still alive. My father had only brothers. All the brothers had already died, only their children were alive. Well, so I went by train in 2003 to Belorussia. My husband said right away, "Get going. Get going. Now that you've found someone, you should go. Every year is precious. Who knows, today they're alive, but tomorrow?" Well, I went with my two daughters that summer to Belorussia. They gave us a warm welcome, of course. We went as far as Minsk, one of my cousins met us there, the daughter of my mother's aunt. Well, and they also took us out to the village, the same kind of backwoods as I had known here. . . . We were there for a week.

CF—And what did they tell you?

VM—So they told me my father worked as a woodsman. They gathered all the woodsmen in a group and told them, "We're giving you a new job." So they all got together, and they sent all of those who came, well the majority, to Arkhangelsk, all of them landed in the Shenkursk region, but one of them remained, but I can't tell you his name. One of them, they said, ran up later and said, "I'm sorry, I'm late." He was told, "It's good you were late." . . . They forced all of them to come here, well almost all of them died, few returned.

CF—And your mother?

VM—My mother went with him. . . . My aunt, the one I just visited in Poland, she says that she was barefoot, and it was wintertime. Someone later brought her felt boots.

IA—And this one was in diapers.

VM—So, they left and wrapped me in diapers. They said they kept a sheep, they wrapped me in a sheepskin, threw me in the sled, and took me that way. There were three of us sisters: Valya, Irena, and I. My oldest sister died there in 1940. Irena and I remained. . . . In 1942, my mother gave birth. . . . No one knows whether it was a boy or a girl. My mother gave birth, but she didn't survive. My father was working somewhere cutting timber also. And so, he didn't come to her right away. It seems she was distraught, my aunt said, so, and she began hemorrhaging. And he, they say, was caught under a falling tree. . . . And he was crushed. His spine was broken. He couldn't . . . And she died because of the hemorrhage. And two days later, he died. He probably found out that she had also died and got upset. And, so, they buried all three of them in one grave.

IA—Her, the baby, and your father.

VM—My aunt says, "I didn't even go to the burial. My legs hurt terribly." She worked there, too. She was also exiled there. Her legs gave way. She says she hired some man, and he buried them, he took them away and that was it. . . . No one knows where the grave is, no one knows anything. Maybe it's just unmarked. . . .

IA—So two little girls remained, Irena and Vera here.

CF—Were you taken together after your parents died?

VM—Yes, right away, my aunt took us right away after my parents died and gave us to the orphanage.

IA—And at the orphanage, they sent you to different orphanages because of your different ages.

VM—Yes, because of our age difference. Well, my aunt had her own two daughters. And, since Irena was older, well she was closer to her, and they were together more. Then she was sent to Stavropol' out of this Shenkursk. She studied there, my sister, in a Russian school, she knows a little. She speaks Russian. And from Stavropol' . . . . after the war . . . . even later, she was still studying during those years in Stavropol.' Later, probably in the 1950s, but she—they were sent to Poland.

IA—The Poles gathered their children from all across Russia. There was a particular special commission headed by Wanda Wasilewska. And they gathered the children and sent them to Poland.

VM—But who looked for me? No one looked for me. . . .

CF—Tell me, when you met your relatives, what feelings did you experience?

VM—Well, of course, anyway, I was with my own people. At first I met that one in Belorussia, my sister also came there. So. Well, we came a day earlier, she came a bit later. There I met all three aunts, my mother's sisters. My mother was born in 1918. . . . After my mother, there was Aunt Maria, who was born in 1920. Aunt Nadya, she was born in 1922. And Aunt Zhenya in 1924. . . . Well, I also saw my cousin. . . . Aunt Nadya has a son. Well, and there were these cousins Irina and Nina, too. Well, of course, there's that impression, that I hadn't seen them my entire life and here they all were. . . . Irena calls now, we call each other.

CF—And did you see any common features?

VM—Yes, I look a lot like Aunt Zhenya. When we arrived, all the neighbors were saying, "Well, you're stuck with each other now, you're family, a perfect copy," they said. And Aunt Zhenya says, "And I would play with you and Valya, we would crawl with Valya under the rocker, under the cradle and rock," she says. "And Aunt Olya would yell at us, tell us we were not babysitting well, since the baby was crying." And she said that we're playing with dolls, we would make dolls, wrap the sticks in fabric, and these were all the toys we had. . . . Well, and they were all calm people. They were all decent. Everyone was decent.

CF—And how did your daughters receive this discovery?

VM—Well, how would they be? They were also happy to have some relatives. . . . My mother's side of the family is not tall, but everyone on my father's side of the family is tall. So, it comes from my father.

CF—Well, please tell me about when your adoptive mother died and after that.

VM—My adoptive mother lived with me her entire life. . . . Yes, she lived her entire life with me. . . . On friendly terms, well, always. Well, she lived to be ninety-four years old. . . . She died in 1999. And so, as long as my mother was alive, Irena was told, "We know nothing," and only after she died did they tell Irena my address, in short.

CF—So that means they had known for a long time?

VM—She knew that I was somewhere in this region. . . .

IA—The issue is that, in Russia, adoptions are legally confidential. . . . They lifted the confidentiality only when her mother died.

VM—My sister would say, "I don't know what else to do, I've made every possible inquiry." And she has this many [*Vera raised her hand at this point several inches above the tabletop*], she has a whole pile of letters.

IA—She looked for you for fifty years.

VM—For fifty years she made inquiries, so that's why she has a pile of these documents. She says, "I would lie down, I would think, well, let me write again. I'll tell them I want to thank this woman who adopted her, and then they'll tell me and let me come." But she was gone. . . . And so that's when they gave Irena the information. She says, "I was so overjoyed that I had found you." . . .

CHAPTER SEVEN

"The feeling of loneliness has stalked me always"

TAMARA NIKOLAEVNA MOROZOVA

Staritsa

June 27, 2005

Transcribed by Elena Vetrova

Introduction

According to family lore, German bombers were flying overhead when Tamara Nikolaevna Morozova was born in November 1941 in a village outside Tver. Her mother, a worker of peasant origin, had fled Leningrad on the eve of the war while pregnant with Tamara. She had received a warning from her husband and his brother that war was imminent. She took her older daughter with her to her mother-in-law's home in the village. Her husband disappeared almost immediately after the German invasion; only in 1943 did mother and daughters receive word that he was in the Gulag, sentenced to ten years in Kolyma. Wartime challenges intensified for Tamara's mother when official word reached the village that she was living there and should be arrested as a wife of a traitor to the motherland, her two children placed in Soviet state institutions. The strategies she adopted to escape this fate illustrate how wartime chaos helped some victims of political repression evade imprisonment and further family separation.

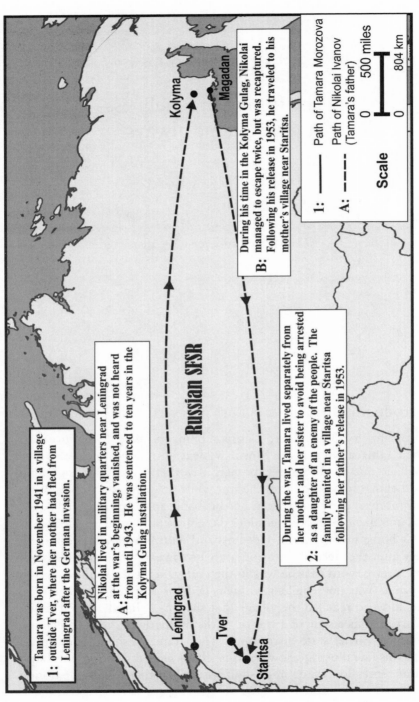

The following text labels appear within the map:

Kolyma

Magadan

During his time in the Kolyma Gulag, Nikolai
B: **managed to escape twice, but was recaptured.**
Following his release in 1953, he traveled to his
mother's village near Staritsa.

Russian SFSR

Tamara was born in November 1941 in a village
1: outside Tver, where her mother had fled from
Leningrad after the German invasion.

Nikolai lived in military quarters near Leningrad
A: at the war's beginning, vanished, and was not heard
from until 1943. He was sentenced to ten years in the
Kolyma Gulag installation.

During the war, Tamara lived separately from
her mother and her sister to avoid being arrested
2: as a daughter of an enemy of the people. The
family reunited in a village near Staritsa
following her father's release in 1953.

Leningrad

Tver

Staritsa

Scale

1: ——————— Path of Tamara Morozova
A: - - - - - - - Path of Nickolai Ivanov
(Tamara's father)

0   500 miles

0   804 km

The journeys of Tamara Nikolaevna Morozova and her father, Nickolai Ivanov, 1941–1953 (Map by Eric Pugliano)

Remarkably, the family members survived and were reunited after Stalin's death. They moved to the nearby medieval town of Staritsa.

Tamara Nikolaevna's interview provides the most explicit linkage between hunger and longing for missing parents among the many such vignettes and references in survivors' interviews; the connection is direct, painful, and emotionally overwhelming. Tamara Nikolaevna speculates that the generosity of peasants in her grandmother's village played as much a role in her family's survival as did the confusion caused by the war. Her interview reveals how the self-discipline this family developed during their experiences with repression guided their behaviors for the rest of their lives. Tamara Nikolaevna described the revival of Russian Orthodoxy in the post-Soviet era and her own personal faith as the wellsprings for her emotional healing.

I interviewed Tamara Nikolaevna in her freestanding, tidy house along a street that was on the very edge of Staritsa. Her front yard and porch planters were bursting with flowers. Her home embodied meticulous homemaking and creative gardening. Through the kitchen window, terraced, raised beds for vegetables and flowers ran from the back porch to the back fence, filling the entire backyard. Inside the living room, the only wall decorations were icons or pictures of Orthodox churches. Tamara Nikolaevna wore an immaculate, well-pressed lavender blouse and a purple skirt, with every hair of her bob haircut in its proper place.

Before we conducted the interview, Tamara Nikolaevna served a lunch of fresh salads and soups, complemented with beer, kvas, vodka, and a sweet red wine I had never encountered before—Kagor. Our companionable lunch, and perhaps the vodka and wine, prepared the way for Tamara Nikolaevna to enter far more rapidly into the emotional memories of her hungry childhood than I would have expected on the basis of the propriety of her demeanor and home. The moments when emotion overwhelmed her were all the more powerful given the emphasis she placed on self-control as the most highly valued virtue she imbibed from her parents.

CF—Tamara Nikolaevna, please describe how you became a so-called child of the Gulag, or a child of the repressions.

TN—They arrested my father in 1941. At first he left for the front at the beginning of the Great Patriotic War, and then he disappeared, vanished. There was no news of any kind from him. He wasn't declared missing. At that time we thought many soldiers had been taken prisoner. Mama waited for him. People thought that this is what had happened to him. And nothing was heard from him for two years. Until 1943. But in 1943, by chance . . . via a person who had been with him—it was impossible via the mail[1]—Mama received a letter from him, saying that he was in Magadan, in Kolyma. He wrote that, "They've given me ten years under Article 58." This was the article for political crimes. And so then we understood that he wouldn't be back for a long time. We didn't know if he would return or not. And at that time my parents, they lived at first in Vyborg before the war, until the war with Finland, but when the war with Finland began, they resettled all the Russians in Leningrad.[2] . . . And just before the very start of the war, my, my uncle, Papa's younger brother, he was in the military, he was a military man and he served in the army. And so sometime before the beginning of the Great Patriotic War, he also, using the same kind of happenstance traveler, sent Papa a note that said, "Nikolai, take the family out of Leningrad. We are expecting the war to begin. Everyone is preparing, and we are waiting, there will be war." Even though in all the sources of mass media they said that Hitler attacked suddenly. But everyone knew about this. So, when Mama and Papa received this note, he tried to get Mama away in 1941. The war hadn't begun yet, so sometime it was just before the beginning of the war. He sent her to his mama's, to my grandmother in the village.

CF—Where?

TN—Here in Tver region . . . . here, a hundred thirty kilometers from Tver. It was considered sinful, I think. They may have put Papa in prison for this. Because maybe he told someone about this, or he warned someone so they would do the same thing and get their family out of Leningrad. And so, Mama was pregnant with me. I was born in 1941 when we were already in evacuation, which is why I was born in the village.[3] . . . But my sister, Galya, she was, she was four years old only, we are separated by four years. And so she arrived in the village just before

1. All correspondence with inmates of the Gulag was prohibited during the war.
2. The Soviet war with Finland followed the signing of the Molotov-Ribbentrop Pact in August 1939.
3. Technically, they had not been evacuated, which was the exclusive domain of the government.

the beginning of the war. . . . I don't remember exactly, whether she left in May or in June. . . . When I was born in November, the Germans were already at Moscow. They told me that I was born when we were already in evacuation, during bombing raids. The Germans had already reached Moscow in November, and that's when I was born. And it was just at that time that Papa was gone, everyone thought that he was missing in action. Because the Germans were everywhere. And so we waited for him until 1943. But in 1943, it already became clear. At first Mama hid the fact that she—Well, people didn't know that she, well, she presented herself as simply being an evacuee, and we even received rations for the children. She received them. In fact, we weren't even especially hungry, because they gave rations for children in evacuation. And later, when they handed down his official conviction and gave him a sentence notice in 1943, they immediately sent an inquiry to the village council, that you must have, in your locality, the wife of the enemy of the people Ivanov, Nikolai Ivanovich, living there with children. And we were saved only by the fact that Mama's friend, as they say, a childhood friend, worked as the secretary of the village council at that time or as the chair of the village soviet. . . . She came to us in tears, "Katya, they are looking for you. An inquiry about you has arrived." And Mama, right away, when they arrived, when Papa went missing, and before this, when they lived in Leningrad, they, so she told us, "We even slept fully dressed." They arrested people every day in their building. She said, "There was never a night when they didn't take someone away."

CF—In Leningrad?

TN—Yes, in Leningrad, it was called Leningrad back then. She said, "We went to bed fully dressed," she said, "we lived in a communal apartment"—there weren't apartments back then—and she said, "You know, in the morning, in the evening we would go to sleep and if a car went past the building, we would listen." . . . Well this was still before the war, approximately still in 1940 and even earlier, in 1937. The very worst years were 1937, 1938, 1939. That's why Mama used to describe it, "We lived in a communal apartment, and so when a car went by, and if it stopped opposite our building," she would say, "we all would freeze, and if the door into our communal apartment slammed, we all waited—now who? Who have they come for?" And in the morning, when the sound of footsteps became distant, there were either screams or deathly silence. And then in the morning, "Everyone," she would tell us, "would come out and," she would say, "we would look to see who was missing." Sometimes one person was missing, but sometimes an entire family was missing, just gone. And everyone was afraid to ask, who had lost whom, who had been taken, what had they taken of whose possessions. Because the next-door neighbor could inform on them, could report that he sympathized with this person, and then he would be next. And this is what she would say: "It was so terrible," she would say, "and we slept in our clothes." She would say, "We expected them every night, we waited. We slept in turns." And later, when Papa disappeared, Mama guessed that they had taken him from home (he worked in military quarters), and if they had taken someone from the building already, that meant that someone was next in line. If they arrested one person, then our turn would be next. And so when he disappeared, evidently Mama already guessed what would happen. And so when Anna Ivanovna, her friend, came to her like that and said, "Katya, they are looking for you." She, of course, before this she worked, when I was born she was working in the village on the collective farm, she was helping. The war had begun, they took away all the men, so she worked on the collective farm.

CF—Despite the fact that she was pregnant.

TN—Yes, She was a city woman and she was pregnant. And later, when I had been born already, and when they found Papa, we already understood what was up; she understood and left the village, leaving me and Galya behind alone.

CF—Were your parents members of the Communist Party? . . .

TN—No. Papa was a worker. Mama was from the village. Of peasant origins.

CF—Despite this, they were very afraid? . . . What was there to fear, that they were searching for her?

TN—Well, everyone knew that entire families, including the children, were vanishing. Entire families were vanishing, and no one knew where they had gone, no one received any information about them at all. Even if they tried to get an explanation, it was useless, everyone kept quiet, and no one said anything.

A person vanished, as if he had never been there at all. No one knew where he went, what happened to him, what became of the children. And so that's why Mama left and began to work ten kilometers from the village felling timber, so she could go into the forest, so that no one would notice her there among the workers. And at that time there were lots of workers, they were clearing the forest, there were a lot of evacuees in the western regions, people who had fled the Germans. It was possible to hide among them. And Anna Ivanovna helped her redo her passport, to find another one, she gave her the passport with her husband's name on it as if it had been lost, and she gave her one under her maiden name. She became not Ivanova, Ekaterina Ivanovna, but Mukhina, her maiden name.

CF—. . . How many people lived in that village?

TN—A lot. The village where I grew up until Papa returned was big. This was a very large and friendly village. There were, I don't know, around a hundred households, even more, a hundred to a hundred fifty houses.

CF—Did your mama leave you with her friend?

TN—No, she left us with our grandmother.

CF—. . . And no one noticed that there were extra children?

TN—You know . . . . in the first place, the neighbors were very kind and friendly. We had a very united village. That was the first thing. And, second, the Germans didn't get that far. . . . And there were a lot of evacuees. For people who were strangers, we were also strangers. No one would ask, are these your own or strangers' children? And anyone who came from outside took me for the daughter of my mother's younger sister. And as for my big sister, they took her for, well, my mother's cousin lived not far away, and he had a son who was just like Galya. The same age. I was fair, but Galya was dark, and this Vitya was dark. They passed for twins. . . . Galya lived with that family, and I lived with Grandmother and Aunt Klava, my mother's sister. . . . Well, I remember that when I was very small, I missed Mama so much.

CF—What were your first memories?

TN—[*Begins to weep*] Loneliness. It is hard to talk about it. [*Weeping, followed by some minutes of silence*]

CF—May I ask, was your mama ever able to come to see you, in secret? Could she?

TN—Yes, she would come very, very rarely. [*Still weeping*] Very rarely. She would come just to bring us something to eat. We were very hungry. We were hungry. She came in secret just to give us something to eat. And so she would come, just for that. I'm telling you, I remember to this day that there was absolutely nothing to eat. . . . And our one cow had to feed six children. How many in all? And there were three grown-ups. So just imagine how much milk there was for the children. . . . And I kept begging, "Mama, take me with you." She would say that she couldn't explain to me as a child why she couldn't take me with her. [*Weeping*] . . . . When I asked her, "Take me with you" [*Begins to weep again*], she would say that she couldn't explain to me why she couldn't, why I was alone. It always seemed to me that she didn't take me with her because she would have to feed me. [*At this point in the interview, Tamara Nikolaevna breaks down into sobbing, followed by another very long silence*] . . . . But my sister was a bit older, smarter, maybe they explained to her why it was impossible. She was older, maybe she could bear it more easily. . . . Well, we were always separated. We pretended that we weren't from the same family and somehow they kept us separate. And then later, I don't know, for some reason or other, maybe there was some new danger looming, they tried to send me to live at the logging camp where Mama worked, they sent me to the boss at the site. They were very good people, I was such a skinny little thing. [*Weeping again, followed by silence*]

How many years have passed, and it is so difficult to talk about. [*Weeping again*] . . . . When they gave me away, I lived there exactly one week. I was probably five or six, and I ran away from them. Imagine, as a five-, six-year-old child I walked through the forest seven or eight kilometers away from them. The road took every form in the forest. During the war, there were so many animals in the forest, there were so many deserters, all sorts. And I walked through the forest by myself. I don't know who led me or protected me. . . . I came home and told Mama, "I won't eat with you, I'll just live with you."

CF—You found her?

TN—I went to Grandmother's. Then when Grandmother—they raised the alarm because a child had disappeared—Mama had run home. She said, "What do you mean, my dear daughter, you'll have more to eat there, no one will touch you there, live there." "No," I said, "I won't eat, only don't give me away to them, I will live here." And so we kept living from hand to mouth until, probably, I had already started school. The war was probably already over here, in 1945, 1946. At that time, Mama started to come more often, because the camps were probably already overflowing, the second wave of arrests started. They were arresting those who had been prisoners of war and they were sending everyone again to Kolyma. It was the second wave of arrests. Papa began sometimes to write us that, "Probably, they'll release us." And this "probably" lasted until 1953.

CF—And you knew, when did you find out that—

TN——that Papa was in the camps?

CF—Yes.

TN—For a long time they didn't tell me. They didn't tell me anything, where he was, evidently to prevent the spread of needless rumors, so that people wouldn't know that, living here, there was, well, a family of an enemy of the people. They didn't tell me for a long, long time.

CF—They believed even after the war that there was still a danger that they would take all of you?

TN—Of course. It didn't make any difference. Once he was sentenced, they could take everyone at any time. . . . So Mama didn't return to the village, she lived there, separately from us, but she began to come more often. [*Long pause*] And then Papa arrived in 1953. I, of course, called all men "Papa." They say that I asked everyone, "Is this my Papa?" "No." Again, "Is this my Papa? But where is he?" "Soon he'll come." I would say, "But when will he come?" And even when he came back, people said, "Here's Papa." And it meant nothing to me, I hadn't ever seen him, I had never known him. I just remember the one thing, that we were all starving like baby wolves. Because if someone came back from the front, they would pay him. If he came back from the front, he would work, help the family. And if he didn't come back they paid the family a pension for the loss of a breadwinner. But as for us, no one paid us anything. Mama did what she could on her own, and relatives did what they could to help us.

CF—Were you in school then?

TN—Yes, I probably started school at age eight.

CF—Were there times when it was uncomfortable for you to say that you didn't have a father? . . .

TN—Everyone knew, yes, everyone already knew at that time that he wasn't there. And everyone knew where he was. I have to give credit where it is due, we had a very good first-grade teacher. I remember her to this day, I can show you a photograph of her. I have a photograph of this first class of "children of the war." Look how we are all in rags, how we were all so skinny [*long pause*]. And the teacher was Aleksandra Pavlovna. [*Begins to weep*] I remember her name to this day. She was very kind, for some reason she was. Perhaps she had a tragedy of some kind of her own. She treated me, us, very well. Well, as for the kids, well they were so, how to put it, maybe the people there were completely different. Even when I would go there as an adult, I would see the difference between the people in the village and the people in Staritsa. They were so well meaning and kind. Maybe they always felt sympathy for Mama, or somehow they respected us in the village, our families, because my grandfather, Mama's father, he was a very good farmer. . . . Well, in the village, as I was saying, we were respected, for some reason. Maybe this partially helped save us, as well. Well, they sent inquiries about Mama several times. So the story is that Anna Ivanovna would come, her friend, well, since she worked in the village council, she came more than once and said, "Katya, they are searching for you." Mama would tell her, "Anna Ivanovna, well, do what you must." But her husband was missing, and she had a son. Well, he, evidently, had perished, maybe he had ended up as a prisoner of war. Mama would tell me, "We would sit, we would cry, we would hug each other, we would cry." That's what she told me. "Well, what can we do?" And the other responded, "Well, if it comes to the camps, we'll be there together." And she wrote that "no such person is residing here." And she sent it back. And just in case, Mama kept on the safe side by living separately, so as not to draw any attention to us. So that's how we were saved.

CF—And what was Anna Ivanovna's fate?

TN—She lived in the village to the end. I went to the village as an adult, she lived in the village to the end. She is dead by now. And Papa sent Mama a letter. He said, "If you want to preserve the family, then do not return to Leningrad under any circumstances." Our apartment had survived the bombings in Leningrad and was still there. It had been sealed; all our belongings were there. . . . And someone wrote her a letter, telling her the apartment had survived, that it was on the other side of the street from the bombardments, it was completely intact. She could return. But Papa wrote a letter, "If you want to preserve the family, don't go to Leningrad, because I'm forbidden to live in capital cities of the republics. I can't live in regional towns, only in a district town." They took away his right to vote for five years. He didn't have the right to vote. And he was in the camps without the right to correspond these ten years. And it turned out to be more than ten years for him. He was in the camps for almost twelve years. That's how we wound up here in Staritsa. Because his mother lived not far from here. My grandmother on my Papa's side. So he picked us up and brought us here. . . .

CF—How did he find work after the war?

TN—All the buildings had been destroyed, builders were in demand, and he went to work in construction. So as not to attract any attention to himself, or anything. He worked, he was a first-rate builder, he could do literally everything. He did every kind of job. . . .

CF—May I ask what recollections you have of your grandmother and aunt, from when you were missing your mama so much.

TN—You know, everyone, of course, loved me, I was the youngest of all the children. They tried to give me extra food. I had very serious anemia. I would faint on the street. I remember this very well. [*Weeping*]

CF—You fainted?

TN—Yes, they cared for me for a very long time. But Grandmother cured me. She, I remember, I remember from that time, I remember that I could fall down on the street, I could, well, I was completely emaciated. And Papa's brother lived in Moscow. He served in the army, and when he was demobilized, he lived in Moscow. . . . And he would send us food, big chunks of sugar once, when there was nothing in Russia, and he tried to provide us with food. And so Grandmother asked him, "Bring us some Kagor [a sweet red wine associated with Orthodox services].

Send some Kagor, I need to save my granddaughter." He sent us a bottle of Kagor. . . . And Grandmother would give me a teaspoon of this Kagor to drink. Evidently, I ate and stopped fainting. Otherwise, they had not been able to do anything to treat me at all.

CF—Do you remember when Stalin died?

TN—I remember very well when Stalin died. Well, so I remember when my parents, at that time the government really did force everyone to weep. They assembled everyone in the village and said, "Our dear beloved leader has died, you must all cry." Can you imagine? To gather everyone in this way in the village council and to say that you must cry and make speeches about how we feel sorry about him, our dear, our beloved leader. And also, how will we live without him? That everyone must sob. And I will never forget this. By that age, I had a good memory, I remembered very well.

CF—You were thirteen years old.

TN—Yes, ... I was at this Grandmother's, the one in Staritsa, Papa's mama. And I remember how the elderly women got together in the club and came to Grandmother's place. They all used to come to her place. From that region, for some reason, all the neighbors who lived here for some reason always gathered at Grandmother's place. So they arrived and said, "Maryushka, praise be to God! Satan has croaked. Maybe now your Kol'ka[4] will come home." In school they said one thing. They said, you must weep, that we must all do so. And this was how the simple people reacted. So this is like litmus paper, revealing the whole attitude of people to our leader. You couldn't say it any more eloquently. . . .

CF—What can you say about your father when he returned? Did he remain silent or did he talk about what had happened? . . .

TN—For his whole life, he kept silent, he did not describe where or what. He said, "A time will come when you will find out for yourself." Because there was no one who would believe him. Who? How was he to describe it to anyone when people were calling him a Fascist behind his back? Whom could he tell?

4. A diminutive of Nikolai.

And evidently they had taught him to be careful what he said, because that's why he was in the camps. I suspect that he also saved someone else's family, the same way we were saved, who got out of Leningrad in time. Maybe it was for that.

CF—But you do not keep silent?

TN—I broke my silence a long time ago already.

CF—Did you usually keep silent in your childhood?

TN—Yes, I never said a word as a child.

CF—And Mama also?

TN—Yes, Mama also. Because it was impermissible to talk to anyone.

CF—And there were no other friends who also were—

TN——right nearby?

CF—Who also had relatives in the camps.

TN—No. No. Nearby there was no one. No one at all.

CF—So this is why you felt lonely?

TN—Yes, the feeling of loneliness has stalked me always. [*Weeps*]

CF—Up to now?

TN—No, now I no longer feel alone. Only because I started going to church.

CF—You said earlier that your father taught you never to be in debt to anyone . . . . always to be your own person. How did he teach you that? . . . .

TN—Well, he knew that there was no quarter from which to expect help. To complain or request something from someone was completely useless. He himself always counted on his own strength. He was a very strong person. And I am struck by the fact that, well, there are people who didn't experience this, this fate, these torments. Two times he attempted an escape from Kolyma. He was young, strong. He twice attempted to escape from Kolyma, not everyone can do that. Not just any person could do that. They held him, he used to describe, in water up to his waist, they would throw him into the punishment cell after each escape. He said, "I was in water up to my waist for days." Afterward his legs constantly hurt. But evidently what saved him was that he was a workaholic. In the first place, he was as strong as an oak. And a workaholic. He could work, so, probably, he also passed this on to me.

It's no accident that everything at this house has been planted in this way. I planted every one of these trees with my own hands. And at home he was always very strong in spirit, too. Here's someone who served such a long sentence in such conditions, and he never used foul language, *never!* He never drank vodka. Only in the last years of his life, evidently his nerves gave way. He never even smoked. He told us, "I would exchange bread for cheap tobacco. Some people smoked, and so they would give me their bread ration in exchange for the tobacco." . . . So that's the only reason that he stayed alive. He used to say that these smokers would have given away anything to get something to smoke. He didn't smoke. He gave his away. So this is how he would get bread. Well, and, evidently, they were grateful to him, those to whom he gave the tobacco. Evidently they supported him, a good, kind person. But here, there was no one to talk to. It seems to me that they were lonely. Mama was always very reserved, there was no one to share a word with. She could never speak frankly.

CF—But she also had to be very strong. . . .

TN—Well, you know, to live alone for ten years, after all, she was still very young. And she waited for him. Evidently they lived well together. He was a normal person, he never drank, he never insulted her. Well, he was a decent, normal person. And so she waited for him for ten years. And I, so, well, it was as if I was always taking lessons from her. Once I was an adult already, I would always remember her restraint, how self-controlled she was. She never said a superfluous word. She never hurt anyone. And so when I married, my husband even said, "I love my mother-in-law better than I love you, because you still need to learn from her how to live." Or I could say something harsh, and she would never have said such a thing. She knew how to get along with people, she knew how to keep quiet, she knew how to get out of some kind of unpleasant situation in time. And to have lived as she did, separated from her children, well, that's really hard, and to know that your children are starving some place. But I ceased to be lonely when I started to, when I began, as I said, I saw how Mama constantly prayed. Evidently for us, for Papa, for herself. And that, probably, stuck with me. And so I began to attend church. There was this difficult situation. I told you that they drove us out of our apartment, maybe that's why. For some reason they treated only me this way.

Maybe it was because I demonstratively did not enter the Party. That really made an impression on them. The first time they came, a second time they came, three times they tried to get me to apply for membership in the Party. Really, such prominent people recommended me. They would even try to scare me. "I would"—how did she put it back then, an instructor with the Party district committee, when she approached me the last time?—"I would not, in your position"—I'm repeating her words exactly—"I would not, in your position, ignore such recommendations, well the recommendations of such comrades." I said, "Well, thank these comrades for me, but I've not matured enough yet to be in your Party." . . .

CF—Why did you decide not to join the Party?

TN—Because I had already learned a lot of the truth. Papa, although very rarely, but in fact we tried somehow to drag the truth out of him. And also, the reason I tried to drag it out of him, because I, I was in the Komsomol, after all, but I was such an exemplary Komsomol member. I was a good student. I didn't believe at first that it was possible to put a person in prison for no reason. We had such an argument. I tried at first to argue with him and said that this could not be. "And why didn't you prove that you were innocent, that they had arrested you for nothing, why didn't you prove that?" He said, "You still don't understand, but a time will come, you will understand that there is no one to whom you can prove it. And no one will stand up for you, and no one will help you. It was such a terrible time," he said, "that I don't want it to happen again."

And when I saw who of the older ones, being an adult, already even when, even in the Komsomol, I already saw that by far not the most honorable people were joining the Party. I didn't want to stand side by side with them. You understand? It was as if a wall separated me, it was something I didn't want. It was precisely this, I thought, "How can I join the Party, when this kind of person would be near me, what do I need him for?" People completely opposite from me. And later I really saw that my parents were decent, hardworking, they had never done anything bad to anyone. They wished no evil on anyone, they never did anyone wrong. And suddenly this dishonest person would pour filth over them, spit on him behind his back and say "You're a Fascist," when he was never a Fascist, he never helped anyone like that, he didn't do anything. And it was not his fault that they had put him in the camps. . . . And this was why it bothered me that this guy was a Party member, that he ostensibly held some kind of position, but I knew that he was a filthy and insignificant little man. And I was to enter the Party next to this person? And, moreover, I saw that my parents were exemplary, and saw that these were two opposites. Well, and on which side should I be? Join this Party and also be worthless, or become a decent person, but a non-Party person? . . . .

At this point in the interview, Tamara Nikolaevna discussed persis-
tent problems she encountered trying to get housing, as well as her
experiences as a mother of a son fighting in the Soviet war in Afghani-
stan (1979–1989).

CF—We can consider this the last question. To what extent do you think that the repressions determined either your life or the life of the country? . . .

TN—You know, I have read a lot, I have tried to figure this out, why all of this happened. In the first place, why the revolution happened. Where did this cruelty come from, really? In fact not only did it appear during the period of repressions, indeed it appeared before that. It appeared, first of all, during the Civil War. And the famine along the Volga was artificial, isn't that so?[5] That was really an artificially created famine. There was grain in the country, there were potatoes in the country. But, it was—they disappeared. So, that's why the repressions were not a separate thing as repression. Repression—that was a continuation of the very same politics that began a long time ago in 1917. My con-clusion is that with the death of the last tsar, the entire policy in the country was directed precisely at destroying the Russian Orthodox population, the most decent and honorable element in the population. That's what I think. . . .

5. She is referring to the famine of 1921–1922.

CHAPTER EIGHT

"I had a completely non-Soviet worldview"

ALEKSANDR NIKOLAEVICH KOZYREV

Saint Petersburg

February 16, 2007

Transcribed by Natalia Kholopova

Introduction

Aleksandr Nikolaevich Kozyrev was born in Leningrad in 1932 to members of the Soviet intelligentsia who were not members of the Communist Party. His father, Nikolai Kozyrev, worked in theoretical astrophysics in the 1930s before his arrest. Neither parent was executed, although both were arrested. His father was arrested in 1936 in connection with the "Pulkovo Affair" at the Pulkovo Observatory outside Leningrad. His mother was arrested as a wife of an enemy of the people as a result of Operational Order 00486 of August 1937. After his father's arrest, young Aleksandr Nikolaevich was able to remain in Leningrad with his mother, aunts, and grandmother, but, anticipating the arrest of his mother, his other relatives took him with them when they were exiled for being related to enemies of the state. They eventually returned to Leningrad, only to be evacuated early in World War II. After the war, they returned to the city permanently.

Aleksandr Nikolaevich's father was freed early from camps so that he could return to Leningrad to resume his activities as a scientist. In the late 1950s, the senior Kozyrev theorized lunar volcanism, which

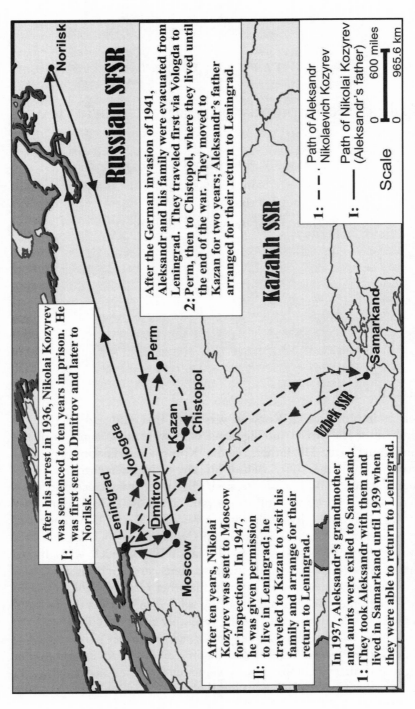

The journeys of Aleksandr Nikolaevich Kozyrev and his father, 1936–1947 (Map by Eric Pugliano)

Norilsk

Russian SFSR

After the German invasion of 1941, Aleksandr and his family were evacuated from Leningrad. They traveled first via Vologda to Perm, then to Chistopol, where they lived until the end of the war. They moved to Kazan for two years; Aleksandr's father arranged for their return to Leningrad.

Kazakh SSR

After his arrest in 1936, Nikolai Kozyrev was sentenced to ten years in prison. He was first sent to Dmitrov and later to Norilsk.

Perm

Vologda

Kazan

Chistopol

Dmitrov

Leningrad

Moscow

Uzbek SSR

Samarkand

After ten years, Nikolai Kozyrev was sent to Moscow for inspection. In 1947, he was given permission to live in Leningrad; he traveled to Kazan to visit his family and arrange for their return to Leningrad.

In 1937, Aleksandr's grandmother and aunts were exiled to Samarkand. They took Aleksandr with them and lived in Samarkand until 1939 when they were able to return to Leningrad.

1: - - - Path of Aleksandr Nikolaevich Kozyrev

I: ——— Path of Nikolai Kozyrev (Aleksandr's father)

Scale

0   600 miles
0   965.6 km

was later confirmed by U.S. astronauts during Apollo missions, earning him international recognition. Aleksandr Nikolaevich profited from his father's scientific reputation and was able to gain admission to Leningrad State University. After Stalin's death, Aleksandr Nikolaevich had a successful scientific career at the Leningrad Physico-Technological Institute. Following the collapse of the Soviet Union in 1991, he was politically active in electoral politics in Leningrad/Saint Petersburg and as a member of Memorial.

Aleksandr Nikolaevich's interview provides a snapshot of the fine living conditions members of the Leningrad intelligentsia enjoyed in the 1920s and 1930s. Their very large apartment on one of the most prestigious streets in Leningrad afforded a comfortable life for many relatives. Having two unmarried aunts and a grandmother in the apartment enabled Aleksandr Nikolaevich to remain at home with family, saving him from the Soviet children's homes that so many other children whose parents were taken away had to endure. Aleksandr Nikolaevich's interview conveys—however laconically—the ways individual Soviet citizens could retain a position of internal opposition to the Stalinist regime and its teachings.

I interviewed Aleksandr Nikolaevich in his apartment in Saint Petersburg. Before agreeing to be interviewed by me for my project, he invited me to supper at his apartment with his wife and their beloved dog. I understood this to be his way of establishing who I was and whether I and my project warranted his participation. Only after that first evening of intense conversation did he agree to be interviewed on another day at his home. During the interview itself, Aleksandr Nikolaevich sat erect at his desk, maintaining cool composure and speaking with conscientious precision. At only one moment during the interview did I detect any display of emotion, and even then I could not be sure whether emotion was what I was witnessing. Available accounts of his father suggest that such polite emotional restraint was a family trait.

CF—How old were you when your parents were repressed?

AN—That's an awkward question, because they weren't arrested at the same time. My birthday is October 30 . . . , and my father (he was arrested first) was arrested October 6, no, that's not true, November 6, 1936. . . . I was just four years old. . . . I have memories from early morning the next day. This is what I remember. Mama woke me up early. I was unhappy about

that, but Mama said, "Let's go into the hall, I will show you
something." And she led me there, into the hallway, lit a match,
because it was dark, and showed me how a seal was hanging
on Papa's door.[1] And she told me, "Do not touch this under
any circumstances, because it will be bad for us if you disturb
something."

CF—And do you remember any feelings?

AN—There was a feeling . . . Mama talked and explained in
such a way that I wanted to stay farther away from this door.
More than just not getting close, I wanted to keep myself as far
away from the door as possible. This is what I remember.

CF—And do you have any memories before that? Do you
have memories of your childhood when your father was still living with you?

AN—Well, of course, of course, a lot. . . . Before his arrest.
Okay. We had a very large family. We had a large apartment on
the Griboyedov Canal. . . . My grandfather died before I was
born. My grandfather was a hydrogeologist, he worked in Kazakhstan in the summer. But the main person in our family was
Grandmother. They had four children. The oldest was my Aunt
Yulya, the next was my other aunt—Lenochka, Elena Aleksandrovna. Then my father, well, and the youngest son, my uncle,
he was born in 1916, and my oldest aunt was born in 1903. My
father married. He worked in the Pulkovo Observatory. He completed university, graduate school, worked at the Pulkovo Observatory, married my mama, whose grandfather was the chief of
the station, the seismic station at the Pulkovo Observatory. . . .

And the apartment was large, it had six rooms. It was on the
top floor. You could see everything well from up there. Below,
under the windows, was Griboyedov Canal, there were trees below. There was one room right on the corner. That was Grandfather's room, next to it was the room where my uncle lived. There
was a large room—the dining room, where we ate. And the furniture was from the nineteenth century. Then came the room

1. In the Soviet Union (in offices and museums, for example, as well as after
searching a location during a police investigation), it was the practice of security
officials to place string across the doorjamb and door, sealed with wax, to indicate that no one but an official or person in charge of the space could enter it. This
is still true in the Russian Federation.

where Grandmother and my two aunts lived, and a hallway that went into the kitchen. Out of this hallway the door led to the room where Papa lived, and another entry, opposite, into the room where Mama and I lived. And then there was yet another room next to the kitchen, a small room where a woman who was a good, very old friend of Grandmother's lived. She helped with the housework. . . .

CF—Was it typical, was it the custom that a mama lived separately with a small child?

AN—We arranged it this way because my father was a scientist, and it is uncomfortable and not good to work on science in the same room where a child is running about. It is true that I sometimes came to his room and played there, with steamships and so on. I had toys in there, in his office. . . .

CF—What kinds of memories of your father do you have?

AN—He was young, very energetic, a member of the intelligentsia . . . A fast-mover, I would call him. And he did move quickly, was responsive, and was very busy. . . .

CF—So let's return to the morning when you found out that the door had been sealed. Did you understand that your father was gone?

AN—This I, of course, understood, but I didn't understand what had happened. I didn't understand why. The only thing was that Mama frightened me, so that I wouldn't touch anything.

CF—What was the ostensible reason for his arrest?

AN—The reason was simple—the so-called Pulkovo Affair. A rather large number of people were arrested in the Pulkovo Observatory, and he, as a member of the staff at the Pulkovo Observatory, was also arrested. . . . He was tried in May, they tried many of them together. This was on May 26. Back then, they didn't try people all at once, back then they tried them one at a time: they would try one person in thirty minutes, another person in thirty minutes, and so on. But my father himself was sentenced to ten years of prison and the camps. At first after this, he was in prison in the town of Dmitrov, this is not far from Moscow, and then—I'm afraid that I won't get the date right—in a year and a half, they sent him to Siberia, to Norilsk. . . .

CF—And he served his full sentence?

AN—Yes.

CF—So, this was until you were fourteen years old.

AN—Yes.

CF—How did your father's absence affect your life, and how did his fate as an enemy of the people affect your life at this time?

AN—This is very difficult to say. But the main thing is—they arrested my mother soon after.

CF—After how much time?

AN—Yezhov[2] was in office then. And on August 15, 1937, a decree was issued over his signature about the arrest of wives of enemies of the people.[3] And they arrested her three weeks after that, after this decree was issued.

CF—Did she know about that decree?

AN—You know, I have the impression now—I've just now remembered this—that she and all the members of our family (Grandmother, my aunts and uncle)—signed a statement that they would not leave the city at that time. I think they signed this statement about not leaving, unfortunately I don't have the exact date. And rather quickly, Grandmother and my aunts received an order to leave Leningrad to go into exile. . . . Grandmother and my aunts, yes, as mother and sisters of an enemy of the people. And they took me with them. Because Mama also had signed the promise not to leave, and they were very worried about, if she were arrested, what would happen to me?

CF—Where did they exile you?

AN—To Central Asia, to the city of Samarkand. . . .

CF—Do you have any recollection of your parting with your mama?

AN—No, I remember that she told me that, unexpectedly for me, Grandmother and my aunts were leaving and taking me with them. And that was all. . . . She was very young, and she was somehow very interested in life, she worked in some kind

2. Nikolai Yezhov, then head of the NKVD.
3. Operational Order 00486; see the introduction and Appendix III.

of community work. She was an instructor in PVKhO, Air and Chemical Defense. . . . She had finished only high school, that was it. She liked to work with people, and for that reason she mastered all of this quickly, and was happy to work in this field.

CF—Okay. So you landed in autumn 1937 in Samarkand. Where did they assign you? I have in mind a place to live and work for the adults.

AN—You know, at first, when we arrived, we were told, "You'll be going outside the city." So this is when Grandmother and my aunts began to resist, simply because they had heart disease, and there was no doctor outside the city in the district.

CF—Did they expect mercy from this government?

AN—They wrote to various offices. They placed a request with the local NKVD to write to Leningrad that they had been sent to Samarkand, that there was a judicial basis for this, but that there they were being told that they had to go to the district. And they wrote—they wrote to Leningrad. The locals agreed to wait for an answer from Leningrad, and finally, the answer arrived, saying that they didn't have to go to the district.

CF—Interesting. This means that you stayed right in the city.

AN—Yes, right in the city. Before this answer arrived, Grandmother and my aunts rented a little house not far from the train station, because, well, so they wouldn't have to live in a hotel! And we began to live there.

CF—Do you think they were very strong women, strong-willed? How would you describe them?

AN—The fact of the matter is that they raised me. And this was not at all easy. Later the war came, and then, evacuation—no, not evacuation, but deportation. All of this was not at all simple, because managing a boy—this is extremely difficult. . . . And the fact that they did this and managed this, is, of course, remarkable.

CF—And when did they find out about your mama's fate?

AN—My uncle brought the news. He was also exiled, and also to Samarkand. He arrived after approximately a month and told us that she had been arrested. They arrested her about a week after we left. . . .

CF—What did the grown-ups do in Samarkand, and how many years did they live there?

AN—Well, my uncle tried to enter the university to continue his studies, but he was not allowed to do so. Well, at least, he didn't study his first year. Later, I think, in a year, they allowed him. My aunts worked in the university. One of them worked in the library, but the other one—also in the university, only I don't remember where. And Grandmother was at home, she kept house. But my aunts helped her a lot. . . .

CF—And how many years did you live there?

AN—Two.

CF—And what did you do there as a boy?

AN—Well, it was very interesting for me. Because, in fact, I had lived in a city, sometimes I had gone to Pulkovo, but that was it. It was interesting for me. But there, the house was on the bank of a little stream, there were various children around. We played there, all kinds of battles and so forth. Well, and then, there were various living things, that was also interesting. There were a lot of frogs. In the evening when the sun set, the frogs began to sing, and everything was just full of their song. And there were dogs. We had dogs. We had two dogs, so that everything was there. I even built them a little house. . . .

CF—And I also wanted to ask you what atmosphere at home you remember. Everyone was working, you were busy. What was the atmosphere like at home? . . . And how did they discuss your parents' fate, or did they simply not talk about this?

AN—Practically, no, but they received letters. . . . Grandmother took charge of me. She began to teach me everything—to read and write . . . so that we studied practically every day.

CF—And what happened to your apartment in Leningrad?

AN—We lost the apartment. When we left, Grandmother sold the furniture very quickly, well, and that was it.

CF—Your mama expected that she would be arrested, therefore they simply sold everything?

AN—It didn't make any sense to leave Mama so much furniture, in any event, even if there were no arrest. Well, so Grandmother sold it. . . .

CF—When and why did you leave Samarkand?

AN—The whole issue was that my aunts and grandmother always wanted to leave, they thought about it, talked about it, what we should do, and so on. They wrote letters to different offices about how hard and bad it was to live there and so on. And, as a matter of fact, they wrote even directly to Stalin. And as a result, they permitted Grandmother and an aunt—both of them—to return to Leningrad on the basis of health issues. But the others said, "We were all exiled at the same time, they've been permitted to return, but we haven't?" And they managed to get permission to leave, too.

CF—Interesting. That means that sometimes these requests met with success.

AN—Absolutely. And not only for us. I think that for propaganda purposes, the government sometimes reacted positively to legitimate requests.

CF—What year was this?

AN—1939. . . .

CF—And how did you find housing in Leningrad?

AN—They gave us completely different housing, they gave us one room for everyone, and that was it. But in the same building.

CF—In the very same building? . . . That was a real return. . . . So, you should have gone to school in 1939?

AN—No, 1939 would have been early. Back then you had to be eight years old. So that I was supposed to start school in 1940, but I hadn't had my eighth birthday yet.

CF—What did you do during all this time? Read?

AN—On the one hand, I read by myself, but then my aunts and Grandmother set me up in a group where I was taught German. So that every day we went there and Grandmother took me there, and later she picked me up at the end of the day. . . .

CF—This is how you spent the last period before the war. . . . Do you remember the start of the war?

AN—The memory that made the biggest impression is that it was a fine, sunny day. Everyone stood listening to the radio. Molotov's speech happened at that time. My aunts had very, I would say, strained expressions. They listened to all of this, and for a long time couldn't pull themselves together. They talked quietly, obviously about what to do then, how to act, and so forth. I should say that the clearest recollection is that when we went for a stroll, Grandmother took me with her to church—my grandmother and aunts were religious—and as we were walking to the church or on our way back, it was very difficult to cross the street, we had to stand and wait. We had to wait because barrage balloons were being carried along the street. . . . This was the most striking impression. And then, they caught a spy on the street, right there.

CF—Right away?

AN—Yes, they shouted, "We've caught a spy!" . . .

CF—What did the grown-ups decide in the end?

AN—The grown-ups—Grandmother decided. . . . She was very gentle, she was in charge, but very gentle. She simply said, quietly, without hurrying, and the more quietly she spoke, the more slowly she spoke, then the more important what she said was. She wore a pince-nez. When she put it on, that meant it was already an official situation. . . . She decided, after about a week, that we needed to leave. Because the Germans were approaching very quickly, and there was the danger that they would make it to Leningrad. And so they did. Ten days, no, two weeks later, it was already after Stalin spoke on the radio, pretty soon after that, we gathered our things and left.

CF—Where to?

AN—We had relatives, distant relatives in the Tatar SSR, on the Kama River. There is a town called Chistopol'. We went there. Through Vologda. . . . But, in fact, it was not easy to leave, because at that time they weren't permitting people to leave the city. The train station was surrounded by guards, they didn't let people enter. But Grandmother found some kind of old pensioner without legs, who led the way in for us. . . . At first the pensioner helped her and one aunt, and then he came back, and took me and the other aunt, that's how he led us. It was a freight car, not a passenger car, but that was fine.

CF—How did you sleep—were there plank beds in it?

AN—There were plank beds. . . . We went by rail to Perm. The train went slowly, we stood on the sidings a lot, it was hard to ride in this kind of train. Mostly there were women, there weren't many men, mostly there were women and children, who were leaving. And I recall how the women went to the bathroom. They would sit just like that, there would be a line of women, they sat and did their "business" right on the railroad tracks. . . .

CF—Well, you arrived at your relatives'. Where was your uncle?

AN—My uncle had been arrested. Just before the war started. My uncle was arrested while he was still in Leningrad. . . .

CF—So, eight-year-old Sasha,[4] two aunts, and Grandmother. You arrived and landed in . . . Chistopol'. And did you spend the entire war there?

AN—Yes, ... In fact, they wanted to leave, but they didn't let everyone return. Even after the war was over, it was very difficult to return to Leningrad. At first we, Grandmother, my aunts, and I, we moved to Kazan. In Kazan, we also had a relative. . . . We arrived in Kazan at the end of the autumn in 1945, and we lived two more years in Kazan. . . .

CF—Did you experience problems getting food during the war?

AN—Many. It was very difficult.

CF—How did you solve this problem?

AN—Well, it was not really solved, because this was a completely hungry time. We didn't live with our relatives. We lived separately. Sometimes my aunts would bring something home from work. Bread was rationed. They also gave out some kind of food through ration cards, but the problem was simply a disaster, especially for me. Because a boy is growing, he needs to eat. I even hit my aunts with my fists so that they would give me something else to eat. In general, I was a horrible child, it was simply some kind of disaster. . . . What I remember is this, that I would make my aunt . . . So, we would be sitting at the table eating potatoes, they would be serving mashed potatoes, how I would insist, I would yell so that they would let me lick the spoon each time they would serve someone. . . . My aunts would shake the spoon so that no potatoes were left on it, and then they would give it to me, because otherwise I would have a fit.

---

4. Sasha is a diminutive for Aleksandr.

Overall, this was an extremely large, a very big problem, really. So how was a boy to grow up without food at such a time? Well, in the summer it was okay, in the summer, you could slip into someone else's garden. . . . Of course, I could do this, but it was dangerous, because if they caught you, the owners of the garden would give you a real beating. . . .

CF—And did your aunts and grandmother know about that?

AN—I think not, because, in fact, they also were suffering from the food shortages, Grandmother was at home practically all the time, and my aunts ran the household. My aunts worked, and somehow they did something around the house. I was out of the house on my own. . . .

CF—You lived for two years in Kazan, so that means that your father returned where?

AN—This is what happened to my father. At the end of the war—in general he was a very good astronomer, and in 1944, Academician Shein wrote a letter, a request to the Presidium of the Academy of Sciences about the fact that astronomy had suffered very large losses during the war, that there were few astronomers left, they had perished in Leningrad from the famine or at the front, and therefore, he asked that, if it were possible, to liberate Nikolai Aleksandrovich Kozyrev so that he could revive astronomy in the USSR. This was in 1944. But after a while . . . Probably in the autumn of 1944. This letter took a lot of time. From the Academy of Sciences, it was sent to the NKVD, they decided the question there and in the end, decided that my father would be transported from Norilsk, that he would be transported to Moscow for a review. . . . This was under Beria.[5] And so my father was in Moscow for approximately a year. Right in the Lubyanka. . . . They freed him December 28, 1947. . . . He was given permission to live in Leningrad, to work at the Pulkovo Observatory, and at the same time, he was permitted to go to the Crimea, to an observatory. There was an observatory there in Simeiz, and he was permitted to work in that observatory, too. . . . As for his family, it was quite simple. He came to Grandmother, there, in Kazan, and to us, and he took us away from there.

CF—And what was the first meeting like?

5. Lavrenty Beria, then head of the security services.

AN—He wrote a letter, and my aunts met him at the station. I was not at the station. It was cold. Well, someone arrived, they said it was Papa. Well, so, fine, Papa. So. Somehow my parents no longer played any real role for me. The people who were dearest to me were right there.

CF—Your father returned. How much time did he spend in Kazan?

AN—He was in Kazan, I think, one week. Maybe something like that. He went back to Leningrad, the Academy of Sciences gave him a place to live, two rooms. He registered us, sent the documents to Kazan, and we were very happy to go back, we went back with great pleasure.

CF—And did he try to get to know you or not? . . .

AN—How did he act with me? He was extremely benevolent. When he came back, when he returned, he came into our room, he kissed Grandmother for a long time, and then he took me and threw me up in the air, saying, "Oy, what a big boy!" . . . That was fine. But he made things clear to me right away. We sat down to eat, and I said, "Let me lick the spoon." He said, he asked me, "Why would you lick it?" I said, "Because the spoon is dirty!" And he said, "Well, if it's dirty, then why would you lick it?" I looked at him for a bit and agreed. And I never asked again to be given the spoon to lick.

CF—Father's first lesson—don't lick a dirty spoon. So, you gradually grew close. As friends.

AN—Yes, especially in Leningrad. Grandmother even used to laugh, she would say, "Sasha comes home from school and says, 'And is Papa home?,' and Papa comes home from work and says, 'And is Sasha home?'"

CF—. . . . But your mama, what news did you have?

AN—Mama received a sentence of five years, in Siberia, and when she was let out, she was let out in 1942, she married someone there. . . . So, our mama was gone.

CF—She never returned?

AN—No. Later she lived near Leningrad. Later, when I was at the university already, we would meet sometimes. And that was all.

CF—. . . . What was this like?

AN—Okay. And the thing is, she had spent very little time with me. After all, she had been very young.

CF—So that means Papa became the main person.

AN—Yes, for me. . . .

Aleksandr Kozyrev discussed his studies in university, and how his father's renown as an astronomer actually helped his career more than his status as a son of an enemy of the people hurt it.

CF—How do you remember Stalin's death? You were a student then.

AN—You know, I used Stalin's death to improve my own reputation. Very much. The thing was that this was when I was at the university already. I knew that Stalin was sick, very sick. But I didn't always go to classes early. . . . I slept late, I usually read at night, so it often happened that I skipped the first classes, but I would go to classes later. And so on that day, one of my friends calls me early in the morning and says, "Get here immediately!" And at home, they already knew that Stalin had died. My friend had called me so that I would come to the assembly. This assembly was organized in the big gym, in the gymnasium. And since I had very little time, the assembly was just about to start, I ran. . . . I rushed, ran there, on the tram in places, on foot in others, however I could. So, I ran into the gymnasium. There were already a lot of people there. Everyone was so gloomy, sad. Someone started to give a speech, started to speak. And I began to feel bad. And I said to my buddies—there were two of them—I said, "I'm going out." They said, "You've lost your mind! Under no circumstances! Under no circumstances! Stay put!" And I fainted. . . . I had run, I needed to breathe, I needed oxygen. I fainted. They carried me out of the gym, put me on some kind of chairs, and when I came to, Party workers were walking around me, waving pieces of paper. . . .

CF—Everyone thought this was a result of your suffering.

AN—Yes, my suffering. I improved my reputation. Because at the university, of course, sometimes we permitted ourselves to be sarcastic about politics. Of course, I didn't have the best reputation. We, of course, were carefully sarcastic, but, all the same, sometimes we were sarcastic.

CF—So you and your friends were not in the Komsomol? Were you a Pioneer?

AN—I was a Pioneer, but I was not in the Komsomol, and my two friends were also not in the Komsomol.

CF—Did you apply?

AN—No, no. We simply avoided it. . . . They tried [to get us to apply], but we told them that we were sick, that we couldn't attend meetings.

CF—So, you didn't tell them frankly why not, you thought up an excuse?

AN—No, no. We thought something up, of course.

CF—How was it at home that evening [of Stalin's death]? How did your father, grandmother, and aunts react?

AN—Overall, it was very tense, because we didn't know what the next steps would be, what would happen next. And therefore I suppose I can't say that I remember our home life at this time, because for me, life was already basically outside the home. University and everything else.

CF—. . . . Your parents' arrest, the loss of your parents—did this influence your worldview, the development of your patterns of behavior and feelings?

AN—The whole thing is that Grandmother and my aunts raised me not on Soviet literature, but on prerevolutionary literature. Foreign literature. And so I read these kinds of books: *Uncle Tom's Cabin* and so on. Good, universal treasures were very dear to me. And, of course, internally, I had an extremely negative attitude toward the fact of my parents' arrest. In any event, I had an internal opposition to this regime. And this was completely clear. Nothing else was possible. It so happened that we lived here under this regime, unfortunately. Therefore, it was necessary not to talk about a lot of things, not to be a blabbermouth. And so on. . . . I would put it this way. It influenced all of it definitely. I had a completely non-Soviet worldview. There were some things . . . In school it was fine. Not only for me. So, in school, what was interesting was that our literature teacher, she explained the behavior of various heroes, the reasons behind their behavior as if they all correlated with the class they belonged to. In class, this was in ninth and tenth grade, when we heard this, the students broke out laughing. But this was a Leningrad school.

CF—Could one say that you were not Soviet, but you did not feel entirely alienated?

AN—Yes, I was not the only one. We had arguments. This was in school, we did not agree with each other about something—this didn't matter. What was important was that in the milieu where I lived, you were expected to think. Having different views. This was very good. And later, there were three of us at the university, we were very close, we had very similar views. . . . So that in this regard, we always had to . . . you would listen to the radio, "Well, so, it's started! Propaganda again." And in books.

CF—And in newspapers.

AN—Well, that's out of the question. We did not *read* newspapers.[6] . . .

CF—What would you say, looking back on the past as a person who lived through both events, which would you say had a greater effect on the history of the USSR—and perhaps to this day has an influence—the war or repression?

AN—Well, I think that there is no doubt, it was the war. On the spread of attitudes in society. Because, very little was ever said about repression, there was practically nothing in the print media, even though millions, tens of millions were there [in the camps]. People said very little about this among themselves. But the war—this was such an event. There are no doubts whatsoever. . . .

CF—I want to ask you. Three times already I have heard this phrase: "genetic fear." Is this a typical phrase now, has this become somehow formulaic? Among members of Memorial?

AN—May I say something? This is the first time I have heard this. From you.

CF—So this is what is interesting. So I've heard exceptional words, I've heard them three times. I've also heard this phrase: "Silence was our salvation."

6. Aleksandr Nikolaevich is referring to the fact that his family, like most Soviet citizens, used newspaper for toilet paper.

AN—That's correct. That is a good phrase, and it is correct. You understand that I, obviously, was young, and I came from a special, not a bad milieu. Because fear, of course, there was, fear, of course, there was. But there was a desire to resist this.

CF—In your family.

AN—Among the guys who were my friends. In my family, too, of course.

CF—So, you consciously decided to resist?

AN—I always had this internal sensation. Not accepting this, and dissenting. Joking about it on purpose, to say "This is all lies." It was like that. Not only because you wanted to present your point of view, but simply because this was a different propaganda. . . .

CF—Which aspects of the history or repression do you believe should be taught in the Russian Federation and in other countries in courses on Soviet history?

AN—This is a very difficult question. It seems to me that the chief thing is to talk about the danger of the consolidation of power. If power is concentrated in one, two, three persons' hands, then the possibility is not excluded that repressions can reappear. Therefore, it is extremely desirable to facilitate the development of democracy in all aspects, so that such a danger won't arise.

CF—To serve as an example . . .

AN—Absolutely. Both Hitler and Stalin. I think there is in this its own internal logic. Simply that when a person strives for power, concentrates it in his hands, he will strive to destroy those persons who would interfere. And then this spreads more and more widely. . . .

CHAPTER NINE

"I have dreamed my entire life, for me this would be a great joy to find my relatives"

MAYA RUDOLFOVNA LEVITINA

Smolensk

November 14–15, 2007

Transcribed by Natalia Kholopova

Introduction

Maya Rudolfovna Levitina was born in Smolensk in 1928 to two Soviet physicians who had joined the Bolsheviks as Red Army soldiers in 1918. Her parents were both from the periphery of the Russian empire. Her mother, Antonina Konstantinovna Nosovich, was the daughter of prosperous Polish farmers. Her father, Rudolf Ennovich Yakson, was the son of a German mother and a Latvian father living in Riga as prosperous members of the bourgeoisie. When the Stalinist repressions began, Maya Rudolfovna's family lived in Leningrad, where Rudolf Yakson was deputy director of Ivan Pavlov's Institute for Experimental Medicine, and Antonina Nosovich practiced and taught obstetrics. Nosovich and Yakson were thus Bolsheviks of non-Russian nationality, with Yakson a prominent figure in Soviet medicine and science who traveled abroad to represent the USSR at international conferences.

Rudolf Yakson was arrested in November 1937 and executed in Leningrad in January 1938. Antonina Nosovich was subsequently

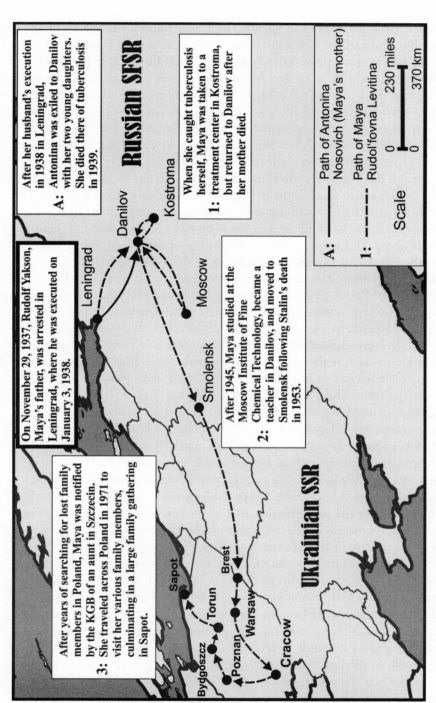

On November 29, 1937, Rudolf Yakson, Maya's father, was arrested in Leningrad, where he was executed on January 3, 1938.

After her husband's execution in 1938 in Leningrad, Antonina was exiled to Danilov with her two young daughters. She died there of tuberculosis in 1939.

A:

When she caught tuberculosis herself, Maya was taken to a treatment center in Kostroma, but returned to Danilov after her mother died.

1:

Russian SFSR

Kostroma

Danilov

Leningrad

Moscow

Smolensk

After 1945, Maya studied at the Moscow Institute of Fine Chemical Technology, became a teacher in Danilov, and moved to Smolensk following Stalin's death in 1953.

2:

After years of searching for lost family members in Poland, Maya was notified by the KGB of an aunt in Szczecin. She traveled across Poland in 1971 to visit her various family members, culminating in a large family gathering in Sapot.

3:

Sapot

Torun

Brest

Bydgoszcz

Poznan

Warsaw

Cracow

Ukrainian SSR

Scale

A: ———— Path of Antonina Nosovich (Maya's mother)

1: -------- Path of Maya Rudol'fovna Levitina

0   230 miles
0   370 km

The journeys of Maya Rudolfovna Levitina and her mother, Antonina Nosovich, 1938–1971 (Map by Eric Pugliano) exiled from Leningrad in spring 1938 as a wife of an enemy of the people. She and her two young daughters were sent to Danilov, a railroad junction north of Yaroslavl. Maya Rudolfovna lost her mother to tuberculosis in 1939 and her younger sister to diphtheria during the war. Her mother's friend, Dora Mikhailovna Minkina—a midwife who had assisted in Maya Rudolfovna's birth—moved to Danilov to care for the orphaned girls when Antonina Nosovich knew her death was near. After Stalin's death in 1953, Maya Rudolfovna and Dora Mikhailovna returned to Smolensk.

Maya Rudolfovna's life illustrates extensive family destruction by the Soviet state, displacement, hunger, and lifelong stigmatization. It also reveals the vast differences between the standards of living she experienced as a child of privileged Bolshevik professionals before their arrest and exile and those she endured as a stigmatized, exiled orphan of enemies of the people living in an underdeveloped region of the Soviet Union. Her reminiscences take us from mirrored ballrooms in Peterhof Palace to freezing peasant houses on the edges of swamps in the Russian north. Her interview also demonstrates the key role Good Samaritans played for those children of the Gulag who survived. In Maya Rudolfovna's case, the remarkable Dora Mikhailovna Minkina was not the only one to provide vital assistance; teachers and other friends of her mother also offered love, food, and shelter. Like the other child with a Polish background in this volume, Vera Mikhailovna Skiba, Maya Rudolfovna eventually experienced the joy of reunion with family members in Poland, whom the Soviet state had kept away from her until middle age. Those relatives' tenacity in searching for their dead sister's child, whom they had never met, against all odds and in the face of Soviet obstructionism, embodies profound familial devotion. Maya Rudolfovna's reunion, like Skiba's, reminds us of the inestimable value of the International Red Cross in assisting repressed, displaced, and isolated victims of political systems to the very end of the twentieth century.

I first met Maya Rudolfovna in December 1989, when I was an unexpected guest in her home during a research trip to Smolensk. Her husband, Mikhail Naumovich Levitin, who oversaw the Smolensk regional archive, invited me to stay at their home. During the night I spent in her spotless, welcoming apartment on that visit, she shared her life story. I was able to return in November 2007 to interview her formally as the last "child of the gulag" for my book *Children of the Gulag*. Over the course of two days, we broke bread together; visited around the table; went through family photo albums; and sat side by side on the narrow convertible sofa in the bedroom of the two-room

Maya Rudolfovna with Dora Mikhailovna Minkina,
mid-1930s (Private collection of M. R. Levitina)

apartment to conduct the interview. I interviewed Maya Rudolfovna
in several sessions, each lasting as long as her failing health could
sustain.

Readers should note how often Maya recalls her parents using terms
of endearment, and how often she herself uses such terms in referring
to her son and dead sister. Finally, I encourage readers to take note
of the multiple ways Maya Rudolfovna refers to Dora Mikhailovna
Minkina, her mother's friend who rescued her from the fate of complete solitude and separation as an orphan of political repression
("Mother," "Grandmother," "my adoptive mother"). This confusing
list of terms reveals how one woman of no blood or legal relationship
filled so many vital, family-oriented roles for Maya Rudolfovna.

In this interview, I have retained the verbal stutters to convey Maya
Rudolfovna's hesitation either as she paused to capture a memory or
because a memory had overwhelmed her.

CF—So, please, we'll start with basic information about you.
What is your family name, first name and patronymic?

MR—I had a double maiden name. Before 1942, I was Noso-vich, Maya Rudolfovna; after '42 I became Yakson, Maya Ru-dolfovna. Then, when I married I became Levitina, Maya Rudol-fovna. The reason I had a double family name was that [*pause*] my parents did not go through the process of formally registering their marriage for a long time in ZAGS [the civil registry bu-reau]. And therefore they registered sometime after 1937, more likely, before . . . '37, when . . . all these horrible events were taking shape, then they registered their marriage [*sighs*] and we could . . . n . . . not find these documents for a long time. Then, it was totally by chance that they were found in '42 [*sighs*] and in '42 they gave me . . . the official name already . . . my paternal family name Yakson, Maya Rudolfovna. . . .

CF—Tell me, please, your birthday and where you were born.

MR—I was born December 16, 1928, in Smolensk.

CF—When did you lose your parents? . . .

MR—My father was arrested November 29, 1937, and my mother died on June 10, 1939 in exile. . . . They didn't arrest her, but they exiled her without voting rights, basically. They de-prived her of all her rights, and she was exiled to the north to the town of Danilov in Yaroslavl Region. That's already considered a rather northern region.

CF—But before we begin to talk about the arrest, I would like to discuss family history from the beginning. Tell me, please, how your parents met each other and what their families were like before the revolution.

MR—My father was born in Riga. He was born in 1897, in Latvia. His father was a railroad officer, he worked with the rail-road. His father was Latvian. His mother was a music teacher, and she was German. They had two children . . . my father and his sister, Maria. My father studied at first in a Russian gymnasium in Riga. Why a Russian one? I don't know. Then he studied in Tartu at the medical school. . . . My mother was born in Radun, that's formerly Polish territory. That's the village Radun in Grodno Re-gion, but now it is Belarus. Now it's called western Belarus. My mother was born into a large family, they had eight children, her father was a peasant, but . . . not poor . . . He was very hardwork-ing and rather prosperous. Her mother was of gentry background,

although, it's true, poor, bankrupt gentry. The children, all eight
children, ah . . . eh . . . they educated all eight children in the gymnasium in the city of Lida. That's where my mother studied. Yes.
And even in . . . mmm . . . before . . . the revolution she was already drawn to revolutionary ideas. And when . . . the Red Army
came there, then Mama was very [*pause*] well . . . excited about
all these events, the revolution called her to battle, so to speak. She
abandoned her family and joined the Red Army.

CF—What year was that, and how old was she then?

MR—. . . . She was born in 1899, so she was, that was in
1918, she was not quite nineteen years old. Here, I have a photograph of her in the Red Army. . . . But Father, when he was
still a gymnasium student, having relatives in Sweden, he traveled
across all of Europe. When he was still a gymnasium student,
he was in Germany, and in France, and in Sweden, and in Finland. When the war began, then my father also joined the Red
Army. He was some kind of technician in defense against chemical weapons. . . .

CF—How do you understand his decision to become a Red
Army soldier?

MR—At that time, they were still students. As gymnasium
students already they were rather revolutionarily inclined. Well
and then . . . how . . . they . . . really . . . somehow believed in
the revolution. When my mama left . . . her father's home, all
her relatives, of course, were really distraught. My grandfather
especially loved her, she was his eldest daughter. He really, really
loved her. And he said to her as "Antosiia, where are you going,
and why are you leaving us?" She answered: "Papa, understand,
I am going to fight so there won't be poor people, for everything
to be fair, . . . so that . . . people will live well, so that it won't be
the way it is in our country, . . . to fix it all. I can't not help taking
part in this struggle." That's how Mama talked. What her father
said, I don't know. Well, so . . . her sisters who were present told
me what Mama said. Well . . . then . . . Father entered the institute to complete his education . . . he graduated from the Second
Medical Institute in Moscow. . . . So, Mama also, when . . . the
fighting ended, also entered the institute, but she entered the first
year, she also graduated from this medical . . . medical academy,
and became, she became a doctor, a gynecologist. . . . Papa was

a doctor, a surgeon. How did they find each other? They sent Mama to work in Smolensk. She worked here as the chief doctor of the maternity hospital. There's also a photograph of her standing in her doctor's white coat with her co-workers. And Papa worked a lot, it's written there [*indicates documents in her possession*] . . . . In 1926 he was assistant to the chief doctor of the soviet's hospital in the city of Smolensk; in 1927 he was the chief of the City Public Health Department here in Smolensk; and here in Smolensk, when he was head of the Public Health Department, they met. [*pause*] And that was precisely in 1927.

CF—But your mama also completed an institute in Moscow.

MR—Yes, also in Moscow, it was part of MGU, what was it called, Second Moscow State University, that's what it was called, Second Moscow State University. The medical school was there, and they both graduated from the same school, well, and they met. [*Pause*] They met in Smolensk . . . in 1928. . . . They were both members of the Communist Party, they were very, very dedicated Communists. Both believed it was necessary to do everything so that everything would be good in Russia. They really tried. Mama was extraordinarily conscientious. When I myself, giving birth to my son, ended up in the hospital, the same staff were still working there who remembered her. They said people like Antonina Konstantinovna are rare. . . .

CF—What are your very first memories? . . .

MR—So, my very first memories were rather late. Because at first my parents lived in Smolensk, then Father entered the Institute of Red Professors. Naturally they moved to Moscow. After that, from Moscow, after Father graduated from the Institute of Red Professors, they assigned him to the All-Union Institute of Experimental Medicine. At first he was assistant to the Director, he was where the famous academician Pavlov worked, that was the All-Union Institute. My parents moved to Leningrad. Well . . . that's what life was like. We lived in the Peterhof Palace. . . . They gave us an enormous room, and there were terribly big mirrors there, like this. And so I remember that as a child I was always walking up to this mirror and looking at myself and being very frightened. . . . That was my first impression. Then, since he was lecturing to doctors, who studied in advanced training courses, the institute of advanced training gave him a good apartment. Well, how "good," in the sense that there were three rooms, but, of course, they didn't have either a bathroom or a decent kitchen, but even so, the rooms were big with large windows on Kirochnaya Street, Number 41. This I remember. At this age, I also remember how Papa had a study, then there was a big dining room, and there was also our room. Mama and I shared the room. *Pause*] So, I remember what was really good was that the Tauride Garden was directly opposite, we could go walk over there to stroll. I had a really good nanny, a gypsy, very good. Her name was Manya. . . .

CF—Did she live with you?

MR—She lived with us, this nanny, she slept in the dining room, on a very, very hard, little sofa. Because we had the kind of kitchen then, then there were horrible kerosene stoves, three primus stoves were burning, and there was not a single window in the kitchen. It was . . . I can't recall if there was any ventilation, but there was no window. So, therefore Manya did not sleep in the kitchen, she slept in the dining room, on the sofa . . . Mama had a friend in Smolensk, a midwife, Dora Mikhailovna Minkina, Jewish by nationality, she and Mama really came to love each other. And when Mama moved to Leningrad . . . she really tried to get her friend to come live with her . . . and then this, her friend . . . . She came to Leningrad and lived with us. Then this Dora Mikhailovna and Manya both slept together in the dining room. Then Dora Mikhailovna moved into our, into Mama's and my room, and she slept with us.

CF—And was that the usual custom, that the child slept with the mama, separately from the father?

MR—It's just that Father needed . . . Father was very busy. He was giving lectures, he participated in various things, in debates, international conferences. He had a lot to do, he needed to be alone. He had this study, I remember it, I remember very well what it looked like. Enormous wooden shelves with books, something like a camp cot, for some reason there was a washbasin in that room, a desk with many, many papers. That's how I remember my father's office and there was also a ficus plant. So, well, and Mama lived in the larger room, it had two big windows, well, naturally, and where else could I sleep, there was no place else for me to sleep, except in the kitchen. So, that's why I shared a room with Mama. Then, when my little sister was born,

my little sister also shared the room with us. Then they hired a
second nanny, and that nanny lived with us in this room, because
there was no place to live. Mama also worked a lot, ... Mama
worked in Leningrad in the Ottovskii Institute, there was such
an institute of obstetrics and gynecology at that time. She was
an assistant professor. She worked there. Mama worked a great
deal. Quite often they even summoned her at night, when there
were urgent cases. . . . That's why our parents, of course, could
give us very little attention, because they were very, very busy.
They were busy up . . . up to the limit of what was possible. And
I remember Papa only sometimes, on Sunday, ... he would give
me some attention, he would take me to the puppet theater, he
would take me to the movies. I remember just now that I saw the
American film *Three Little Pigs* . . . so . . . sometimes he would
take a walk with me, but Papa was the one who did that. Mama
was somehow so busy, that she could not even be with me. She
would be with me only when I was sick. . . .

CF—What do you remember about their personalities?

MR—. . . . Papa was . . . a very . . . open . . . person. A very . . .
generous by nature, so very . . . tender, so very kind, Papa was
very good, such a cheerful person. By the way, since his mama
was a music teacher, he played very well. We rented an upright
piano. And so, something else I remember from my childhood,
that sometimes I would be falling asleep and I would hear just a
bit, and . . . the dining room was quite a distance across the hall,
I would hear Papa playing the piano. He played all the classics,
and all kinds of folk songs. Well, Papa really loved people, people
often gathered at our house. There was a Latvian community in
Leningrad, these Latvians would come over. They were the ones
who had gone over to the side of Soviet power and were very devoted to Soviet power. . . . Mama was a somewhat different kind
of person . . . she was . . . very fair . . . very, she had an exceptional conscience, well, and she was a bit more severe. Somehow
she even rarely, I can very rarely recall Mama's caress. But Papa's,
often. I remember that even when he was talking to me, I even
remember, oft- . . . often, his caress often. . . . Papa was a typical
Latvian, he had such a very, very kind face, and he tried to be
kind to people. Like, for example, when he, these years were after all very hungry years in Russia, and he received a professor's
ration. . . . He shared that ration with the brother of that friend

of my mother's. He sent it himself, himself, in spite of how busy he was, he packed up this package and sent it to Belarus. And I can tell you another interesting fact. Papa essentially worked two jobs. He was at one point the assistant of the deputy director and also he was somehow some kind of . . . well I don't know what the position was called, in the institute of advanced training he was the curator or something, and he received two salaries . . . at one place and the other. And Mama did not even know about this, because he always brought home one salary, the second he did not bring home. Mama, when she found out, of course, Mama was very unhappy. She said, "Since you work so much, since you give so much of your energy to this, you have the right to this money." And he answered her, my adoptive Mama told me this, he would answer her this way: "Tonechka,[1] but people are so poor, and well, you and I wanted to help people." . . . So that's what Papa was like, that's what Papa was like. . . . My little sister was born in 1934. . . .

CF—So was it primarily the nanny who took care of you?

MR—The nanny, and then when that same friend of my mother's came, Dora Mikhailovna, she did. She was also a midwife. She took us on, basically. And then later, when my little sister was born, she herself took us on to raise, so to speak. She loved us very . . . very much. She loved me so much, more than life itself. She knew me even back from when I was born. . . . I was born, in fact, in her apartment, because in Smolensk, Mama lived with her and I was actually born in her apartment. . . . She was also a very generous, very good person. She was a very, extremely noble person.

CF—Was she also a Bolshevik?

MR—Nooo, she really disliked the Soviet government, she disliked it very much. She was from a Jewish family, and all of them, her brothers also, all of them disliked the Soviet government, from the very start in 1917. In that regard, I don't know how they got along. . . . She also worked as a midwife in Leningrad, in a clinic at a textile factory.

CF—That means that in one apartment lived you, Dora, Papa, Mama, two nannies . . .

1. An affectionate diminutive for Antonina.

MR—And a little girl . . . . Here, here [*shows a family photograph*] is what my little girl was like, that was, that was not long before she died. [*Pause*] She was ve- . . . also a very good girl . . . She, for one thing, sang very well. . . . This is my little sister, Innochka.[2] Innochka, Inessa. Here, this is my little sister, who died in 1942. . . .

CF—And did you start school in Leningrad?

MR—I started school when I was eight years old. I didn't go to first grade because . . . Why didn't I? Because when they took me to first grade, they looked me over, they talked with me, and said that I didn't need to go to first grade, "Let the child play for another year, and then she can enter second grade directly." Moreover . . . even then . . . I started school in nineteen thirty- . . . what year? [*Long pause*] In 1937. . . . When 1937 started, at the beginning of the year, they still hadn't touched Papa. They even gave him a very fine apartment somewhere on, on some, I no longer remember, on some Prospekt, and we were all supposed to move to that apartment, but they were still painting and decorating it. They gave him a personal car, a personal driver. That was all at the beginning of 1937. But Papa somehow did not believe that these repressions were so terrible, that they could touch him, that all of this was very unjust. In this case, he displayed some kind of foolishness and enormous naïveté. But Mama, she turned out to be smarter than he was, she said, "Rudik[3] . . . leave, go somewhere to the provinces, far, far away and hide, because . . . you will certainly fall . . . into this net." . . . She already sensed that . . . they took that one, they took this one. Not far from us, next door, was a military community, Red Army commanders lived there. So, well, on one fine day . . . it was revealed that in all three of these large apartment buildings, all the apartments . . . had been sealed, that is, every single one of these Red commanders was locked up, and their children . . . were taken, who knows who went where. This net of repressions . . . . fell on almost every other person in Leningrad who held any kind of responsible position and had anything to offer. And then there was the additional factor . . . that Papa was Latvian, and he had come directly from Latvia, and in his dossiers, he wrote that he had been abroad,

2. An affectionate diminutive of Inessa.
3. An affectionate diminutive of Rudolf.

and then later, when he was director, he had also gone abroad to conferences, that is, he had a passport to travel abroad. All of this, all of this went against him. That of course they would . . . liquidate him, but he didn't believe it.

CF—And do you remember these conversations?

MR—I remember, *that* I remember already, there were such conversations already, and then suddenly . . . at some point they moved us out even from that apartment on Kirochnaia, which we rented, and moved us . . . into one room with a kitchen. All of us! At that time there were two nannies, two children, Dora, and Papa and Mama. . . . When they moved us out, Mother already understood that this was already the end . . . On this point, she and my father disagreed sharply. My father was constantly trying to persuade her that this could not be, that nothing of the kind would happen, that, "I am not guilty of anything, I have served the Party very loyally and I truly believed in the correctness of Soviet power. This cannot happen, that they would arrest me." Well . . . then they expelled my father from the Party . . . that was in the summer already. . . . But Mama they didn't touch . . .

Mama was working. Mama was working as an assistant professor, and she continued to work. Then . . . this I remember very well, when they arrested Papa. I had tonsillitis and wasn't going to school, and I was lying in bed sick. By then, we already had, of course, only one nanny, because there was nothing to pay the second one with and no place to put her . . . So I was at home with the nanny, and Papa was home. And since he was no longer working anywhere . . . he was sitting next to my bed and holding a globe in his hands, and he was telling me about . . . well, some kind of countries, which rivers, which cities, to distract me somehow from my being sick.[4] Then suddenly the doorbell rang, and three people appeared. [*Pause*] And they were in civilian clothes . . . one woman and two men. [*Pause*] So. They came up very sweetly to me and said, "Oh! Little one, you are sick, you're in bed, why aren't you in school?" And I answered, "Yes, I'm sick." And that was all. But I understood immediately, instinctively somehow, that this was something very bad. But my father held himself together with such dignity, well, they began

4. As Maya Rudolfovna began to recount this scene, her words became broken and elongated.

to carry out the search . . . They ransacked everywhere, I even got out of bed, and they picked up that little mattress, they all looked there . . . so. . . . Nyura was there as our housekeeper, and Nyura was such a brave person, she said, well, basically, she began almost scolding them, "Why did you come here, what do you need from the professor?" and so on and so forth. . . .

This Nyura started in on them, and they said, "Woman, be quiet, or we'll take you, too." [*Pause*] Well, she, of course, was frightened and clammed up. Well, they rummaged about for a long time . . . they took whatever we had of value, we had almost nothing of value. They took the most valuable books. Well, we had books, they weren't bad, it is true, they were Academica editions of Pushkin, and . . . there was the Great Soviet Encyclopedia, it was beautifully printed then. So this is what I . . . so this is what I remember. Then they left only certain little children's books, and several pamphlets and the like. At that time Papa sometimes traveled to those international conferences and sometimes they gave him . . . remnants, for him to sew together somehow, so he wouldn't look so terrible. So they gathered these suits. Papa was in such a . . . simple suit. Then Mama . . . even before this . . . for a year she had received packages from Papa's sister Manya from Estonia. This sister loved my father very much, and she understood what Soviet Russia meant and what it meant to live there. She sent outfits, but she sent outfits primarily to Mama. And they took whatever Mama had of these outfits. She had such a beautiful wool suit, some nice shoes. All that they seized . . . Then they sent for someone to write up the list. Then the commandant came, they summoned the commandant.

And then, the most interesting thing is that the commandant was a woman, and later she was the mother of one of my students when I was already back in Smolensk. You understand, she and I met in Smolensk. That was such a terrible, tragic meeting. She told me, she said, "I so worried about you and your papa then, when I signed the certification of the search having been conducted and everything." So that's how life sometimes brings people together. Her name was Vladimirova.

And so this Vladimirova signed the certification, and they made the nanny sign the certificate. They signed the certification that they had been present during the search, that only Father's personal things had been removed, and that was all. Well, and so that's how Papa disappeared. It was November 29. [*Weeps*]

CF—Forgive me for interrupting. What did your father say to you in parting?

MR—He said to me, "Mayechka,⁵ get well, be healthy, stu- . . . study well." And I . . . I asked, "What is this? Papochka, where are you going? Where are they taking you?" And he answered, "Well, I am going on a long business trip." [*Pause*] And that was it. So. Well, then Mama came home, but Mama didn'- . . . didn't cry. Mama was so very, very steadfast. Everyone on that side of the family, the Polish side, they were all very courageous. I later learned about that, they told me our family's entire history, everything. Well, and so she did not cry at all, not at all. . . .

Maya Rudolfovna describes how the Red Army destroyed her maternal grandfather's farm and livestock in the Polish borderlands after the Molotov-Ribbentrop Pact.

MR—Mama came home. I don't even remember how that was. Mama came home. But I remember only that I never saw Mama cry, she *ne-e-e-ver* cried. So, then, when they took Papa . . . what should we do? We decided to take him parcels . . . to Kresty prison.⁶ At that time, they took them primarily to Kresty. . . . Nyura put this parcel together and left. Mama had to work, because we had to live on something, there were still four of us all the same, and she [Nyura] went to Kresty. Well, and the most interesting thing was that they took the first parcel from her [*pause*], and later, no matter how many times she went there . . . they wouldn't accept anything. . . . They gave the parcels back to her and said that this prisoner has been deported . . . this one is not listed here. He wasn't there for long, it is true . . . they liquidated him very quickly. [*Pause*]

And as for his liquidation, if necessary, I can describe it all in detail. Here is his personal case file. [*Looks through documents*] Here they are, here. So they wrote this, "the Eighth Department" . . . it was opened on November 30, and on December 15, the case was closed. [*Pause*] That means that they deprived a person of his fate in the course of fifteen days. [*Sighs*] Who was in charge of this case? Sergeant of State Security [*pause*] Ivanov.

5. An affectionate diminutive of Maya.
6. The main detention center dating to the imperial era.

That means that the fate of a director and professor, one can say, of a world-famous institute, was decided by Sergeant of State Security . . . Ivanov, so. And they had issued the order for my father's arrest on November 28. In the warrant it was written that enough had been exposed to prove that he was a participant in a revolutionary organization. [*Pause*] How was he exposed? They never summoned him to any kind of interrogations before this . . . nothing . . . they never took any kind of evidence, nothing. But this Sergeant Ivanov [*long pause*] passed this case down the line. At first he . . . ran the investigation, but he apparently couldn't get anything out of my father, and then they passed this to Junior Lieutenant Bashko [*pause*].

Here it says that the director of the Institute for Experimental Medicine, here's his dossier, in 19- . . . [*pause*] . . . from 1935 through 1937 [*pause*] was unemployed as of October 16. So, I was correct when I said October. [*Looks through papers*] Here it is written: In 1919–1920, a doctor with the Red Army." [*Leafs through papers*] . . . "Nosovich born in 1899." In prison, he was in Section Nine. Here are the notes of the interrogation. The first interrogation took place on the eleventh. So, they detained him on the twenty-ninth, the first interrogation took place on December 11. Nothing is stated, nothing, in this interrogation, nothing. A blank page, which means my father didn't sign anything." [*Pause*] And if only you could see this file. The file looked like this: two terribly dirty sheets of paper, like these, like these here. Here, and here, there's more personal information, it's written that they took from him at the time of his arrest a fountain pen with a gold nib, a wa-a-atch with his name engraved on it, something else, it was all written here, then information about the family, here, here it is all written down. Here it says [*long pause*] there's nothing written here, but here there was . . . there was more on these two terribly dirty sheets of paper. It had such an effect on me, that I don't even know how to . . . how to tell you what it was like. . . .

Well, to continue . . . evidently, they beat these terrible . . . they horribly beat these terrible statements out of Papa. And so, they say to him . . . it continues by saying that "he was connected with enemies of the people in the Institute of Red Professors, there it lists names, that is, everyone, everyone who was already in prison. . . . [*Goes through papers*]

So, here we have a top secret document. [*She looks through papers*] Here, now it says, the decision, that he was sentenced to execution by shooting by the military tribunal of the Leningrad military district, that he was sentenced to execution by shooting for treason . . . for . . . and for espionage. And now the "Top Secret" decision. These documents were secret. [*Long pause*] So, and they shot my father on January 31, but the certificate was issued on January 4, 1938. So, and they even recorded who did the shooting, some kind of Polikarpov. And the People's Commissar of Internal Affairs signed these documents. He signed the documents on December 31. They shot him on January 3, and on January 4, they signed the death certificate. The bill of indictment was issued on the fifteenth. [*Long pause*] . . . .

Maya Rudolfovna describes seeing these documents for the first time in the 1990s.

CF—After Papa's arrest, your mama kept working?

MR—Mama kept working . . . and she continued to work, no one fired her.

CF—Perhaps this will sound stupid, but anyway, what was the atmosphere like at home?

MR—So, wel-l-l, with her, this is what they did. Soon after they shot Papa, they summoned her to the security organs. Well, they also expelled her from the Party, of course. She was expelled from the Party . . . sometime in December already, they expelled her sometime shortly after the arrest . . . [*sighs*] they summoned Mama . . . and said that she had to immediately . . . leave the city and that she was being exiled to the north and deprived of all her rights, that is, she was deprived of her job, deprived of her right to vote. . . . Well, by that time, Mama had fallen very seriously ill, she had . . . in her early childhood she had had tuberculosis, then they cured it. But, apparently, when all these terrible things began, apparently, her condition became active again . . . and Mama presented her documents, that she was very sick and that she had two young children. And she said, that—she told me this herself—this clerk, the one she had approached, turned out after all to be a humane person. He said, "Well, since you are so sick, don't go during the winter, because it's the winter"—that was a ferocious winter—"you can't go in January, but when can you go?" And she said, "Well . . . , in May, in April, or May." And he said, "Well, no later than May, leave Leningrad." So, where did they assign her? At first, they assigned her to Cherepovets . . . so . . . well, Mama . . . Mama agreed to go to . . . Cherepovets. Then, after some time, they summoned her and said, "No, you won't go to Cherepovets, you will go to Danilov." . . . So, we went to Danilov. Our nanny still lived with us, she was such a good person, that Nyura, that she did not abandon us. Back then . . . people were very kind. She was such a simple woman, she did not abandon us . . . Although, of course, she received no salary at all from us, she just lived with us. And she even said, "Antonina Konstantinovna, if they put you in prison, I will take the children." And . . . my adoptive mama, when they arrested Papa, she was very . . . upset. And my mama said this to her, "Dora, leave . . . go to your brothers, because you will be taken, too, and then you'll perish. Go to your brothers." And she went to her brother in Belarus, in Orsha. But she was also very worried about how, how we were and what was going on with us, she never stopped writing us, she ceaselessly worried about us, but she left. She left for Orsha.

We moved in May to Danilov. Well, at first we went as far as Moscow. Our nanny accompanied us, we put together what we could carry. We couldn't take any furniture, nothing. In Moscow we stayed with my adoptive mama's brother. He was also such a fearless person. He was not frightened by the fact that my father had been arrested, that they were exiling my mother. They welcomed us, we even lived with them for a while. Then we went to this Danilov. We arrived at a peasant's house, a terrible little wooden house. There were drafts from all the chinks, even though it was May, but it was a very cold May. And as I recall just now, I used to lie on the bed and they would lay another mattress on top of me, so that I wouldn't freeze.

Well, so we had to figure out how to live. They had taken Mama's work away. Well, to Mama's, as they say, to Mama's good fortune, but it is difficult to call this good fortune . . . There, in the maternity hospital, the doctor, the chief doctor died. And they hadn't been able to find anyone there for half a year, and they said to her, "Work, Antonina Konstantinovna, well, in a sense, illegally. And then we'll see what we can do." There was a very good director of public health there, he was a simple stoker, whom they had appointed director of public health in the district. As I recall now, his name was Upalkin. Well, he had such sympathy for us, he was just a simple Russian man. He said, "Konstantinovna, work until we can, maybe somehow we will figure out how to set you up officially. Well, we'll pay you a salary, you will live at the hospital, we'll feed the little ones, we'll feed you whatever we feed the people in the hospital." So, we settled in the hospital. But we also lived in the hospital . . . we lived in an addition. And in the winter . . . it was so cold there that water spilled on the floor would freeze. That's what kind . . . the cold is very harsh there . . . in the winter there, temperatures of minus 30 to 32 degrees centigrade happen, and we were in the same clothes we had left Leningrad in, we had practically nothing. . . .

CF—And did you go to school there, too? . . .

MR—In Danilov, yes. I entered third grade there in school . . . Well, it was the kind of almost rural school there that I, of course, did extremely well. [*Laughs*] They gave me certificates for excellence, but . . . I was already, to a certain degree, a pariah. The little boys, there, fought and swore, they called me . . . this is what they called me: "Akh, you, our little Pole—excuse my language—akh, you, little pisser." They didn't just swear at me, abuse me like they did to the girls in general by pulling their hair, they would, because they must have seen my nationality in the class register where they recorded even both parents' nationalities. . . . I recall there was one redheaded Solovyov, who for some reason really did not like me. And when he was pulling my hair, he always shouted: "Akh, you Polack girl, akh, you little pisser."

CF—And did they know your father was in prison?

MR—Up to then, probably, they didn't know, because . . . it was such a backwoods, it was such a *ba-a-a-ckward,* backward region, there . . . half of the population was illiterate, although they said even then that we had universal literacy, but half the population there was illiterate and half the population even in the town . . . people lived there only around the railroad junction, there was a junction station. There was nothing else, no industry, nothing, people lived on subsistence farming, they kept cows, goats, pigs, chickens, and they cultivated a little land, and they lived off that, because the people were very backward.

CF—And what did your mama do?

MR—Mama worked in the maternity hospital as a midwife. And they gave us, whatever they gave to the patients, whatever kasha, whatever soup they had, they gave it to us, too, to eat. Because Mama was also extremely devoted to work. She was here and there, there was one maternity clinic for the entire district, so, she had plenty of work, of course. Well, and the most important thing is that she had already become very sick that summer already, by the fall, her illness got so much worse that she already had active tuberculosis, and the worst thing is, that they permitted her to work with active tuberculosis. . . . She even worked with pregnant women and women giving birth. And, of course, she also spent time with us, even though she did not spend much time with us, but still she was with us. So, she requested permission, she approached the KGB with a request that they permit her to move somewhere with a warmer climate, because she was very badly off with active tuberculosis. There was really nothing there to treat her with, there was no medicine. . . . But they didn't give her permission . . . Well, and so, by the fall she already was becoming seriously ill, and then she wrote to this friend of hers, Dora Mikhailovna Minkina, that . . . "I will be gone soon, somehow, do something, so that the children somehow don't perish altogether." And then the director of district public health took great pity on her, on Mama . . . he took the trouble to get her permission to go to Yaroslavl for treatment. They even took her, by then she could hardly walk, they took her on a stretcher to the station, and they took her to Yaroslavl. They put her in a tuberculosis hospital there, but her case was already hopeless. They did not cure her there, she stayed there about a month, but they returned her home to die. She already had tuberculosis in her lungs, tuberculosis in her intestines, and, generally, her entire body was consumed with tuberculosis. Well, and this is what the doctors said, that, on the one hand, it was an infection, of course, that had been dormant for some time, but on the other hand, her very acute emotional stress provoked such a, well, severe crisis. Mama tried not to spend time with us once she was very sick. They gave her a separate room in the clinic. . . . a tiny room. She lay in there, and we, children, would only come to see her, my little sister and I . . . Well, and, of course, our life, you can imagine what it was like . . . Papa was gone,

Mama was gone . . . Mama was lying at death's door. But we, we didn't really understand that she was dying, but we did see, of course, that she was very ill . . . so. And we were still waiting . . . for this Dora Mikhailovna. But, all the same, she came, she also . . . she was living with her brother. He had three children, and her brother, of course, was very much against it, and her other brother was opposed. He said, "Where are you going? You are a midwife, you earn only a few kopeks,[7] what are you doing taking on these children to raise, what can you do for them? Nothing." But, even so, she didn't listen and she c- . . . came. Since she didn't have any experience, they made her the district traveling midwife. She would go out to the villages for births, she rode to births on sleds and the like. But she also moved into the clinic, they gave her something to eat, too. That was already 1939, it was a very . . . very difficult year . . . and . . . no, that was in 19- . . . when [Mama] . . . what am I saying . . . she became very ill in 1938. She was already doing poorly when she moved in the spring, she got sick in the fall, she was sick all of 1938, and in June 1939, she died already.

And by that time, both of us girls developed tuberculosis, because she had infected us. I didn't even see . . . and didn't say a final good-bye to Mama, because Mama died without me, because they sent me to Kostroma to a tuberculosis sanatorium for children with the active form of tuberculosis. I was there for six months. So I didn'- . . . didn't see them bury Mama, or anything . . But Innochka . . . but Innochka, well, stayed with . . Mam- . . . at first they didn't take her anywhere, then . . . Grandma . . . Grandma—that was our adoptive mama, she started to try to arrange for her to be assigned somewhere else, because she was also deathly ill. They took her—her brother's wife was a pediatrician, she took her, and she managed to get her into some kind of sanatorium near Moscow. They took her, too, to the sanatorium. As for Mama . . . Mama died.

But Grandma, our adoptive mama told us this: she died very peacefully. . . . She called out to . . . her friend, hugged her and said, "Dorochka, I'm passing, let's kiss . . . If you are not afraid, but this is it, I'm counting on you, that, no matter what, you won't abandon my children." . . . Well, and she didn't abandon

7. A kopek was equal to a hundredth of a ruble; the equivalent of a penny.

us, despite the fact that she . . . earned . . . it's terrible to say . . .
in the money of that time three hundred fifty rubles, which later
was thirty-five rubles, and how much that is now, I don't know,
that was her salary. Well, if she went out into a village, someone
would give her ten eggs, another, a slice of pie, someone else, a
few potatoes . . . because they understood that she was actually
destitute. Well, and for us, for two children, they gave assistance,
since we had become complete orphans, they gave us seven rubles . . . for two children, so . . . Well, I came back from the
sanatorium, that was sometime . . . already, I think, at the end of
July or even the beginning of August, I don't remember precisely,
well, and came in and saw that Mama was no longer there. . . .

No one had told m-me anything, they didn't write to me that
Mama had died . . . nothing . . . They hi-hid it from me, they
didn't want me to . . . But, then, they buried her, so to say, with
great honor. She was very respected there. The women cried a
great deal, those, all the hospital attendants there, and the cleaning women. One of them there . . . Auntie Sonya, she got very
drunk and cursed Soviet power at the funeral, using terrible language [*laughs*], but for some reason they didn't arrest her. She
really cursed, she said, "So, well, why did they destroy such a
woman?" Mama died, she was thirty-nine years old . . . thirty- . . .
it was her fortieth year, she was already in her fortieth year, she
was already in her fortieth year . . .

CF—Excuse me, I am interrupting. During these last months,
when you were with Mama in this little room, how did she act
with you? Do you have any memories of that?

MR—You know . . . I have memories, but very dim . . . Well,
first of all, Mama, somehow, she knew that she was very ill, she,
first of all, tried to spend very little time with us, because she
understood that she could . . . could infect us. Second, she was
hiding from us that Papa had been destroyed, she knew that Papa
had been destroyed.

CF—And how did she know?

MR—She simply instinctively knew this, because . . . but she
didn't know, she didn't receive any kind of documents. I received
a document . . . already after, when . . . they rehabilitated Papa,
a document, false documents about his death, saying that he died
of a brain abscess . . . in 1942, and as for where he died . . . they

had put a line through it. I have his funeral, his, even a funeral document. Well, this was a terrible lie, he didn't live to any 1942, and did not die from any kind of brain abscess. . . . But anyway she knew that he had already died. Well, and she was deeply distressed by the fact that there was no way for her to get in touch with her relatives. Beginning in 1935, she had no contacts of any kind with her family, because . . . . already somehow . . . someone forbade her or she decided this herself, or her relatives had written her. But she did not correspond even with her father, or her mother, or her sisters, she had four sisters, three brothers. She did not correspond with any of them or have any contact with them. And, of course, this was very painful for her, because she loved her family very much, and it was very painful for her. And she knew that her father was very upset, too, and that her mother was upset, my grandmother. And the sisters recounted that they . . . . my grandmother often wept, and was constantly asking where my mama was. And moreover, my mother also lost touch, she also had contact with my father's sister, with Aunt Manya, as we called her. Well, she no longer had any contact with Aunt Manya, no correspondence, nothing. Well, that's how it was. And thus she felt so intensely that she was, so to say, alone in the world, that she had no friends, no one.

Well, we were for her, after all, still little children when she died. . . . I was nine, nine and some years old. . . . And my little sister was of course small, ... she was six years old. . . . I don't know, something warned me, I never asked where my father was, *ne-e-e-ver* . . . never. I never asked that question . . . But in school, I remember, I was once very worried. We had this kind of reader for reading. It had been published long before. And there were prints in it of all these marshals: Tukhachevsky, Blyukher, Yakir.[8] And even in school they made us black them out. Well, and the bolder—I didn't ask a thing—the pluckier children asked, "But why?" "These are enemies of the people." So then I thought, probably, probably, my papa is also an enemy of the people, because he is . . . gone. But I knew that he couldn't be, he simply couldn't be in his human nature, he could not be, never in his life could he be.

8. Mikhail Tukhachevsky, Vasily Blyukher, and Jonah Yakir were senior officers of the Red Army, purged in 1937.

Well, and Mama was very taciturn. She had already seen
through Soviet power sometime in 1935, 1935. Grandmother
said that she already understood, but from the Party . . . she
wanted to leave the Party. But then she thought that this was really frightening, that they would immediately punish her, if she
withdrew. So she was officially in the Party until they expelled her.
But she already deeply disliked Soviet power and really regretted
that she had left Poland, that she had left Poland behind. And
so, when we were left behind, she never said anything about this
either. She only, well, showed us—we had photo albums—she
showed us photos of our father and said, "Here . . . here is your
papa, here, he was a professor." . . .

CF—So, she preserved something for you?

MR—She kept something, yes, she preserved certain papers.
And she showed me and my little sister. My mother's friend told
me even more about my father. She told me what he was like,
how he behaved. . . . Mama was somehow very reserved, she
really was terribly distressed. She endured dual sorrows: first,
that my father . . . that she had lost her husband, and second,
such terrible disenchantment with all her ideals. That was probably a major blow for her, too, because she was such a highly
principled person and very firm. . . . She was buried there in
Danilov . . . During . . . during the war, there, where she was
buried, they buried victims of the Leningrad Blockade, whom
they transported out of the blockade. They evacuated them all
via the northern railroad line, and they died ten at a time, and
they dug common graves for them, and now there is not even a
grave marker for my mother. . . .

CF—So you were about eleven years old when you came
back?

MR—No, I was still ten. . . . Well, and then I understood that
Mama was gone. And . . . her friend said to me, my adoptive
mother, she said, "Why aren't you asking anything about your
mama?" . . . Dora Mikhailovna asked me, "Why aren't you asking anything about your mama?" [*Pause*] I said, "But I ca-can't
ask anything, because I know that Mama is gone." And then
she told me, "Yes, your mama died." And then she told me how
strong she had been while she was dying, but that . . . she had
experienced very great suffering, because there were no painkill-

ers of any kind then, nothing. But she remained very stoic, and just as she had lived courageously, so had she died."

CF—Maya Rudolfovna, I want to ask you, was being tough and stoic a major and desired trait for the Bolsheviks and for the Soviet people? . . .

MR—It was. Of course. It was supported by Soviet ideology, reinforced by Soviet ideology . . . they even used to say, "Let us go into battle for power to the soviets and all die as one. Let's all die in this struggle." . . . Kirsanov[9] wrote, "One should make nails out of these people, there would be no tougher nails in the world." . . . So, people were supposed to be nails. Wel-l-l-l, my papa was not a nail, he . . . he didn't know how to become a nail, but as for Mama, probably, she was like a nail after all.

CF—And you, as her daughter, did you also believe that you should be tough?

MR—Yes, and by the way . . . I was very self-contained in those years. To tell you the truth, I never cried either, like Mama. And in general, I was such a, how can I put it, such a . . . I knew how, I tried, . . . it's not really that I knew how; I tried to defend myself at every opportunity, somehow to defend my dignity, but this was a long time ago, now. But *now,* starting about after I turned seventy, I became different, now I already . . . can cry a little, I can even become depressed. I'm no longer that woman now. I tell you, I was like a tightly wound spring, that has been wound up for a long time, and then is released, and it all comes unwound. [*Uses her hands to demonstrate a once-tight spring that comes undone, opening her hands and letting them flop into her lap in a helpless gesture*]

Well, I was also such a very, very strong woman. Well, first of all, I was a hiker, and a mountain climber, and I even went into the mountains. Even being as frail as I was, I climbed fairly high summits, all of this . . . this was all considered . . . the guys would feel sorry for me, they would say, "You shrimp. [*Laughs*] Why do you have such a backpack?" And I would answer, "No, I will carry the same backpack that everyone else carries." . . . This is the way my family is, my grandfather was the same. . . . Our grandfather was like this. . . . My mama's father. He was very sturdy. He died at eighty-four, while he was scything grain in

9. Semyon Kirsanov, a popular Soviet poet.

the field . . . At eighty-four, he was scything grain . . . And when they . . . the Bolsheviks in 1939 dealt with him that way, they expropriated all of his property and beat him, and they came into the house and broke all the mirrors. They tore everything apart . . . they took photographs out of bureaus or somewhere from a chest, and stomped on them all with their feet, and all of this Grandfather . . . Grandfather endured, Gran- . . . Grandmother for her part fainted, some . . . she had a kind of heart attack. But Grandfather, no, no, no—nothing, he held himself together so steadily. And then they deported them from there, they deported Poles, do you know?

CF—Yes, yes. And where did he go?

MR—Stalin, Stalin removed them . . . Some he, . . . some of those Poles who were Legionnaires and fought against Hitler, they were the first to liberate Vilnius.[10] They . . . . deported them to Siberia. Half of them didn't make it all the way there, so. Well, and those Poles who remained, like our family, for example, in Radun, they showed up there, and they took my uncle . . . my uncle himself did time for ten years in Vorkuta.[11] . . . . He was imprisoned in Vorkuta. He worked in the mines and was in the camps at Vorkuta. . . . He was in the camps for ten years. He was in the camps for ten years. . . . One of my uncles was in the camps in Vorkuta, where they had a horribly tragic fate. His father, my uncle's father, and their three brothers, were all Legionnaires, only he, this uncle of mine, wasn't a Legionnaire. He, when the Germans were there . . . he . . . dressed in a peasant shirt, he was dirty, as if he were the shabbiest one possible, although he was a scholar of agronomy, then later he was a professor, he worked the land. But the Germans came, they kept summoning him, but he said that he didn't understand anything, acted like a village idiot [*laughs*], and they didn't touch him. But these brothers all fought, they fought as partisans. Then when our . . . our Red Army, the Soviet army came, they came there for a second time, they killed them all. There remained only this very youngest, the

10. During World War II, Vilnius was occupied by the Soviet Union from September 1939 to June 24, 1941; by the German army from then until July 1944; and again by the Soviet Union from July 1944.

11. A major Gulag forced labor camp in the far northern region of European Russia.

youngest brother remained alive of the brothers, they killed two brothers and their father.

CF—Let's count, how many persons from your mama's family—

MR——Perished—

CF——perished at the hands of the Soviet government?

MR—By my count, from Mama's family, my uncle perished, then my uncle's father and two brothers—four people.

CF—And Mama.

MR—Well, and Mama—the fifth. Five people. . . .

CF—Yes, but we will return now to you as a little girl. How many years did you live with Dora Mikhailovna and your sister in Danilov in the maternity hospital?

MR—We lived in the maternity hospital. We lived in the hospital. In 1942 . . . Grandmother was very afraid that the Germans would come to Danilov. And they really did start to evacuate certain things, they started to evacuate people. . . .

We lived through 1939, 1940, 1941, 1942. By that time, my little sister was in the sanatorium, and she returned, she was home already. And so she, . . . Dora Mikhailovna, supported these two children on her own. [*Pause*] . . . . In that place, in general, it wasn't possible to buy anything except what people planted and grew on their own. They gave us only horrible bread, like putty. And this was still before the war, in peacetime. It was half potato, with husks, and everything in it. As for the rest, one could, well, it was possible to buy milk there, eggs, potatoes, and beets. There was nothing else there, no sugar, no . . . nothing. Yes, and the people there were so primitive, they didn't make butter, well, it was possible to buy cottage cheese there, some sour cream, it was possible to buy that there. Well, and also this wasn't cheap, therefore Grandmother . . . I don't know what she bought us there, very little. But we ate only because the cook there in the hospital was nice, she . . . even though she was a drunkard, she still felt very sorry for us. She could prepare something a little bit better on the sly and bring it to us. And we ate it, the children. So. So, the world was not without good Russian people, well, so. In 1942, they suddenly arrested Grandmother. . . . All of a sudden, they arrested her. They accused her of performing illegal abortions. She never performed a single abortion in her entire life! And so, imagine, we two children are sitting there, and she was sitting in jail. [*Pause*] The chief doctor denounced her because she would not let him, as they say, shake people down for money. He, for example, for some money, would release someone from the labor front, or from something else. But our grandmother took it upon herself to act against that, this Dora Mikhailovna. Well, and he wrote a denunciation about her, and they arrested her. [*Long pause*] That was in 1942.

Again, it's like a detective story. But I, a girl, in 1942 I was twelve and some years old. I took it upon myself to write a letter, to Molotov, for some reason.[12] [*Chuckles*] Because of all our leaders he somehow impressed me the most. I looked at him and thought that he looked like a teacher, that he was like that . . . And I wrote him a letter, that, well, they had accused my mama, that she was completely innocent, how old she was, that she had been working even before the revolution, she worked, she, ah, she was born in 1899. So she had already worked as a midwife before the revolution, everything. I wrote this letter. The most interesting thing is that I wrote this letter, and in three days it landed in the office. Two days later, they wrote up an order, to Danilov, to release her from jail. Just imagine! And suddenly, I arrived . . . they summoned me there, to this jail. I come in, my grandmother—Mama—comes out and bitterly . . . Mama hugs me and cries bitter tears. I say, "Why are you crying?" She says, "I can't even believe my own happiness, they are releasing me." Can you imagine? And now when I tell this story to a lot of people, people don't believe that in Stalin's time it was possible to write a letter to a completely wrong address. And what did Molotov have to do with this story? Well, it, this letter, passed through that office, obviously, well, and . . .

CF—Question: when you say "office," where was the office?

MR—Molotov's office.

CF—You believe it reached Moscow?

MR—Yes, it reached his office. The most interesting thing is that, evidently, it reached the office and this decision arrived, because they released Grandmother and apologized, and all that. But Grandmother didn't want to work after that.

12. Viacheslav Molotov, then Commissar of Foreign Policy.

CF—Well, of course, with that doctor.

MR—With that doctor. And . . . and they sent her even farther to some small village hospital, to a rural clinic . . . . in 1942.

CF—And you went with her?

MR—And I went with her. She took us two children with her. These were completely wild places, way out, on a swamp, surrounded by forest. There were bears roaming around; I even saw real live bears when I would go to the swamp to gather berries there. And that's where my little sister, I don't know where, she caught diphtheria. [*Pause*] And there, imagine it, a rural first-aid station . . . there was iodine, bromide, camphor, and nothing else, and it was forty kilometers to Danilov. [*Pause*] So they put her, in such terrible shape, on a cart, and I couldn't even sit on the cart, I walked forty kilometers behind the cart.

CF—A marathon.

MR—Of course I walked with Dora Mikhailovna. It was nothing for me to walk, I so loved to walk and knew how, but she was really falling down, and held onto this, onto this, onto the, well, and the driver sat on the box there . . . We took her to the hospital . . . and there was no electricity there, they needed immediately to, how to say it, to perform an insufflation, to remove the phlegm. But there weren't any lights on. No one was there, no help of any kind. She rushes here and there, to the main building, there was one doctor in the main building. He says, "I don't know anything, I don't know how." And she died. [*Pause*] In the morning, Grandmother returns, my, my Dora Mikhailovna comes home, not herself and says, "That's it, Innochka is no longer with us." So, that's how we two were left together. So, those were terrible things that happened.

Well, even before that, we, generally, had been through a great deal. And then they started to bring these Leningraders. And she, Dora Mikhailovna, took care of these terrible dystrophy victims, and after all, among them there were a lot of pregnant women, those who had just given birth, with newborns. So, when she would come back from there, she could not speak at all. She could not even speak. . . .

So that's how she and I lived together until 1945. In 1945, I finished school, well, . . . I finished school without a medal, although I earned only one grade of four (all the rest were fives, the highest grade, for which students received a medal) For some reason, they didn't give me a medal, even though they gave everyone who had only one four a silver medal. But they didn't give me any kind of medal, but that didn't matter to me. I really loved chemistry and studied chemistry. . . . And, there was a very good chemistry teacher, very good. . . . Well, so, this teacher, her name was Valentina Petrovna, advised me to go to Moscow State University, to the Chemistry Department. . . . I had to submit my documents. . . . Then we had to take ten exams. . . . I missed by one point going to MGU. But they invited me to the admission commission, by the way, it was done very well at MGU, they invited me to the admissions commission very politely and said that, well, unfortunately, it's like this, "You are one point short . . . . We offer you the Institute of Fine Chemical Technology, that also involves a lot of chemistry. You can be admitted there without any exams, of course, and by the way, there is a dormitory there. At MGU, if you had been admitted there, it's not certain that you would have received a dorm room or not, because we have a very bad situation with dormitories." . . . . [*Pause*] I went to that dormitory, the dormitory was outside the city, you had to go there on the commuter train, probably thirty or forty minutes. It was a horrible concrete building, there were ten people in each room. I took one look and thought, "How ever am I going to live here?" . . . . And I thought, "But Dora Mikhailovna's brother and his wife said, 'Live with us.'" They let me live with them. In their dining room there was a kind of . . . little couch, a kind of bunk, because when I lay down to go to sleep, I put a chair or a stool, so that my legs had somewhere to fit. Well, I began to live with them, well, this was when there was rationing, imagine what kind of life it was. . . .

CF—And what year was this?

MR—1945, 1946, 1947, and the beginning of 1948. Well, and what was it like there . . . this was an engineering institute, there were many engineering disciplines, and in our province, we didn't have any instruction in drafting whatsoever, I had no concept of drafting at all. . . . Well, and all the subjects, for example, math, well, I no longer got fives there, but I did get four. But in drafting, I couldn't do it at all. . . . Well, so, I passed the first year, moved on to the second, and then I passed the second year, and moved into the third year. And then in the third year, one had to submit a project. This was an engineering discipline. I understood that I wouldn't be able to do it, I wasn't up to it. Yes, and there was another interesting factor: when I was studying in Moscow and lived with this uncle, but later . . . at first I lived at that uncle's, but then the next year a friend of my mother's took me in, a friend from Mama's institute days, who at some point studied with her again somewhere, at that time they had been that kind of friends. She had her own three children, and she took me in as a fourth. . . . The second year and the beginning of the third, I lived with them. Well, and it was better for me to live with them, because they fed me there, whatever they had, they would give me. Sometimes, it is true, just a potato with pickled tomatoes, but, all the same, they would give it to me. . . . Well, and I left that institute. The institute gave me, I still have this document, saying that I had completed two years, two years entirely and was studying in the third year, so. And where did I go? I decided that I would transfer to Yaroslavl. . . . I thought about it, I thought, as always, how was I to live? What could Dora Mikhailovna send me? In the best case, she would send me ten rubles, and that was the very best-case scenario, and there were months when she couldn't send me even ten rubles. And then I went to the Pedagogical Institute. . . . And I began to work in Danilov, in the same school where I had once studied. And I worked there, I taught math and, very interestingly, I taught German language. Why did I teach German? Because, when I was a child I hadn't gone to a kindergarten, and even though my nanny was raising me, my parents believed that this was not enough, so they took me to a German language group. . . . And I spoke German completely fluently, and even wrote well, I learned the basics even more quickly in German. . . . I knew a lot of little songs, fairy tales in German. So it was easy for me to do well in German in school, and in the institute, I never had any difficulties. And then, when I came to Danilov, they gave me math. And there was no one there who could teach German language for half a year, and they gave me German *laughs*], and I taught German too. . . .

CF—May I ask you? This, such a chronicle from 1937 to 1942, five entire years of losses and deprivations . . .

MR—It wasn't only these five years, I would say that it was until . . . this lasted until 1947 even. . . .

Break to give Maya Rudolfovna a rest. We ate lunch with her husband, Mikhail Naumovich, and her son, Rudolf Mikhailovich ("Rudik"). Maya Rudolfovna continued to reminisce during lunch. In the following segment of the interview, I asked some questions referring to comments she had made during lunch.

MR—When I studied in Moscow in the second year, that was in 1946, my aunt, who had lived in Estonia, she . . . during the war, she had fled to Sweden with three children. And all this time she was searching for me through the Red Cross. And she found me and wrote me a letter and sent me marvelous photographs of . . . of all the children and of all . . . of everyone, who . . . who . . . who existed. And I was so happy, and I even showed everyone in the institute. Then one unfortunate day, I was called to the dean's office, a man also in plainclothes, and he says, "Are you carrying on correspondence with someone abroad?" I said, "Yes, I correspond with my aunt." He said, "Show me your correspondence." I said, "Well, I don't have it with me." And he says, "But you know that this is not permitted, that your aunt lives, she fled Estonia, that means she's a traitor, she is a Fascist, she is a traitor to the motherland, and correspondence with her is impossible. If you want to be in the Komsomol, and if you want to be a student, then you must cease this." And that was it. He says, "I order you to destroy all this, completely." And I destroyed all of it . . . That was that. So . . . it was like that. That was in 1946.

CF—Do you consider that to be the final loss? The Soviet government gradually stole . .

MR—It stole everything it could. It stole my mother [*coughs*], it stole my father, it stole all my mother's many relatives, it stole this, this, my father's only sister. . . .

CF—Well, I want to ask anyway, but were there any happy moments among all these losses?

MR—You know, happy moments, of course, youth is youth, this was a happy time. And then, too, where I lived, there was wondrous nature. And in childhood, I grew up in the forest. I really loved the forest. When I was a child, my friend and I would walk, we would walk many kilometers into the forest. And then, when we were in school, they used to send us . . . Oh, yes! and I haven't told you yet how during the war I worked on the rail-

road. . . . During the war, they made all of us work. They made
some do the weeding, ... and they made us fertilize the cabbage
with human excrement. I couldn't do that. I asked to do a different job, and then they assigned me to count trains. . . . A train
would arrive, and you needed right then to . . . . the counters go
out to the train junction and write down how many train cars
there were, how many loads there were on these cars, what kind,
what kind of steam locomotive, everything. . . .

CF—And did you feel that you were making some kind of
contribution to the war or no, none at all . . .

MR—None at all, somehow, you know, that people say that
they had some kind of great patriotism, and all that. I want to tell
you that, on the one hand I somehow, I was probably very stupid, and somehow I wasn't even afraid of the war. We even had
bombings there several times. For some reason, I wasn't afraid,
during bombings, I would go out and stand on the porch. Everyone was hiding, but I'm standing on the porch. [*Laughs*] So
there. But, to say that I was particularly worried about the war,
well, of course, when they began to liberate cities, one after another, then this, of course, was very joyful, this was joyful. But,
then again, so, we really loved . . . I loved the forest, and then I
was with that other train counter, that . . . hmmm . . . well, even
so, I was very young, and it was also very dangerous there: we
would record one train, it would begin to move, and immediately
we go under the wheels of the next train to record—how we
weren't crushed, I don't know. Then some director of the station
came and took me away from there, he understood that this was
impermissible.

Then they ordered us to prepare things for the Workers' Supply Office, to pick mushrooms. We were supposed to hand in a
certain number of mushrooms, or so many kilograms, I no longer
recall. We would go into the forest, into such distant forests for
mushrooms. So we would walk, we children, of course, would
sing, pick berries, and there were lots of all sorts of animals there,
all kinds, and moose, and there were rabbits, and small deer, you
could see anything! That was really joyous! Later, when I entered
the institute, I began . . . I joined the hiking group. I also really
loved this, these hikes, all of these . . . tents, you could be cut off
from all life anywhere. Now that was a joy. That was fun. . . . I

was a, as we say here, a woman "on the go." I would go somewhere every year, and sometimes even to two places.

*We broke here for the evening and overnight. When we began again
the next morning, I asked Maya Rudolfovna to return to the topic of
nature, because she had talked about nature at length at supper the
evening before.*

MR—I really love nature. I spent my childhood and adoles-
cence among the forests in the northern Yaroslavl region, in nature. The forests there were marvelous. There, you walk in the
forest and then there's a kind of little . . . a little clearing. . . . It's
planted in, it might be oats or it might be barley, or something
like that. Aah . . . y-yes . . . I don't know how it is now, but the
rye grew so tall there, it almost reached my ears. And I really
loved to walk along the path through the rye. And such tall rye
all around. And usually on the edge of the path some cornflow-
ers always grew, such little dark blue ones. . . . The sun would be
so clear, such a clear day, and so, you would walk through this
rye field, and it was so joyful, so comforting somehow. But then,
in the spring, for example, when the earth was just thawing, the
larks began to sing, and we would walk in the field just to hear
the larks singing. In childhood we also really loved not only . . .
the forest itself, but we really loved any living thing that was
there. My girlfriend and I really loved to find birds' nests, but
we *never* destroyed them or touched them *ever.* But we liked
them so much, that at first we would find eggs somewhere, some
speckled or smooth ones. We would remember the spot. Then,
after some time, we would come, and there would be the baby
birds sitting already. We would watch them. Then later we would
come, and there the grown birds would already be sitting, and
they would even peck at us with their beaks, and they would go
"op-op," they would trill, reacting to us, we really loved that.
But then there was the kind of forest there where there were a
lot of cuckoos. For some reason, they were usually in the pine
woods, so, for some reason, you would find them less often in
the leafy forests. And so, whenever we would come to a pine
forest, a cuckoo was always going "cuckoo." And we always
asked her, "How many years do we have left to live?" We have
such a superstition in Russia that if you ask, "How many cuckoos?," you will live as many years as the number of times the

cuckoo goes "cuckoo." . . . We also went out for mushrooms, and we even knew all the mushrooms in childhood, absolutely all of them, there are places there filled with mushrooms. Boletus mushrooms grew there, and butter, milk-agaricus cap, and, and orange cap boletus, and brown cap boletus, and saffron milk cap mushrooms. We really loved to gather mushrooms not only because this was food, but because it was so interesting. It was like this, boletus mushrooms grow this way. First you find one slightly bigger mushroom, as if it were the head of the family, and next to it you walk along and find a bit smaller one, then still smaller, and still smaller, and it's like a whole family. Well, and later, when we were already teenagers, they sent us to pick mushrooms for the Workers' Supply Office, for the railroad, for the canteen at the railroad. We would go out early in the morning with baskets into the forest. . . . Also, when we were still children, we had to do such a terrible job. The school was heated with firewood, and the children themselves had to prepare the firewood for the school. We, already at age thirteen, went to the forest with a two-handled saw, my friend and I. The two of us would saw . . . We didn't know how, of course, we tried to saw dead wood, but that was the kind of area where, for some reason, there was very little dead wood. It was very hard to find this dry wood. We would find a live tree, just the same. We tried, of course to find not very thick ones. And so, we two would cut it down. Of course, it was terrible, the saw would stick, we were afraid we would pull it out, well, and then we wouldn't know how to pull it down. Sometimes we would pull at it so badly that it would just fall . . . we didn't know how this tree would fall. Then it would fall, and we still had to saw it up into pieces like this, and then out of these pieces, we had to stack a cord like this. The two of us had to prepare two and a half cubic meters of firewood. . . . Well, on the one hand, of course, this was very difficult and even dangerous work, but on the other hand, it was interesting. At times, it was joy, truly, truly extraordinary. And then, I also went with Dora Mikhailovna to births in the villages. This was also very interesting. On low sledges, but in the winter on . . . in the winter on low sledges, the kind, you know, of sledges, the kind of sleds, low here and there on top a little taller, well, and such . . . We would put on, she would put on a sheepskin, and we would also take some kind of sheepskin for me, because we had to ride for thirty kilometers, for forty kilometers, pulled by a horse along what you could hardly even call roads, in the winter on a sledge. In the summer we road on a cart, we simply sat on a cart.

CF—Just the two of you?

MR—No, we had a driver, there was always a driver, a little, old, lame peasant. He was assigned to the hospital, the water there . . . he delivered water, he was the water carrier, and he was also this, the driver. He took us to the villages. In the villages, for example, it was very interesting for me. . . . Generally all the farms in that area were subsistence farms. The peasants at that time were still, this was before the war, there were still rather a lot of peasants. They lived very . . . how to say this, disconnected, they were even disconnected to a certain extent from Soviet power. They lived far from the railroad, far even from any district center, in the forests, and it was rare that any authority ever got that far. . . . Once I . . . . had a very close encounter with a bear. When Grandmother and I lived in the rural hospital, in that place where she was working as a physician's assistant in the local hospital, there was an enormous swamp, a terrible swamp. And around that swamp there was forest, a section of the forest. The raspberry patch was very big, such tall, tall branches and a whole lot of raspberries. And, so, once I was going to pick raspberries. I was picking raspberries. And I heard something, *right there,* rustling, something wasn't quite right, a rustling and some kind of noise, as if something were breaking. I looked around and I saw that it was a bear, and the bear, the bear was treating himself to raspberries, I . . . Well, the bear saw me. Well, so he's looking at me and I'm looking at him. Well, then I got scared, I didn't know how I got out of this . . . out of this raspberry patch, . . . And after that, after I had already encountered that bear, I saw him a second time, but I wasn't alone that time, I was with the cleaning woman of this hospital. . . . But this woman wasn't afraid of bears, she said to me that, well, "Don't be afraid." This is what she told me: "Don't be afraid! In the summer, bears are full and they won't touch anyone. They'll only, well, tear up some oats in the fields, different kinds of berries, and they'll eat little animals, but they won't attack a person." So, that's about nature.

CF—You said that when you are feeling very good now as an adult, you dream about the nature there.

MR—Yes. You understood me perfectly. I dream . . . and I dream especially about one very beautiful place: it's a mixed forest, and in the middle there is a clearing overgrown with oats. And I dream that I have, it is as if I have come to this clearing, I have sat down on the edge, and I am watching, I am watching there. There are small leaves, and there are lindens, and maples, and birches. I sit and a breeze stirs up, it's the north after all, and a breeze rustles the leaves, and so the field also is rising and falling, all the oats, all of it. And even in my dreams, I am simply so happy. Then I wake up and think, "How sad it is that I will never be able to see any of this again."

CF—Well, now we will return to prosaic life. Here is a question that I ask everyone. How do you remember Stalin's death?

MR—Stalin's death . . . I learned about it in Danilov . . . By the way, almost no one had a radio there. There were very few radios around there, of course no one received any kind of newspapers. I was in a class . . . with my pupils . . . and suddenly the door opens, another teacher comes in, all in tears, in anguish, and says, "*Oy!* Josef Vissarionovich has passed away!" . . . And right there in the class there arose such a howl . . . and I went numb. [*Pause*] Then all the children were crying, and I started to cry. But, why was I crying? From some kind of shock or . . . and I even . . . I simply couldn't grasp how it could be that suddenly such a luminary . . . and . . . and despite my family I already knew that this was a luminary, how it could be that he was suddenly no more. Well, then I cried for a bit, I calmed down . . . I calmed down. Then the next day, there was a meeting. There, around the train station there was this railroad square, there was a club there. They ordered everyone they could to go to that place. The teachers were there, and the children were there, and the railway workers were there, well, and they put on such a grandiose meeting. But just then I remembered myself [*laughs*], just then, when they began with these words—this glorification started, I stood and thought, "How can it be, that even if this had been a good person, how could you put on such pomp on the occasion of his death?" There were so many people—and this was March by the way, it was bitterly cold, it was probably thirty degrees below zero centigrade. We stood there for an hour and a half, and after this standing . . . . to honor the death of this villain, I was very scantily dressed. . . . I got so sick then, that I was in bed sick for

two weeks after the death of this Stalin. The simple folk said
various things. While we were standing there . . . in the crowd, a
very old, very old railway man was standing with me, who had
probably seen tsarist power, and had been a railway man back
then. And so he says, "Ha, is this someone to feel sorry for or cry
over?" Well, we, of course, were no longer crying. The children
all wanted, they already lost interest, they would rather go home.
Well, so that's how I received the death of Stalin . . . . somehow
with complete indifference. But even so, there was one thing that
I was glad about. Because the Doctors' Plot[13] was closed. And
the Doctors' Plot was just before Stalin's death. And . . . and
then they made my Dora Mikhailovna and all the medical workers go into the outpatient clinic, and they were all supposed to
curse the enemies of the people and to praise this same—what
was her name, Milkalenchuk or God knows who—who had unmasked these enemies of the people to Stalin. Well, and when this
all happened, and they asked everyone to say something, to say
what they would. But my Dora Mikhailovna said, "I don't believe this." [*Pause*] Then she came home and said to me, "They'll
probably arrest me, because I couldn't contain myself and said
that I don't believe it." But they didn't touch her, because then . . .

CF—Well, wasn't she Jewish?

MR—She was Jewish, yes. She, and she even knew, there was
another Jew there when we were in Danilov . . . . So, it was
this [Jewish] pharmacist who told Grandmother—he evidently
had some channels of information, connections—that "Dora
Mikhailovna, get ready for them to deport everyone Jewish."
Therefore she was very afraid of this. She was afraid that they
would exile Jews. But I said to her, I said, "I'll go with you." She
said, "No, you will not go with me. Somehow you will stay here.
You'll move into an orphanage or somewhere, but you will not
go." . . . and when that . . . Grandmother was so happy, well, I
was also very happy, because I thought, "It's over, since he has

13. The Doctors' Plot was a fabricated conspiracy that led to the arrest of Jewish doctors who allegedly had plotted to kill Soviet leaders. Announced publicly
in January 1953, the Plot signified a major feature of accelerating official anti-
Semitism. On the "Doctors' Plot" see Jonathan Brent and Vladimir Naumov, *Stalin's Last Crime: The Plot Against the Jewish Doctors, 1948–1953* (New York:
Harper Perennial, 2004).

died already, then this case won't happen. There'll be no deportation of Jews to anywhere." . . . . So that's how I reacted to Stalin's death.

CF—Did you try to join the Komsomol when you were in the institute?

MR—I entered the Komsomol even before the institute. I was still a schoolgirl. I was fourteen years old. You could enter the Komsomol from age fourteen. And back then it was like this: everyone in the class was supposed to enter the Komsomol. . . . Those who *didn't* enter the Komsomol? I don't even know what would have happened to that person, because there was no alternative: either you entered the Komsomol or who knows what? . . . Well, and when we all . . . submitted applications that we wanted to serve the Party, the government and all, and they invited us to the district committee of the Party, a group of children, there were several of us. The school director came with us and the secretary of the Party organization [*chuckles*] . . . . When they read my file there in the district committee, I had written there that I . . . . well, there was no way for me not to write it, because everyone knew I was repressed, because I had been exiled there. I wrote that I was repressed, that my father . . . I didn't write that my father was an enemy of the people, I wrote that I didn't know where my father was, that he was probably in a camp. That's what I wrote. Then, when they started to admit everyone into the Komsomol, there were four or five persons, they admitted everyone. But for some reason they made me last in line. I thought it was because of my last name, that I was the last in line because I was named Yakson, I thought, well, "Ya," well, "Ya" is the last letter in the alphabet. But then, this girl there, the secretary of the district committee, said, "Well, but we will not admit Yakson for now, because her father is an enemy of the people." But our school director was such a tiny woman, she was very fair-minded and had a very sharp tongue. She spoke out, "What do you mean you won't admit her? According to the law, the daughter does not answer for her father. And this girl is a very good student and so active in school life." She's talking as though I'm practically the ornament of our school. "How will it be, if you don't admit her, think about it. What will the other children say if you don't admit her to the Komsomol?"

CF—And how did you feel when this was happening?

MR—I myself sat there, listening to all of this, and all the children were sitting there listening. . . . Everyone sat there, listening. . . . Well, and that's what she said . . . and the other woman thought about it and said, "Well, of course, we can admit her." And they admitted me to the Komsomol.

CF—And do you remember your emotions when you were sitting there listening to this?

MR—I listened . . . In the first place, for some reason I was not very frightened, I thought, "Well, how can it be that they will admit everyone, but I will be left outside the Komsomol?" . . . And then this really hurt me; I thought, "How can it be that my father is an enemy of the people?" Because I had never heard that in my life at all, no one had ever said that about him anywhere, not there among the people we spent time with or anywhere else, they never uttered such words, that he was an enemy of the people.

It was the first time I heard this. . . . I blushed easily as a child. Later the children said to me that I was as red as a beet. My . . . cheeks were burning, and my ears were burning, and my face. I was completely, well, shocked. Then I could barely recover . . . I came home and told Dora Mikhailovna. She began to cry . . . and she cried very, very hard and was very stricken in grief. And she hugged me so tight, she was a very loving person, and said, "You poor, poor girl." That's what she said to me. . . .

CF—And how did you view Soviet power overall at that time? . . .

MR—[*Pause*] It is hard to say, really. Personally, I kn-knew, that Stalin was a scoundrel. That I already knew, . . . probably, . . . well, maybe from the time I was sixteen, well, maybe from age fifteen, I don't recall exactly. But, on the whole, I trusted Soviet power. In general, I had no such notion that this was all so wrong . . . that this was all, all of this was very bad, although, life had been very horrible, but I didn't think that way. And I . . . didn't think that, until the time when that guy at the institute made me destroy all my letters and documents, so that's when I came to hate Soviet power.

CF—Immediately?

MR—Immediately. When I came home, I was then living with my mother's friend. She had a son, Vladik. I told him. And he says, "You didn't know until now that they are all scum, that they are all slimeballs!? . . . You don't have any brains, if you didn't recognize this until now!" So from that point I already understood that this was all not right. That was probably in 1947.

CF—And when did you begin to correspond with your aunts in Poland?

MR—Oh! That's a whole long story! With my aunt in Poland, how was it? I myself wanted to find the Poles. But how? Somehow I couldn't figure out how to do it. Well, I went to Poland as a tourist in 1961. I was there in Zakopane, in Cracow, everywhere, I traveled around all of Poland, so. And then I decided, I'm thinking, "Aha, well, since I'm in Poland, I'll go to the embassy . . . to the Russian embassy. Well, in order to . . . to the Russian embassy, because I didn't speak a word of Polish then. . . . Well, so, I thought, "I'll go to the Russian embassy and ask them to find my relatives." . . . And when I arrived in Warsaw, I immediately, I had a friend named Seryozha,[14] and we, I was afraid to go to the embassy by myself [*laughs*], and this Seryozha accompanied me. We arrived at the embassy, and I wrote an official statement that, so, I was looking for my relatives. I listed them all: my grandmother, my great-grandmother—although I feared that she was no longer alive. She . . . her name was Telentiia, and she was no longer alive. Well, I named my grandmother, these four aunts, and two uncles. Back then I knew all their last names . . . . They said to me, "Yes, yes, we will . . . arrange a search, and we will try to find your relatives." This was . . . this was in 1961. So, he says, "We'll find your relatives, at the very least, since your uncles have the same last name, and they live in Poland, then we will surely locate them." I was so happy when I left. After that, I traveled around all of Poland, and then returned through Warsaw. I went to the embassy again, again with this Sergei, I was afraid. I arrived and they told me, "You know, unfortunately, we didn't find anyone. There is no one in Poland. But, you know, probably, your relatives . . . there were some people who immigrated to England. After all, Poles . . ." I say, I even said, "That can't

14. A diminutive of Sergei.

be! Because, I say, my aunts lived in such an out-of-the-way little place, from which there is no way they would have gotten to England." . . . Somehow this got all mixed up, and I forgot about it. Then this . . . 1970 [*pause*] what year? 1971 . . . 1971, 1970 or 1971, I don't recall exactly. One day I'm sitting at home, the telephone rings . . . we had a telephone there, the telephone rings, and they say, "Are we speaking with Maya Rudolfovna?" I said, "Yes." "You know, you are invited to the KGB . . . for a conversation." [*Pause*]. Well, I even started panicking. I'm thinking, I still have a son, he was so little, I think, "Well, that's it. Someone wrote some kind of denunciation about me and they are going to lock me up." So, I arrive, some petty officer is sitting there, in civilian clothes. I sat down. He says, so very politely, he says, "Tell me, Maya Rudolfovna, do you have relatives in Poland?" I say, well, it was already useless to hide it, I say, "Yes, probably," I say, "but I did not locate them." He says, "You did not locate them, but they have found you. [*Pause*] Your aunt Maria Konstantinovna Leskovskaya located you through the International Red Cross." . . . . He says, "Well, so, we found your aunt, there, your aunt has been found, she is looking for you. Well, what do you think, will you keep in contact with them or not?" [*Pause*] I say, "I have dreamed my entire life, for me this would be a great joy to find my relatives." He says, "Well, if that's the case, then of course." And that was all. He says, "So here is her address for you, her telephone"—she lived in Szczecin—"get in touch with her." Well, I came home, I was beside myself with joy and called Szczecin immediately. At that time, it was rather difficult to call, but all the same, I reached her. Well, and when my aunt took the receiver, she says, "Mayechka!" and began to cry. She couldn't even speak. She says, "We so want to see you! We have all been looking for you. I searched for you." By the way, every time she came to visit the graves, well, Soviet authority had permitted her to come for two or three days to the graves in Radun, to the grave of my grandmother, great-grandmother, and her husband's relatives. . . . And each time that she came, each time she looked for me there in Russia. She says, "Mayechka, come to us right away." I say, "Aunt, soon," this was winter, it was winter, it was already, I think, October, and I said, "Aunt, I have a small son and I can't come in the winter." She says, "Well, then, at least, come as soon as you can. We so want to see you, it's just impossible to wait." Well, after that, we started to call each other by phone, and after that, I received a stream of letters, they all wrote me.

CF—How old were you then?

MR—Well, how old was I? This was in 1971, probably, and I was born in 1928. So I was forty-two years old, probably, approaching forty-three. Well, and so, I could hardly, hardly wait for warm weather. Then I call my aunt and say that I didn't have anyone with whom to leave my son. I couldn't leave him with Grandmother, after all, with Dora Mikhailovna. The child, Rudik was five and a half years old. . . .

Maya Rudolfovna describes how they decided she would travel with her son, and how she got a passport and tickets for the two of them.

We arrived in Warsaw . . . . My aunt is standing there, she was so beautiful, a lady with such presence, she's holding, . . . she knew that I was traveling with a little boy, she's holding a bunch of balloons and she greets me. Well, I was so happy that she met me. We stayed for two days in Warsaw in a hotel, two or even three days. Then all the relatives started to telephone: one uncle, another uncle, one aunt, another aunt [*laughs*], asking me to come visit them as soon as possible. . . . The uncle who would be second to host us was the one who had been imprisoned in Russia in a camp, I told you that he was in the camp in Vorkuta for ten years. He lived in Cracow, he was a professor, chair of the department of Russian literature in the pedagogical university. . . . Well, I was his guest for a full week. Then he put me on a train, he and his daughter, and I went to Szczecin [*laughs*], no, from there I went to Poznan first, to Poznan, so, to that, my most beloved cousin. She lived there. There they also met me, they gave us a very warm welcome. Their children came to the station. . . . And her husband also bought Rudik presents, all kinds, all kinds of presents for the child, all kinds of toys. . . . Then we went to a different aunt. [*Laughs*] Another aunt lived in Bytgoszcz . . . They gave us a very warm welcome there, too. . . . We went to Torun, from Torun to Szczecin. Overall we traveled for two whole months. . . . A family had materialized, everyone. . . .

CF—How do you think the status and experience of your childhood as a child of enemies of the people affected your life?

MR—Two factors influenced my life . . . the first factor was
that I wasn't Russian. And although they endlessly talked about
the friendship of peoples, still I always felt during my entire life
that I was not Russian. . . . That was the first factor, which I
felt even, at some point, I told you, in Danilov in school I began to sense that I wasn't Russian. . . . If my father had not
been repressed, then, of course, my life would have taken shape
completely differently. For that reason, I understand that, having
lost my parents, and so terribly, and ooooh, so terribly. They
didn't simply die. Having lost my parents in that way, I could
not ever forget that for my entire life. I *NE-E-ver* forgot! Not for
one minute. For that reason, wherever I was—even on vacation,
let's say I'm having fun, I'm enjoying myself, I'm sitting with a
group of friends—then, when I am left by myself, immediately
the thought would come to me that this had happened. . . . I
myself always felt that I was not, as . . . Gorky's[15] hero says,
"I live on the wrong street." And for my whole life, I have felt
that I live on the wrong street. I live with this feeling, probably,
well, it's even difficult to say since what age I have lived with this
feeling. Probably since age eleven, since ten, or eleven. Then, of
course, this also sometimes affected me even professionally. For
example, they used to give teachers awards . . . all kinds. And
so that first school director, under whom I worked at School
No. 6, nominated me for an award, she wanted to give me a
token of honor, a kind of small order as a respected teacher.
So, but at that time my father had not been rehabilitated yet.
I had to write down my biographical information, I wrote it.
"Don't," the director said to me. "Don't write this, no one will
know about that. Don't you write it. Simply write that you have
lost your parents, your parents died, and that's all." But I wrote
that my father was repressed in 1937. Then they gave awards to
the teachers, but they didn't give me one. Later, well, I did a lot
of work beyond the framework of my . . . even beyond my job
responsibilities. For example, the Academy of Pedagogical Sciences was examining the work of School No. 1, and I worked in
School No. 6, and they invited me to be on this commission, and
I worked in the morning at my school, and during the second
shift, I worked in that school. Well, and later when this work

15. Maxim Gorky, a prominent Soviet writer. The quote Maya Rudolfovna
has in mind comes from *Foma Gordeev: The Man Who Was Afraid*.

was finished, they told me, "Well, we'll give you an award for this." But they didn't give me any kind of award. None at all. . . . Well, and I should say that a few people, for example, the dean of the faculty under whom I worked, he simply despised me to a certain extent. He was always saying, "Oh! Maya Rudolfovna," if for some reason I raised some question, he would say, "Oh! What of it? Who do you think you are?" And I always said, and I say, "I so regret that you did not sit in a camp, like my father, they should have put you there!" . . . . So that's what I would say to him, and then he would shut up. He was a little afraid of me and my tongue, he was afraid. Then my director really wanted to admit me to the Party, he would say, "If you join the Party, then Maya Rudolfovna"—or "you," he even used the informal "you" form with me—"if you join the Party, you'll have a good career and so forth." Well, I, of course, had no thought whatsoever of that. That same Sergei Andreevich and that secretary of the Party organization would say to the director, "Well, how can we admit her into the Party, if her father was repressed?" And by that time my father was already rehabilitated. . . . Why did I need the Party? But the secretary of the Party organization basically said this to me, when we were talking once, she says, "I don't consider any of the people who aren't in the Party to be people!" Therefore, of course, I felt this. But the most important thing is that the person himself felt internally, felt internally that he was awful. How can I put this? That he was cheated by fate. Such is the forest, as the Poles say, such is fate.

CF—Well, and now the last question of our interview: What are you most proud of in your life, or what has given you the greatest satisfaction?

MR—The most important thing, all the same, I don't even want to say that I am proud—proud, probably that's not the right word. I so loved my work . . . that's one thing. It wasn't a burden for me, although I worked rather a . . . lot—that's one thing. Second—that, even so, I had a beloved person with me, because Dora Mikhailovna died only in 1983. . . . She loved me very, *very* much. I always, I even always used to think, why does she love me so much? And so, I would always think, "My God, well, however hard it is for me, still, at least I have her." . . . This was always a great consolation for me. It gave me a certain equilibrium. Most of all, of course, I was proud of my work.

M. R. Levitina with her husband and son, Smolensk,
2007 (Photograph by Cathy A. Frierson)

Well, then, I would also [*laughs*] boast a little for being, well, a
hiker, that I was so daring, that I could go with the children, that
I walked across all of the Smolensk region on my own two feet.
I would think, no one . . . and there were teachers even younger
than me, even men . . . I would think, "No one else is hiking, but
see how I can, see how I can." . . . I would think, "Well, so, no
one can do this, but I can." Well, and then there is the fact that
when I was in those mountain camps, I was also very, generally,
so frail, but even so I tried never to lag behind the others. Always, I would think, "Well, so, everyone is going up, . . . we were
always tied to ropes with carabiners, here would be a carabiner,
there a rope, and I would think, "Oh, look how I can even do
rock-climbing with ropes, and nothing is happening to me, and
I am going up such tall peaks." That made me very happy. Well,
so, there were these three things: work, this hiking and mountain
climbing, and the fact that Grandmother was with me. . . . She
always gave me some kind of support. That was a consolation for
me in life . . . a great one. Well, and then, of course so was Rudik.
I also had with Rudik, we have, you could say, a boundless love,
a love that knows no boundaries. It, of course, I want to say, is
not good, neither for him, nor for me. This is even a harmful love
[*laughs*], if it is possible to put it that way, that sometimes love

also is, when it is very great, is not good, that it should be moderate. So, that's why I even often think, I think, "And if something happens to me," then eh . . . eh . . Rudik tells me, "Mama, I won't survive that." So, therefore, I would, of course, like to live longer [*laughs*], that's why.

CF—Thank you, Maya Rudolfovna, for this interview, for the fact that you could pass all of this on to me. This is very significant for history and for me personally. Thank you very much!

MR—Thank you, that you are doing this work, because in Russia, very few people are interested in this. And the fates of these children interest few people, few people.

CHAPTER TEN

"Well, probably, essentially, they destroyed my life, of course"

VLADIMIR VALERIANOVICH TIMOFEEV

Vologda

July 4, 2005

Transcribed by Anna Manoilova

Introduction

Vladimir Valerianovich Timofeev was born in 1937 in the medieval city of Vologda in the Russian north. He described himself as a descendant on his father's side of noble military servitors to the tsars, from Ivan IV (the Terrible) in the sixteenth century through World War I in the twentieth century. His mother came from a prosperous merchant family in Vologda. Vladimir Valerianovich's father was arrested in 1940, accused of spying for Poland, for no apparent reason other than that he had learned Polish in his prerevolutionary military school. Timofeev, his older brother, and their mother subsequently endured grinding poverty. His mother was silent on the subject of his father's arrest, leaving young Vladimir Valerianovich in ignorance about his family roots into his early teens. By then, he was malnourished and wearing rags. It is difficult to imagine the scene of such a degraded youth learning from an elderly neighbor that he was the descendant of noblemen who had served the tsars for over three centuries. As relatives of an enemy of the people, Vladimir Valerianovich

236

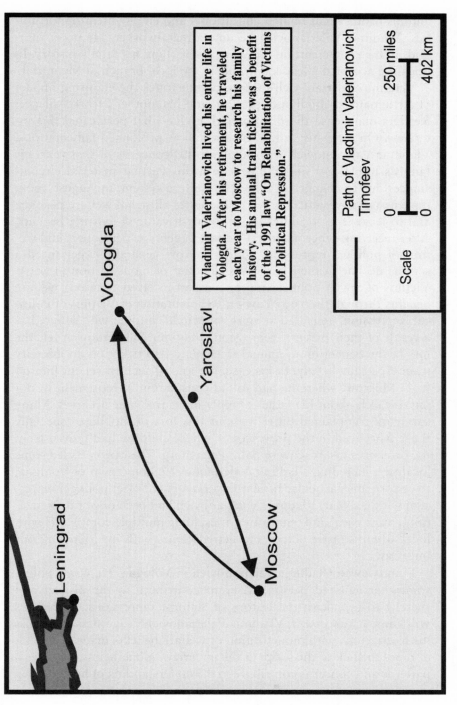

Vladimir Valerianovich lived his entire life in Vologda. After his retirement, he traveled each year to Moscow to research his family history. His annual train ticket was a benefit of the 1991 law "On Rehabilitation of Victims of Political Repression."

Leningrad

Vologda

Yaroslavl

Moscow

Scale

Path of Vladimir Valerianovich Timofeev

0   250 miles

0   402 km

The journeys of Vladimir Valerianovich Timofeev, 1937–2005 (Map by Eric Pugliano) and his brother had limited educational and employment opportunities. Vladimir Valerianovich became a metalworker. He never married. In his retirement, he turned to researching his family history. In 2005, he accepted a leadership role in the local branch of Memorial.

Vladimir Valerianovich's interview illustrates the enduring impact of a stigmatized childhood, poverty, and his mother's fearful silence. Readers may sense the distress and anxiety that permeated this interview. On tape, his words rise and fall as prolonged lamentations. Vladimir Valerianovich was captive to his concerns of that year: his family's noble past and the decline in his current material circumstances due to changes in the social welfare system. In August 2004, the Russian government voted to monetize all social welfare benefits, and to leave it to localities to set the cash value of existing benefits. After receiving generous social welfare benefits as pensioners and victims of political repression, child survivors generally experienced a serious decline in their benefits as a result of monetization in 2005. Victims of Soviet political repression had received generous welfare benefits through the 1991 Law on Rehabilitation of Victims of Political Repression, amended in 1995 to include children who suffered as a result of their parents' repression. Vladimir Valerianovich felt the loss of the benefit of an annual free round-trip ticket on an intercity train especially keenly. In his case, the loss of such travel cut him off from Moscow, where he had found consolation in retirement in doing research about his father's family in central state archives. Many survivors complained bitterly about this loss of mobility, especially those who lived in the provinces or whose children had moved from the provinces to Moscow or Saint Petersburg. Their protests led some localities, including Vladimir Valerianovich's hometown of Vologda, to restore this particular benefit to survivors of Soviet political repression within a year. Vladimir Valerianovich had been one of monetization's most vocal and tenacious critics, filing multiple complaints with local administrative offices. He shared copies with me following our interview.

I interviewed Vladimir Valerianovich in Vologda. He was a polite, somewhat agitated person, eager to contribute to the project and thereby to broadcast the history of Stalinist repressions. As readers will immediately detect, Vladimir Valerianovich's eagerness to discuss his frustrations with monetization of welfare benefits made it difficult at times to stick to the script of the interview. Nonetheless, his speech patterns and concerns contribute to the understanding of how lifelong loss, confusion about one's family history, and stigma may affect one's understanding of the world.

CF—Please explain how you became a child of the Gulag.

VV—Well, maybe, I would start a bit earlier. That is, with my ancestors. So, our family has been notable from the sixteenth century. My ancestor was a prominent official in the government of Ivan IV. But my ancestor, my great-great grandfather Timofeev Vasily Ivanovich, achieved the greatest success. He is buried in the necropolis of the Novodevichy Monastery.[1] He was that kind of person. So anyway, of course, his service was easier for him, because he was related to the counts Vorontsov, and to the Dashkovs, and to the Kropotkins.[2] So, at twenty-nine years old, he was already, better to say, he began his military service from childhood, in essence. He completed the Cadet Corps, then his service was in the army. So, from diapers to death. He was born March 27, 1783. In '99—1799—he graduated from the Cadet Corps, where his service as an ensign began. At twenty-nine years old, he was already commander of the second battalion of the Life Guards, he was a colonel. The regiment was formed in October 1811. Almost the entire regiment fell at Borodino.[3] My great-great grandfather was wounded and in treatment for more than a year. And, so, he received the Order of St. George the Victor, Fourth Degree. And consequently they immediately gave him command of the Latvian division. Well, then, after that, his service was up and down, but not so bad, because he had all those medals, such as St. Vladimir of the First Degree. His title was General of the Infantry, Commander of the Sixth Infantry Corps, now it's not the Infantry, but the Army Corps. He was the Governor-General, later, so, here in Russia the regiment was made precisely into the Lithuanian Life Guards in 1834 in the Moscow Legion, the Moscow Regiment, so my great-great

1. Novodevichy Cemetery is one of the most prestigious of all historical cemeteries in Russia. Located in Moscow, it is adjacent to the equally famous sixteenth-century Novodevichy Convent. The necropolis is the gravesite for many of Russia's most elite military and cultural figures of the nineteenth century.

2. Famous noble families from the eighteenth century forward.

3. The battle at Borodino is considered the first major engagement in the Napoleonic invasion of Russia in 1812. Leo Tolstoy immortalized Borodino in *War and Peace.*

grandfather, that was later, really, and so, it was like this, so, the Lithuanian Life Guards Regiment was partially expanded, one battalion went into the formation of the Gotfield Legion, and a new Legion, a new Moscow regiment was formed. Why do I stress the importance of the Moscow regiment guard? Well, at that time, the chief of the Life Guards of the Moscow regiment was Mikhail Pavlovich, Nicholas I's brother. When Mikhail Pavlovich died, Nicholas I made my great-great grandfather the chief of this regiment. Well, so, this was a great honor. He had another great honor, many persons had the Order of Aleksandr Nevsky, but only a very few had the diamond version of it. In 1843, he received the Aleksandr Nevsky, but in 1846, he received the diamond badge to add to the medal. He died on January 5, 1850. He was buried at the Novodevichy Cemetery, in this monastery's necropolis. The tsar's family is buried in the monastery itself, but the army, on the grounds of the necropolis. . . .

CF—May I ask—

VV—So, to continue, why were all of our ancestors thereafter in the military? I, when I had special welfare benefits, used to go to Moscow and work in the archives.[4] I had a pass for indefinite access to the archives, I found a few things, and learned about a few things, but since they stripped me of all my special welfare benefits, I haven't gone now for eight or nine years. That is, when before I used to travel to Moscow for free twice a month, now I have to pay 552 rubles to go to Moscow, and my entire pension is 2,500 rubles. So that you can't go, all the more so since they've taken away all, all my special welfare benefits. . . .

CF—May I ask you about your family? When did you find out about your family history? Did your parents discuss this with you during your childhood, or not?

VV—No, somewhat later. This is how it happened. Well, my father had a certificate of nobility, he was registered in the official genealogical record of the nobility, and photographs. All of our antiquities were seized, all, all, all, the photographs, the certificate of nobility, the genealogical registration. But my neighbor saw all of this. He told me, I was already somewhere in my teens, I was

---

4. He is referring to the provision in the 1991 Law on Rehabilitation of Victims of Political Repression granting victims one free round-trip intercity train trip per year.

fourteen or fifteen, when he said to me, "So, your ancestor was buried in Moscow, in a monastery." But he couldn't remember in which monastery. . . . So, a bit later, I started to travel to Moscow quite frequently, for work. And so, I looked around in all the monasteries. And I found him in the Novodevichy Monastery.

CF—Well, good. So, let's go to the twentieth century. Tell, me please, what your family history was immediately before the revolution, during the revolution, in the 1920s and so on.

VV—Understood. So, this was the history. My father was born on April 20, 1890. He married at age twenty-four. When he was a year old, his father died—my grandfather, that is. Well, so, my grandmother married a major excise tax collector. They traveled around to different cities. In the end, they stayed in Tashkent. He, my father, graduated from the Tashkent gymnasium, then, he went to Moscow and graduated from the Alekseevsky Military Institute in 1914, a military institute. And so, he was slated to be a lieutenant, in a school of ensigns. He was a professional military man. He received a purely military education. But in the war, in October, he was very seriously wounded in the shoulder, with injury to his kidneys, and a contusion in his head. He received medical treatment for more than a year. But at the same time, he was sent as an army officer, they sent him at first to the Simbirsk Cadet Corps to teach, and then they sent him directly to the Khabarovsk Cadet Corps as a teacher. He knew . . . . five languages, including German, French, English, Mongolian, Polish, which was also his undoing just a bit later. So, and he, so, he taught four subjects: mathematics, Russian, German, and drafting in the Cadet Corps. . . . He was married to an Uskevich. Mama was his second wife, his first wife was Uskevich. I don't know much, just what was in the transcript of his interrogation. . . .

When the Bolsheviks came to power, the Cadets Corps was transformed into a military high school. And he and three other officers stayed on to teach. . . . So, Kolchak[5] arrived and drove all these four officers out, he expressed his distrust of them, even though they had done nothing; they were occupied solely with

5. During the Russian civil war following the Bolshevik October Revolution, Admiral Aleksandr Kolchak of the imperial navy established a competing government in western Siberia in alliance with other opponents of the Bolshevik regime.

studies. So, and then, when the Japanese came, my father joined in the defense against them. In 1922, when they drove out the Japanese, the Bolsheviks had already arrested my father, but then, after torturing him, he was all but dead, they let him go. In 1929, there was a persecution of officers. He was arrested again in 1929. They gave him three years; he served out a year, then, they released him after a year. . . . The first time he was in prison somewhere in Khabarovsk, they released him, too. I don't know exactly where, because when they arrested my father, and they arrested him . . . August 14, 1940, I was only a year and seven months old. So, I didn't know because I was so little. Later, then, when they let me see the KGB files, then I found out a little, I understood a little. Later, the third time already, when the Polish campaign ended,[6] and he had known the Polish language his entire life, then someone squealed on him, and he was arrested as a Polish spy. During the arrest, they took away all documents, all photographs, all notes, they took away everything, everything, everything. After numerous searches, I found none of this, neither photographs, nor the certificate of nobility, nothing. I went to the very top of the security organs in Leningrad and Moscow.

CF—Where was he living when he was arrested in 1940?

VV—So, he was born in Kherson Province. His father was also in the military, so, ... My mother met him in the year she finished her philosophy degree; this is interesting. My grandfather was a senior salesman in Vologda in the merchant Sergei Vasilievich Perlov's store. This Perlov was a very successful tea merchant. My grandfather was, of course, very well off—he earned three hundred rubles a month. A cow cost eight rubles, so he rented everything, there were lots of all sorts of things, which later were sold, because we had nothing to live on in those years. And after the revolution, my grandfather with his education in economics worked as a stoker for some boss, overall, my grandfather also had a rough time of it, regardless of the fact that he worked a lot. And when they arrested my father, then we, five people, essentially lived solely on my mother's salary—I, my brother, old Lyudochka, my mother—we lived on one salary.

6. The Soviet invasion and occupation of eastern Poland following the signing of the Molotov-Ribbentrop Pact in 1939.

CF—Well, okay. You were about to describe how they met each other.

VV—Yes, my mother graduated from a cooperative technical school and worked near Stalingrad, she worked in the city committee of Red Army soldiers. She met my father there, and they married in 1933. And they came to Vologda. So, my brother was born in 1935, I was born in 1937, both of us were born in Vologda already. So, my father had a degree in economics, but it was rather difficult in Vologda, so he worked as the chief accountant in civil enterprises, in one place, then another. That's how their acquaintance began, my mother worked as a junior bookkeeper, he was the senior bookkeeper. So that's how they met and got married. His execution was also in Vologda.

CF—You were describing how many people there were in your family?

VV—So, we were, so, my mother and father, the two of us—my brother, now deceased, and I, my grandfather and grandmother. Well, so, six people. When they arrested my father, Grandmother had no income at all, and as for Grandfather. . . . In essence, we lived, already, the five of us . . . . We were in rags, we wore whatever fit, things, a bit of a dress, all this kind of thing. Well, and of course, we were hungry.

CF—May I ask, what were your first memories? As a child?

VV—Ah, you mean childhood memories, . . . My relations with the neighbors were okay. . . . We lived in a two-story wooden house. My grandfather rented this house at first, but then they kept reducing, reducing, reducing our allotted living space, and three small rooms remained, three small rooms, in which five of us lived.

CF—You mean that at first you possessed the entire house?

VV—Yes, my grandfather rented it, my maternal grandfather.

CF—And he rented the entire house?

VV—Yes, the entire house.

CF—And after this, so, you gradually lost your . . .

VV—Yes, against our will, they reduced, reduced, reduced our allotted living space, and so, well, they utterly reduced our living space. We were left with three small little rooms.

CF—In the same house?

VV—In the same house. So, well, I started school. Well, as far as I recall, I helped soldiers too, I helped dig garden rows, to clean up and all that. Well, and already in about the seventh grade, from age seven, from the second grade, there already began to be summer vacations. All the children relaxed, there, they had children's camps, Pioneer camps, but my brother and I sawed firewood, split it. That is, well, I remember this perfectly, when I was ten years old and my brother was thirteen, the two of us sawed with a hand saw, split, and stacked five cubic meters of firewood, I would not be able to do that now. You would come home dead tired, sleep, and in the morning head out to work again. This was during summer vacation.

CF—Were you paid for this or were you doing this to have fuel to heat your house?

VV—I sawed and split firewood for other people, for other people for money, I was a lowly paid hired hand. . . .

CF—Did you ever have any questions such as "Where's my father?" . . . .

VV—. . . . My mother was terrified about her fate, and for that reason, she maintained a spirit of loyalty, allegiance. And that is why she was bringing us up in an atmosphere of loyalty. I was in the Pioneers. They accepted me to be a Pioneer. I became a Pioneer. I have not been in the Komsomol for a single day. The children of the enemies of the people were not really welcomed. So I was not in the Komsomol.

CF—When did you find out that you had a father and that he was an officer?

VV—. . . . I waited with my questions, but then no one said much of anything. Well, later already, sometime in the early 1950s, when I was already twelve or thirteen.

CF—Did you know this earlier, but not understand?

VV—Neither my grandfather nor my grandmother said that he had been repressed, where he was, why, nothing . . . Later already when, well, when things began to . . .

CF—They told you that he had been arrested. But when you were small, how did they explain your father's absence? Didn't you notice that you didn't have a father?

VV—Well, how could I not notice, of course I noticed. Everyone has parents . . . well that was life already. At that time, the war was going on, many men were at the front. I also thought that my father was at the front, that he had perished there. But no one told me anything. My mother was afraid, Grandfather and Grandmother did not say anything about this. It was later already that I found out my father had been repressed.

CF—And how was it with your older brother?

VV—My brother was older. . . . Three and a half years older. . . .

CF—So, three and a half years older, that means he must have remembered . . .

VV—Yes, but he was also small. That means that when father was arrested, so, he was born in 1935—in 1940 he was five years old, which he also remembers. He remembers practically nothing. So, there. . . . By the way, I can't complain about the neighbors. The neighbors treated me very well. . . . My brother also completed seven grades and, so, our life was really hard. An uncle on my mother's side lived in Yaroslavl, and my brother left, moved to live with my uncle's family in Yaroslavl so that our situation would be easier. When he finished trade school, he was sent to Lvov to serve, and from there, they took him right away into the army. He participated in the Hungarian events of 1956.[7] Well, he said so, and he began to drink, he began to drink. He was so smart, he worked, of course, as a trade school graduate, in supervisory positions.

CF—Well, this means that at around twelve years old you found out that your father had been repressed in 1940?

VV—At the beginning of the 1950s, Stalin was still alive.

CF—And you said that there was an atmosphere of loyalty in your family. Does that mean that you were loyal to Stalin?

VV—I used this word, that is, loyalty to the Party, and all that, she was afraid [his mother], that, well, . . . But when Stalin

7. In October–November 1956, reform-minded socialists and students in Hungary called for major governmental reforms to replace Soviet-imposed, Stalinist-style rule. They staged major street demonstrations. Ultimately, the Soviet Union responded by sending in Red Army tanks, resulting in the deaths of thousands of Hungarian citizens and hundreds of Red Army soldiers.

died, akh, it was like, Praise God! I kept playing with the other kids, I did not sob about Stalin's death. I accepted this "sorrow" calmly. . . .

CF—Why?

VV—I already knew. My father . . . when, so, my grandfather died in 1930. He was already seventy years old—he was a professional military man, he had fought in the First World War, . . . There was no reason, for no reason. Well, it was already obvious, that there was no reason for the arrest.

CF—I see, for no reason. When you found out that your father had been under suspicion, that he was an enemy of the people, did you feel any kind of discomfort?

VV—I did. . . . Well, we lived in very, very severe poverty. Therefore, when I was sixteen years old, I had to find a job. So. Well, what kind—I was small, puny. Well, so, they set me up as an apprentice to a mechanic, a German. This German was very competent, smart. Everyone in Vologda took their motors to him, and he repaired them very well. . . . Well, he was so strict, it was very hard with him, of course, very hard. So, well, I was his apprentice. Well, I'll say this. They didn't especially spare us. Like, the KDM-46 engine—that was from a Stalin tractor—it had a hundred-fifteen-kilogram (two-hundred-fifty-three-pound) flywheel. So they would put it on my shoulders, it weighed almost three times as much as I did, but I, so, was bent over—I carried it. Then I was close to being army age, I was already a half-invalid from such backbreaking work. . . . The work was hard, so dirty. I think, well, I need to study. I entered evening school. Back then, so, there weren't any accommodations for students. You went to work by eight o'clock in the morning. At seven o'clock, around seven p.m., you came home from work. So, from seven o'clock, school. Classes lasted until eleven o'clock, but, so, you had to go to work. I went to school, but I didn't set the world on fire. I abandoned my studies. Well, I wasn't even in any condition to work, and then I had to study too.

CF—I want to go backward with a question. . . . Did you understand yourself that you needed to apply to join the Komsomol?

VV—I tried, I tried, but the most interesting thing turned out to be, well, so . . . I went to work for the Northern Communal Worker [*Severnyi Kommunar*], well, as an apprentice milling machine operator. I qualified as a milling machine operator, after that I landed at an auxiliary workshop. At first as an apprentice metalworker, then as a metalworker. Well, I was the very best metalworker, I was on the "Honor Gallery"—my photograph was on the Honor Gallery. And this, the Party organizer comes up to me and, well, "Enter the Party. So, you're our best specialist, write up your biography, we'll give you a recommendation." I write, "My father was arrested under Article 58." "Oh, no, no, no, no, we can't, we can't, we can't, we can't—such a background." Then, when rehabilitations started . . .

CF—How did you feel?

VV—I felt spat upon. From my head to my toes. Exactly like that. How could they do that? So, I took this very hard. Later, when rehabilitations started, this very same Party organizer comes up to me and gives me an application to join the Party. I looked at him and sent him down the staircase. I was exactly the same person I had been before. Nothing about me had changed. Before, it was impermissible, but now it's possible? Now I don't want to. I completely removed myself from any association with the Party. . . .

CF—Please say, if you recall the moment, when exactly did you find out that your father had been repressed? . . .

VV—Well, in essence, it was my neighbor, Shishigin Vladimir Aleksandrovich, who told me, he lived next door . . . It was he who told me—Later I was able to pull it out of Mama's lips. She wouldn't say anything. So. Well, and what was there to say, what. When I—all doors were closed to me. There were limitations on everything. . . . "Not allowed. Not allowed. Not allowed." My brother wanted to attend a military school. "Not allowed"—they forbade him. Well, overall, so, they didn't destroy his life, but at the same time, he did begin to drink. Well, nothing interested him anymore—not just military school—in general. Probably he wouldn't have been admitted because he was a half-invalid—his legs were injured. So. That he had a hard time. So I'll say this . . . all of this left its mark—"Not allowed. Not allowed. Not allowed." There were absolute limitations on everything. Like, as I said, I wanted, for example, to study in Vologda. At that time there was a Cooperative Technical School and a Veterinary Technical School. And a Railroad Institute. I didn't even consider the Railroad Institute because of my health. I didn't want to go to the Veterinary School. But I didn't want to go to the Cooperative School either. So where then? It was possible to go to a different city, but Mama couldn't give me any help at all. I couldn't go to another city. I couldn't leave. I had no other option but to do the hardest kind of work. So, I worked, I stuck to it. It got to me, it really got to me when I was a handyman, it's dirty work. . . . Overall, it was very hard.

CF—And your mother, when did she die? At what age?

VV—My mother . . . . She died August 15, 2000. Literally in my arms. For six months I was with her night and day. Day and night I spoon-fed her, changed her bed three to four times a day. I bathed her and cleaned the linens. So . . . and she died in my arms. She no longer recognized anyone.

CF—How would you describe the most important, chief consequences of her status as a wife of an enemy of the people? . . .

VV—Well, there's the fact that she essentially worked at one job. Yes. Later, already, later—in the 1960s—she changed jobs twice. And her last job was with the railroad. She was a senior bookkeeper for the railroad. Well, she, so, retired at sixty-three . . . and already, so, there weren't any kind of repressions. . . .

CF—Were there times when you discussed your family's history with your mother?

VV—Not many.

CF—Not many?

VV—Not many. Mother tried to avoid conversations. She avoided serious conversations. She was afraid. . . .

CF—Then how did you learn about your father?

VV—Well, first of all, the neighbors told me bits and pieces. Especially the neighbor who had been my father's friend. A lot. Well, so. I wanted to find something interesting. Well, and he showed me my father's personal case file . . . my brother asked for it at the KGB. And there's a paper that my father was rehabilitated in 1965 in the absence of elements of any crime. So. That means she had already found something out. But I decided to go further, to really get to know. And, so, I wrote a letter to the KGB. A piece of paper arrived. So, on such and such a date, signed by someone. I went, I asked. They gave me my father's case file and a separate room. There was also a staff person and his assistant present. And so I looked at the notes of all the interrogations and his biographical data.

CF—By the way, how many hours did it take to read the entire case file?

VV—There was no limit on how long I could take. I just read one set of case materials. The questions. One question—then the answer. There was nothing of the kind in it. People I didn't know. Well, so, Petrov, Ivanov, I didn't know who these people were, or what—So, well—I read it—who dumped on my father, that's also not exactly clear. This didn't particularly interest me. As for biographical information, there was nothing. An interesting thing was that there wasn't a single photograph. Only my father's labor book and a family photograph. As if into thin air. And my brother was also there. . . .

CF—What were the main consequences for you of all this?

VV—Well, probably, essentially, they broke my life, of course. My life was broken. I couldn't get started. I wanted to see my father's file earlier, but it was all classified. Then later they gave permission. But then it was closed, closed, I couldn't find any answers. I wanted to find out more—"Not allowed." So this neighbor of mine—I told you that I was already working—I harrowed, I mowed. I worked. All day long I worked hard in these years, somewhere. . . . Well, and I finally managed to dig down to my great-grandfather's grave, that is, my great-great-grandfather. I liked it. It was as elegant as could be. Of the very, very, very first order. There were fifty graves. My great-great-grandfather. There were fifty graves. Well, his was generally . . . like a king's. . . .

CF—And when did you, yourself, marry?

VV—But it turned out that I didn't marry. . . .

Timofeev continued to talk about problems with his benefits, complaints against bureaucrats, how unfair the system was, and all the efforts he was making to get someone to listen to him.

CF—I thought that you might want to add something about the repressions, about their significance, about the fate of the repressed. Do you want to add anything for American students? For our American students, what would you like to tell them?

VV—I just want to tell them not to forget about us, not those only who are in Russia, but also abroad. For people to know what happened here in Russia. Well, I believe that genocide, it even now continues. Do you understand? I'm telling you that they don't have enough conscience to treat us right!

Appendix I: Amendments to Criminal Code (Decree of December 1, 1934)

Decree of December 1, 1934: "On Amending the Present Union-Republic Codes of Criminal Procedure," in *Ideas and Forces in Soviet Legal History: A Reader on the Soviet State and Law*, ed. Zigurds L. Zile (New York: Oxford University Press, 1992), 304.

The Central Executive Committee of the USSR decrees:

To amend the present union republic codes of criminal procedure with regard to investigation and trial of cases of terrorist organizations and terrorist acts against the functionaries of Soviet power:

1. Investigation in these cases shall be concluded in not more than ten days

2. The indictment shall be handed to the accused twenty-four hours before the trial.

3. The cases shall be tried without the parties present.

4. There shall be no cassational review of the judgments or acceptance of petitions for clemency.

5. The sentence of the supreme punishment shall be executed immediately upon the rendering of the judgment.

Appendix II: Excerpt from NKVD Operational Order 00447

Excerpt from NKVD Operational Order 00447 (J. Arch Getty and Oleg V. Naumov, *The Road to Terror. Stalin and the Self-Destruction of the Bolsheviks, 1932–1939* [New Haven: Yale University Press, 2002], 473–77).

July 30, 1937

Moscow

4. The families of those sentenced in accordance with the first or second category are not as a rule subject to punitive measures. Exceptions to this include:

a) Families, members of which are capable of active anti-Soviet actions. Pursuant to the special decree by the three-man commission, members of such families are subject to being transferred to camps or labor settlements.

b) The families of persons punished in accordance with the first category, who live in border areas, are subject to expulsion beyond the border area within the republics or regions.

c) The families of those punished in accordance with the first category who live in Moscow, Leningrad, Kiev, Tbilisi, Rostov-on-the-Don, Taganrog, and the districts of Sochi, Gagry, and Sukhumi, are subject to expulsion from these centers to other regions of their choice, except for districts near the border.

5. All families of persons punished in accordance with the first and second categories are to be registered and placed under systematic observation.

Appendix III: Operational Order No. 00486

Operational Order No. 00486 of the People's Commissar of Internal Affairs of the USSR No. 00486, "On the Operation to Repress Wives and Children of Traitors to the Motherland," Informatsionnyi biulleten' Pravelenia Mezhdunarodnogo istoriko-prosvetitel'skogo, blagotvoritel'nogo i pravozashchitnogo obshchestva, "Memorial" No. 12, 1999: 19–21, in S. S. Vilensky et al., compilers, *Deti GULAGa, 1918–1956* (Moscow: International Democracy Fund; Hoover Institution of War, Revolution and Peace, Stanford University, 2002), 234–38.

15 August 1937

Upon receipt of this order, begin the repression of wives of traitors to the motherland, members of right-Trotskyite espionage-diversionary organizations, convicted by the Military Collegium and military tribunals in the first and second categories, beginning from August 1, 1936. . . .

11) The Special Board shall review the cases of wives of convicted traitors of the motherland and those of their children older than fifteen years of age who are socially dangerous and capable of committing anti-Soviet acts.

12) Wives of convicted traitors of the motherland shall be subject to internment in camps for terms not less than five–eight years, depending upon the level of social danger they represent.

13) Socially dangerous children of convicts, depending upon their age, their level of danger, and the potential for correction, shall be subject to internment in camps or NKVD corrective labor colonies or

253

to settlement in special regime orphanages of the People's Commissariats of Enlightenment of the Republics . . . . details about reporting and storing case files, transportation of wives to camps

Placing Convicts' Children

19) All child-orphans remaining after convictions shall be placed as follows:

a) children aged from one to one and a half years up to three full years of age—to orphanages and nurseries run by the People's Commissariats of Health of the Republics at convict residential centers;

b) children from three full years to fifteen years of age—to orphanages run by the People's Commissariats of Enlightenment of the Republics, region and districts (according to their assigned distribution) and outside Moscow, Leningrad, Kiev, Tbilisi, Minsk, coastal and border cities.

20) The cases of children over age fifteen shall be decided individually. Depending upon their age, their ability to support themselves independently by their own labor or to live as dependents with relatives, such children may be:

a) sent to orphanages run by the People's Commissariats of Enlightenment of the Republics in conformity with Art. 19, pt. "b:"

b) sent to other Republics, region and districts (to centers excluding those cities listed above) to be placed in jobs or to study.

[The articles prescribing the fate of very young children displayed the extremes to which the Soviet party-state was willing to go to separate children from the influence of their "criminal" mothers. The decree offered detailed instruction on how to isolate each such young child from anyone he or she knew.]

21) Nursing children shall be sent with their convicted mothers to camps, from which, when they reach the age of one to one and a half years, they shall be transferred to orphanages and nurseries run by the People's Commissariats of Health of the Republics.

22) Children from three to fifteen years of age shall be supported by the government.

23) In the event that other relatives who have not been repressed wish to take on the orphans that remain as their full dependents, this shall not be hindered.

[The order also defined what became of children separated from their parents. Children's reminiscences sometimes include their own or their relatives' experience with these procedures.]

Preparing for the Reception and Distribution of Children

24) In every city where this operation is being carried out, there shall be specially equipped:

a) Receiver-distributors, to which children shall be taken immediately after their mothers' arrests, and from which children will then be sent to orphanages; . . .

27) . . . distribution of lists of the children's names and ages, etc. In the lists children shall be indicated in groups, constituted so as to ensure that no children who know each other or are related to each other shall land in the same orphanage.

28) . . . communications among NKVD offices and orphanages

29) During the arrest of convicts' wives, children shall be taken away from them together with their personal documents (birth certificates, school documents), . . .

35) The operation to repress wives of traitors to the motherland who have already been convicted shall be completed by October 25 of this year.

36) Henceforth, all wives of traitors to the motherland who have been unmasked [and] of right-Trotskyist spies shall be arrested simultaneously with their husbands, in accordance with the procedures established by this order.

People's Commissar of Internal Affairs of the USSR
Commissar General of State Security YEZHOV

Chronology

1914	August	Imperial Russia enters World War I
1917	February	February Revolution; Tsar Nicholas II abdicates throne; provisional government established
	April	Vladimir Lenin returns to Russia and calls for revolution led by Bolshevik Party
	October	Lenin and Leon Trotsky lead Bolsheviks in revolutionary overthrow of provisional government
	November	Elections to Constituent Assembly
	December	Security police—Cheka—established under leadership of Feliks Dzerzhensky
		Lithuania declares independence from Russia
1918	February	Estonia declares independence from Russia
	March	Bolshevik Russia signs Treaty of Brest-Litovsk with Germany, ending its participation in World War I
	April	Civil war rages inside Bolshevik Russia
		White Armies intervene against Bolshevik Red Army
	July	Bolsheviks execute Nicholas II and his family
		Communist Russia adopts first constitution
	August	Military food requisition squads begin to seize peasants' grain
	November	Latvia declares independence from Russia

1919	Council for the Defense of Children established
1919–1920	Civil war turns in Bolsheviks' favor
	Poland invades Ukraine, beginning the Polish-Russian war
1921	Bolshevik Red Army secures victory in civil war and war against Poland
	Tenth Congress of the Russian Communist Party (Bolshevik) held
	Introduction of the New Economic Policy
	Outbreak of famine in Bolshevik Russia
	Council for the Improvement of Children's Life established
1921–1927	New Economy Policy in force
1922	Criminal Code issued
	Show trials against Socialist Revolutionaries and Orthodox Church figures
1923	Concentration camp established on Solovetsky Islands
1924	Lenin dies; Succession struggle ensues
	Constitution of USSR is ratified
1926	Trotsky removed from Politburo
	Family and Marriage Code ratified
	Census of the USSR carried out
	Electoral instructions issued
1927	Trotsky expelled from Communist Party
	Peasants' grain deliveries to state contract
	Joseph Stalin triumphant in Communist Party leadership
	Local campaigns against wealthy peasants—"kulaks"—emerge
1928	Fifteenth Congress of Communist Party launches First Five Year Plan, calling for collectivization of agriculture and rapid industrial development
	Urals-Siberian Method of heavy fines and taxation imposed in some areas to extract grain from peasants
	Trotsky exiled from Moscow
	Shakhty trial of engineers
1929	Stalin breaks with Bukharin
	Trotsky is exiled from the USSR

	"Voluntary" collectivization becomes forced collectivization; target set for 85 percent collectivization during First Five Year Plan
	Stalin's fiftieth birthday; the Cult of Personality begins
	Politburo decides to launch a campaign to liquidate the kulaks as a class
1930	Mass deportation of kulaks and their families to uninhabited regions to establish "special settlements" begins
	Trial of the Industrial Party
1931	Liquidation of kulaks continues
	Collectivization continues
	Trial of the Mensheviks
1932	The Riutin Affair
	Famine breaks out in Ukraine and North Caucasus
	Internal passports introduced for urban residents
1933	Famine in Ukraine and North Caucasus continues
	Cleansing, or "Purge," of the Communist Party
1934	Seventeenth Party Congress
	Criminal Code includes Articles 6, 7, and 35 on "socially dangerous elements"
	Establishment of Special Board of NKVD
	Murder of Sergei Kirov
	Stalin decrees summary justice and execution
1936	Show trial of Old Bolsheviks Lev Kamenev and Grigory Zinoviev
1937	Terror launched through Order 00447
	Decrees on fate of wives and children of enemies of the people
	Mass deportation of Koreans from eastern coastal areas
1937–1938	Mass arrests of enemies of the people; NKVD seizure of their children
1938	Show trial of Nikolai Bukharin, Karl Radek, and other Old Bolsheviks
1939	Molotov-Ribbentrop Pact (Nazi-Soviet Non-Aggression Pact)

		German invades Poland from west
		USSR invades Poland from east
		USSR annexes areas of western Poland
1939–1940		USSR war with Finland
		Many Red Army soldiers captured by Finland sent to GULAG after Soviet Union wins the war
		First waves of deportations from newly occupied territories
1940		USSR occupies and incorporates Latvia, Lithuania, Estonia, and Bessarabia
1941	Mid-June	Mass deportation of citizens from Latvia, Lithuania, Estonia, and Bessarabia to Siberia and Kazakhstan
	June 22	Germany invades Soviet Union
	September	Mass deportation of Soviet citizens of German descent to special settlements
		Leningrad under siege
	October 16	Moscow panic as Germans approach city
	December 5	Red Army begins counteroffensive at Moscow
1942	July	Order 227—"Not one step back!"
	August	Germans reach Stalingrad in Operation Blue; five-month urban Battle of Stalingrad begins
1943	February	Germans surrender at Battle of Stalingrad
	July–August	Soviets win Battle of Kursk
	November–December	Mass deportations of entire national groups in North Caucasus and Crimea
1944	January	Siege of Leningrad ends
	August	Red Army moves into Polish territory; Warsaw uprising
1945	April	Red Army takes Vienna
		Red Army begins assault on Berlin
	May 8–9	Germans surrender to the Allies
	May	Filtration/repatriation of Soviet POWs and slave laborers from German-occupied and German territories begins
1946–1947		Famine strikes USSR
1948		Solomon Mikhoels murdered
		Andrei Zhdanov dies of heart failure under disputed medical care
		The Leningrad Affair

1949	Rearrests of wives of enemies of the people Arrests of adult children of enemies of the people Stalin's seventieth birthday: climax of Cult of Personality
1953	Public announcement of Doctors' Plot Stalin dies Party-state issues amnesty for many nonpolitical prisoners All Doctors' Plot defendants rehabilitated Georgy Malenkov becomes Chairman of Council of Ministers M.V.D. Chief Lavrenty Beria arrested Nikita Khrushchev becomes First Secretary of the Communist Party Special sentencing board abolished
1954	Rehabilitation of the repressed segments of the population expands
1955	Party-state issues amnesty for persons accused of collaboration during World War II Party-state issues amnesty for special settlers Central organs of the Procuracy order regional and local procuracies to improve and speed up review of cases/applications for rehabilitation
1956	Nikita Khrushchev delivers "Secret Speech" to Twentieth Party Congress
1964	Nikita Khrushchev removed from office
1964–1982	Leonid Brezhnev rules as General Secretary of the Communist Party
1982–1985	Yury Andropov, then Konstantin Chernenko, rules as General Secretary of the Communist Party
1985–1991	Mikhail Gorbachev rules as General Secretary of the Communist Party
1991	Supreme Soviet passes law "On Rehabilitation of Victims of Political Repression" Gorbachev resigns USSR disintegrates Boris Yeltsin assumes power as president of the Russian Federation

1995   Constitutional Court of the Russian Federation
                      rules that children of victims of political repres-
                      sion also qualify as "repressed" and worthy
                      of formal rehabilitation and accompanying
                      benefits

Selected Glossary of Names, Places, and Institutions

Akmolinsk Camp for wives of traitors to the motherland: Prison camp in Kazakhstan for wives of arrested enemies of the people/traitors to the motherland. Also known by its acronym: ALZhIR.

Lavrenty Beria: Director of the security police/internal affairs, 1938–1953.

Butyrka: Central transit prison in Moscow.

Collectivization: Policy in which individual peasant farming was eliminated in favor of collectivized landholding, agricultural labor, and ownership of livestock and equipment. Imposed at an accelerated rate under Joseph Stalin.

Dekulakization: The elimination of prosperous peasants—so-called kulaks—through expropriation, arrest, forced resettlement, and, sometimes, execution. While the early Soviet state under Vladimir I. Lenin attacked kulaks, the wholesale assault was declared policy by Stalin in December 1929.

Gulag: Acronym comprising the first letters of the administrative department—Main Administration of Camps—which has come to refer to the entire network of penal institutions managed within the Commissariat or Ministry of Internal Affairs.

Kolyma: Major Gulag labor camp complex in the far northeastern corner of Siberia in the USSR.

Komsomol: Communist Youth League. A youth organization of the Communist Party for teenagers and young adults.

Lubyanka: Headquarters of the security police (NKVD, KGB, now FSB) in Moscow.

Pioneers: The Communist Party youth organization for children in primary school.

Vorkuta: Major Gulag labor camp complex, primarily devoted to mining, above the Arctic Circle in European Russian area of the USSR.

Nikolai Yezhov: Director of the security police/internal affairs during the Great Terror of 1936–1938.

Index

BOOKS IN THE ANNALS OF COMMUNISM SERIES

Stalinism as a Way of Life: A Narrative in Documents, edited by Lewis Siegelbaum and Andrei K. Sokolov

The Stalin-Kaganovich Correspondence, 1931–36, compiled and edited by R. W. Davies, Oleg V. Khlevniuk, E. A. Rees, Liudmila P. Kosheleva, and Larisa A. Rogovaya

Stalin's Letters to Molotov, 1925–1936, edited by Lars T. Lih, Oleg V. Naumov, and Oleg V. Khlevniuk

Stalin's Secret Pogrom: The Postwar Inquisition of the Soviet Jewish Anti-Fascist Committee, edited by Joshua Rubenstein and Vladimir P. Naumov

The Unknown Lenin: From the Secret Archive, edited by Richard Pipes

The Voice of the People: Letters from the Soviet Village, 1918–1932, by C. J. Storella and A. K. Sokolov

Voices of Revolution, 1917, by Mark D. Steinberg

The War Against the Peasantry, 1927–1930, edited by Lynne Viola, V. P. Danilov, N. A. Ivnitskii, and Denis Kozlov